# CHINDIA

*How China and India Are Revolutionizing*
*Global Business*

Edited with commentary by

## Pete Engardio

**McGraw·Hill**

New York   Chicago   San Francisco   Lisbon   London   Madrid   Mexico City
Milan   New Delhi   San Juan   Seoul   Singapore   Sydney   Toronto

Copyright © 2007 by The McGraw-Hill Companies, Inc. All rights reserved. Printed in the United States of America. Except as permitted under the United States Copyright Act of 1976, no part of this publication may be reproduced or distributed in any form or by any means, or stored in a database or retrieval system, without the prior written permission of the publisher.

1 2 3 4 5 6 7 8 9 0   FGR/FGR   0 9 8 7 6

ISBN 13: 978-0-07-147657-7
ISBN 10:      0-07-147657-1

McGraw-Hill books are available at special quantity discounts to use as premiums and sales promotions, or for use in corporate training programs. For more information, please write to the Director of Special Sales, Professional Publishing, McGraw-Hill, Two Penn Plaza, New York, NY 10121-2298. Or contact your local bookstore.

This book is printed on acid-free paper.


**Library of Congress Cataloging-in-Publication Data**

Engardio, Pete.
    Chindia / by Pete Engardio.
    p. cm.
    ISBN 0-07-147657-1 (alk. paper)

1. Globalization—Economic aspects—China.   2. Globalization—Economic aspects—India.
3. China—Economic conditions.   4. China—Economic policy.   5. India—Economic conditions.
6. India—Economic policy.   I. Title.

HF1604.E54 2006

330.951—dc22

                                                              2006027601

# Contents

# Preface

## Chindia: An Overview of the Issues

China's rise as an economic giant has seemed preordained ever since Deng Xiaoping began unshackling the nation's economy in 1979. Each spurt of reform sparked a new wave of "China fever" by foreign corporations. The international media trumpeted each new manifestation of Chinese capitalism—the appearance of private businesses, affluent consumers, humming export factories, stock markets, Communist Party officials in business suits. Every new sign of China's growing global economic might, such as its rising trade surpluses with the U.S., high-technology advances, and acquisition bids for American companies, have elicited shrill warnings by Washington politicians and think tanks of a major threat to U.S. economic and military leadership. The hype over China has been so intense that it also spawned a cottage industry of cynics who warned, time and again, that the boom was about to end in financial or social calamity.

The economic rise of India, by contrast, has been a much quieter story. Little more than 15 years ago, this other Asian giant was virtually off America's radar. Although India had an established democracy and huge private sector, diplomatic relations with Washington were cool, its economy remained suffocated by bureaucratic controls, and most industries were off limits to foreign investors. Indeed, as the economic gap with authoritarian China grew wider, India's feisty democracy was regarded as a handicap to development. Business was so jaded that the dramatic reforms proposed by Prime Minister Narasimha Rao were greeted with skepticism abroad. Even India's industrial successes, such as in software, semiconductor design, and back-office call centers, were barely visible until recently. Few Western corporations openly discussed such "offshore outsourcing" of skilled work.

The era of skepticism is over. The era of awe, for better or worse, has begun. China and India now are widely acknowledged as the planet's next economic superpowers. Having expanded by an average 9.5% annually for two decades—and a stunning 9.9% in 2005—China already has surged past most European nations in economic size and overtaken Japan as a world trader. India's economy has been expanding at a 6% annual pace over that period, and growth is accelerating as investment rises and more economic sectors open to competition. With their massive populations, swelling supplies of young workers and consumers, and still a lot of catching up to do with incomes in industrialized nations, India and China should be able to sustain 7% to 8% annual expansion for decades to come by most projections—even assuming that there will be many nasty bumps along the way. By 2015, domestic spending in India could double to around $700 billion and in China it could nearly triple to $2.6 trillion, predicts Global Insights Inc. By mid-century, India and China's share of global output is expected to mushroom from 6% now to around 45%. They will be much bigger in terms of domestic purchasing power. By any measure, both China and India likely will dwarf every other economy except America.

Few companies any longer can afford not to engage in China or India. As consumers, suppliers, competitors, innovators, investors, and sources of skilled labor, they are reshaping the world. China has become arguably the most competitive manufacturing platform ever. Its exports have risen more than 850% since 1990, while its share of world trade in manufactured goods has swelled from 2% to 11.5%, notes Oxford Economics. India is a rising power in software, design, and back-office services. Bangalore is becoming perhaps the most important technology and corporate innovation hub outside Silicon Valley. Because India and China are becoming formidable players in both low-cost manufacturing and in high-tech and services, long the bastions of advanced nations, they are even prompting mainstream economists such as Paul Samuelson to rethink long-held assumptions of free trade and comparative advantage. They also have stimulated far-reaching anxiety and debate over the future of America's global competitiveness. As *BusinessWeek* asserted in its Aug. 22, 2005, special issue titled "China and India: What You Need to Know":

> *Rarely has the economic ascent of two still relatively poor nations been watched with such a mixture of awe, opportunism, and trepidation. The postwar era witnessed economic miracles in Japan and South Korea. But neither was populous enough to power worldwide growth or change the game in a complete spectrum of industries. China and India, by contrast, possess the weight and dynamism to transform the 21st century global economy. The closest parallel to their emergence is the saga of 19th century America . . . But in a way, even America's rise falls short in comparison to what's happening now. Never has the world seen the simultaneous, sustained takeoffs of two nations that together account for one-third of the planet's population.*

Understanding the comparative strengths and internal dynamics of China and India, therefore, is essential for the global business community and policymakers. It is equally important to understand the risks. Corruption remains rampant in both nations, and the air and water pollution accompanying rapid industrialization threaten ecological and health disaster. Because China still lacks a rule of law and transparent policymaking processes, resolving cases of broken contracts, embezzlement, and intellectual-property theft through the courts can be extremely difficult. India has a Western-style legal system, but it moves at a snail's pace—and long-term investments can be sidelined by political opposition or unexpected policy shifts. China's financial system is loaded down by hundreds of billions of dollars in bad debt and prone to a financial crisis, especially if Beijing's move to remove currency control goes badly. Indian governments at the federal and state level are running up unsustainably high budget deficits.

This book, comprised of *Business Week*'s groundbreaking coverage of these emerging giants over the past five years, aims to provide a broad portrait of the rise of India and China. As these pages will show, we have been at the journalistic forefront of the search to understand and analyze the market opportunities, business cultures, economic models, and social challenges of both nations. *Business Week* has extensively covered every step of China's evolution toward a modern market economy, getting inside the reform agendas of top leaders, profiling pioneering foreign investors, assessing the fallout of the 1989 Tiananmen massacre, and exploring the impact of China's arrival as a full member of the global economic community with its 2001 entry into the World Trade Organization. *Business Week* also was early to recognize the economic awakening of India and its potential to redefine technology and service industries. We were among the first to profile India's remarkable success in producing abundant top-flight engineering and management talent. Our Dec. 8, 2003, report "The Rise of India" marked the first time India had appeared on the cover of a major U.S. magazine as an economic force.

The inspiration for this book comes from *Business Week*'s recent award-winning special issue on China and India, one of the most comprehensive journalistic efforts ever to assess the economic implications of these budding superpowers in tandem. In articles appearing in the magazine and on the *Business Week* Online Web site, this report examined their emerging corporations, technologies, and financial systems. It also scrutinized the many serious social, political, and environmental challenges both nations must overcome to sustain their burgeoning growth and attain their potential. These include severe poverty in much of India, looming health and environmental crises in China, and the urgent need to upgrade education systems at all levels in both nations.

Perhaps the biggest contribution of this special report is its comparative analysis of the two nations' widely divergent economic models and roles they are playing in the global economy. It helped touch off heated debate by asking the question of which nation is better positioned to sustain long-term growth: China with its impressive ability to mobilize capital and workers to build infrastructure and its massive manufacturing scale? Or is it India, with its more frugal, but entrepreneurially driven focus on engineering and delivery of high-quality goods and services at very low prices to its impoverished masses? Another intriguing question is what would happen if these two Asian behemoths were to merge into one giant Chindia, a term coined by Indian politician Jairam Ramesh. For now, however, this issue is largely academic. As the report shows: "In a practical sense, the yin and yang of these two immense workforces already are converging . . . Thanks to the Internet and plunging telecom costs, multinationals are having their goods built in China with software and circuitry designed in India."

For a richer understanding of the major issues, this book also includes seminal articles *BusinessWeek* has published in previous years. They include the award-winning special report "The China Price," which explains the many factors behind China's domination as a manufacturer. Also included are "Is Your Job Next?" and "The Rise of India," the award-winning cover stories that revealed the extent of the offshore shift of skilled service and engineering work and ignited the national debate on this megatrend. Plus, the book includes landmark pieces on India's IITs and rural development efforts and China's trade strategy and counterfeiting epidemic.

—PETE ENGARDIO

# CHINDIA

How China and India Are Revolutionizing
Global Business

# CHINA

| | |
|---|---|
| 25-21 BC | The Old Silk Road (really numerous routes) connects China with Indian oases and Arabian Sea ports. |
| AD 650 | Arab traders establish outposts in China's coastal cities. |
| 1229 | The Mongol conquest of China furthers commerce and development. |
| 1500s | A Chinese trading company spreads across Asia. |
| 1600 | The East India Company ships opium to China in exchange for tea. |
| 1759 | Chinese merchant families centered in Guangzhou (Canton) are commissioned by the government to act as brokers with European companies. |
| 1800s | In China, urban areas and handicraft workshops flourish. |
| 1842 | Britain's victory in the Opium War leads to the opening of trade to Guangzhou and four other ports. China cedes the barren island of Hong Kong to Britain. |
| 1890s | Japan, Britain, Germany, Russia, and France carve up China. |
| 1914-1920 | WWI allows a wave of industrialization into China and an annual growth rate of 13.8%. Modern banking begins. |
| 1949 | The Communists win China's civil war and initiate land reform and a collectivization of agriculture. Major advances take place in health care and education. |
| 1958 | The Great Leap Forward, a mass mobilization to effect economic transformation, proves disastrous. Millions die in famine. |
| 1960s | U.S. aid helps Taiwan develop. Production for export soars, especially in consumer electronics, steel, computers, and military hardware. |
| 1970s | The Communists' economic program allows some free-market activity and small-scale rural industry. After Mao Tse-Tung's 1976 death, leaders, including Deng Xiaoping, begin emulating the market economies of China's Asian neighbors. |
| 1979 | Foreign investment is legalized; Special Economic Zones are established along the Southeast Coast and the Yangzi River. |
| 1990 | The first stock exchange since 1949 opens in Shanghai. Capitalism begins changing the face of Shenzhen. |
| 1997 | The Communists announce that state-owned industries are to be phased out. China's economy is growing faster than almost any other in history, says the World Bank. A transition to Chinese rule begins in Hong Kong. |
| 2001 | China enters the World Trade Organization, committing itself to sweeping liberalization in virtually every industry. |
| 2003 | A fourth generation of Communist leaders takes over, led by Hu Jintao and Wen Jiabao. |

# INDIA

| | |
|---|---|
| 2600 BC | Trade between the Indus Valley and Mesopotamia. |
| AD 712 | Arabs invade India and trade begins between the two regions. |
| 1500s | The Portuguese are the first Europeans to restore trading links to India that were blocked by the Ottoman Empire; the Dutch and British soon follow. |
| 1600 | Britain grants a monopoly over India to the British East India Trading Company, which focuses on spices, cotton, silk, and sugar. |
| 1700s | The sale of Asian silks and printed or dyed cottons is banned in England. A highly developed preindustrial Indian textile industry collapses due to both the embargo and industrial competition. India is becoming an agricultural colony of Britain. |
| Mid-1800s | The British introduce irrigation canals, railroads, modern banking, and a system of commercial law in India. The export trade sees a steady rise. |
| 1869 | The new Suez Canal lays the basis for the integration of the Indian economy into the world market. |
| Early 1900s | Constitutional reforms allow India an increasing level of fiscal independence, including tariffs that encourage industrialization. In 1912, Tata Co., financed and controlled by Indians, begins to produce steel, hydroelectric power, and textiles. |
| 1940s | Indian industry grows rapidly during WWII. |
| 1947 | British rule comes to an end in India. Under Congress Party rule, the public sector dominates in manufacturing and banks are nationalized. Corporate dynasties such as Tata, Birla, and Bajaj grow to account for 15% of the economy. |
| 1950s | Civilian space research begins in India. |
| 1982 | Beginning as a 12-person outfit, Infosys Technologies develops software for global corporations. The outfit grows at a rate of 40% per year for a decade. |
| 1984 | Rajiv Ghandi, Prime Minister from 1984-1989, encourages high-tech development. |
| 1991-1997 | A balance-of-payments crisis—due largely to Gulf War–related oil price shocks—leads to borrowing from the IMF and World Bank. Economic reforms follow, including opening state-controlled sectors to private investment and a liberalized trading policy. Between 1993 and 1997, economic growth averages 6.8% per year. |
| 2000 | Indian software firms blossom as the Y2K scare ends. General Electric and other multinationals build R&D facilities in Bangalore, which becomes a global hub. The auto-parts industry, pharmaceuticals, and chemicals become major exporters. |

# Introduction

DUE TO THEIR RADICALLY DIVERGENT ECONOMIC models and business environments, China and India are transforming the global economy in different ways. To get started, therefore, it is helpful to understand the fundamental differences between these emerging giants.

## Investment

The most visually obvious difference between China and India is the quality of buildings and public infrastructure. Chinese megacities such as Shanghai, Beijing, Guangzhou, Dalian, and Tianjin boast dazzling office towers, hotels, luxury villas, expressways, container terminals, airports, shopping malls, and public parks—with more arising at breathtaking speed. Industrial zones up and down China's eastern coast are jammed with factories in all directions as far as the eye can see. Enormous petrochemical complexes and high-tech zones that took decades to develop in the West are built on rice fields or reclaimed land in less than two years. In India's major cities, by contrast, one feels stuck in a time warp. Ramshackle huts and fading colonial-era buildings line the narrow, hopelessly congested streets. Few new manufacturing plants are found outside big cities.

The reason is that China's economic model is designed to mobilize massive amounts of capital. Government bureaucracies from Beijing down to the smallest townships set ambitious industrial and property-development goals. They then stimulate heady investment with generous incentives by directing banks to channel China's mountain of private savings into favored projects. Domestic investment in China averages 40% to 50% of gross domestic product (GDP) each year—an extraordinarily high rate surpassing even the go-go years of East Asia's boom prior to the 1997 financial crisis. India's dysfunctional officialdom has neglected infrastructure, saddled its banks with onerous controls, shunned industrial policy, and obstructed foreign investment. Investment rates in India have averaged 22% to 23%, low for a developing nation in rapid growth mode. India attracts only around $4 billion in foreign investment annually, China more than $60 billion. This openness to foreign investment also makes China's economic model fundamentally different from Japan and South Korea during their takeoffs.

As a consequence of its high investments, China has enjoyed a nationwide construction boom rivaling that of postwar Europe. Because China is now one of the few nations on earth building modern, multibillion-dollar plants to produce petrochemicals, silicon wafers, digital displays, automobiles, steel, ships, and other capital-intensive goods, it also is quickly becoming a player in a whole new strata of advanced industries, spreading development to poor regions and adding tens of millions of new jobs. The downside is that much of this investment also is wasteful: A good 20% of bank loans are nonperforming. That figure could spike once the economy slows. And it takes at least $5 in investment to generate one dollar's worth of growth in China, well below world standards. Beijing's control of its banks and currency has spared China from the kind of financial crises that struck neighbors such as South Korea and Thailand in the late 1990s. But such controls prevented the development of deep capital markets that would make its financial system more sound and its development more balanced.

India's financial system also is underdeveloped, with most bank loans going to government enterprises and favored projects. Still, banks are in private hands. And overall, India's financial markets allocate capital more efficiently than does China's—and favor higher-margin industries like information technology and services. Some economists, therefore, think India can sustain high growth longer, especially as savings and foreign investment increase. The cost of low investment, however, has been slower economic growth, fewer people lifted out of poverty, and an industrial base a fraction of China's size.

## Market Power

For many years, cynics sneered at foreign investors smitten with visions of selling everything from cars to cosmetics to China's "one billion consumers." In reality, such critics noted, a tiny portion of Chinese earned enough to afford such luxuries. Prospects of selling much in India, with its per capita income of less than $500 a year, seemed less remote.

Today, China and India are among the world's most important consumer markets. China already is the world's biggest consumer of wireless phones, with 350 million cellular subscribers. It is the world's third largest car market and on pace to become the biggest market for PCs, broadband telecom services, digital TVs, and numerous other goods. Due to its construction and manufacturing boom, meanwhile, China has almost single-handedly driven up world prices for cement, steel, copper, and other materials.

Less noticed is India's rapid rise as a mega consumer market. The number of cell-phone subscribers exploded tenfold, to 55 million, between 2000 and 2005, putting India on the same growth trajectory as China five years ago. It is expected to pass 300 million subscribers in three years. India's auto and consumer electronics markets also are surging. Like China, India has a fast-growing middle class that is independence-minded, optimistic about its financial future, and views luxury goods as status symbols. While open to foreign brands, Indian consumers also insist on quality for the money.

But there are also major differences between Indian and Chinese consumers. The first, of course, is market size. Because China's per capita income is triple that of India, it has legions of more well-heeled consumers. China already has some 300,000 millionaires. Credit Suisse

First Boston predicts 151 million Chinese urban families will earn at least $10,000 annually by 2014, up from 3.8 million in 2003. There are cultural differences too. Many upwardly mobile Chinese are willing to pay $300 for a new top-of-the-line cell phone several times each year, for example. India's consumer class prefers quality goods at low prices. The poorer masses are also an important growth market. India is a proving ground for companies selling 5-cent packets of shampoo, 2-cents-a-minute cellular service, and $100 PCs.

## Industry Strengths

The pace and breadth of China's ascent as a manufacturing juggernaut has been astonishing. By the end of 2006, China expects to export more than $800 billion worth of goods—triple the level of 2002—and pass $1 trillion in 2008. With the end of international textile quotas in 2005, China now accounts for half of all garments imported into the U.S. It also makes most of the world's toys, shoes, watches, and tools. What really sets China apart from previous Asian export machines is that it is still gaining share in labor-intensive light manufacturing even as it is becoming a leader in heavy industry and advanced electronics. In 2000, China exported $30.5 billion worth of high-tech products. In 2005, that reached $220 billion, 28% of China's exports. By 2008, China is expected to double its passenger car capacity to more than 8 million units and begin exporting to Europe and the U.S. China's semiconductor industry, still in its infancy, also will soon be a world player, with 22 new silicon wafer plants planned within three years. Some 50 different chemical plants, each involving at least $1 billion in investment, are under construction. The U.S. has one.

The idea that China will continue to assemble low-end products while high-end manufacturing will always remain in advanced nations also is becoming outdated. From multimillion-dollar computer-controlled factory equipment to $200,000 networking routers, production is shifting to China fast—along with most of the components, materials, and mechanical engineering work. With prices of Chinese-produced goods generally 30% to 50% below those in the U.S.—whether they be rolls of tissue, metal castings, 30-inch LCD TVs, or fine bedroom sets crafted from Canadian hardwoods—companies have little choice but to source from the mainland.

China's critics in the U.S. tend to focus on a few reasons for the so-called China Price. They cite labor practices, state subsidies, and trade rule violations that give Chinese producers an unfair advantage as well as Beijing's policy of pegging the yuan to the U.S. dollar. Critics claim the yuan is undervalued by at least 30%. There is some truth to these charges. Intellectual property theft and dumping at below fair market prices are rampant. China does not tolerate free trade unions, allowing many manufacturers to pay as little as 30 cents an hour to the seemingly inexhaustible supply of young female factory laborers willing to toil up to 100 hours a week.

There is far more to China's overwhelming advantage in manufacturing, though. The low costs of China's immense labor pool apply to first-rate engineers, managers, cargo handlers, and office staff as well as factory laborers. As already mentioned, massive capital investment has furnished industrial-scale and super-efficient infrastructure that Mexico, Indonesia, and other manufacturing havens cannot match. China's supply base of components and materials for everything from electronics to garments is unparalleled. The mainland's economic integration with Taiwan and Hong Kong supplies other enormous advantages. Taiwanese tycoons have been the architects of China's computer, consumer appliance, and semiconductor industries, providing the technology, capital, and managerial expertise—and control 70% of electronic exports. Hong Kong companies, meanwhile, built up Chinese light manufacturing and manage the export trade of everything from dress shirts to jewelry.

All of these factors laid the foundation. Going forward, however, China's chief advantage as a production platform is that it will become both the world's biggest export base and domestic market for many industrial products. Combined with its huge engineering workforce, China is destined to also emerge as a driver of innovation and technology trends in an array of industries.

India is a manufacturing minnow compared to China. But it is carving out industrial terrain that may be even more valuable—software, design, and services. India's economic role also is better hidden. A hot Motorola wireless handset, Cisco network switch, or Philips imaging device may read "Made in China" on the back, but much of the software and integration of multimedia technologies that yield the real profit margins may have been developed in India. Cities such as Bangalore, Pune, and Hyderabad are mission-critical engineering hubs for General Electric, Microsoft, SAP, Intel, Texas Instruments, and other high-tech giants.

While most of America sleeps, Indian finance, marketing, and technical professionals perform the gamut of skilled work for U.S. corporations. They crunch the latest financial disclosures of listed companies, calculate risk ratios for new insurance policies and mortgages, tweak the designs of future tractor engines, research legal cases, scrutinize promising molecules for drug makers, design Web pages for consumer e-commerce sites, help dispatch trucking fleets to factories, answer technical queries from American computer buyers, and conduct market research for consumer product companies. Five years ago, India's exports of software and tech-enabled services, which includes outsourced research and development (R&D) and call-center work, was miniscule. Exports reached $22 billion in 2005 and could hit $148 billion by 2012, as projected by McKinsey Co. and NASSCOM, India's IT services trade association.

India is the first developing nation whose export takeoff was based on services rather than factory and mining labor. It also is helping usher in a radically new stage of globalization. As *BusinessWeek*'s Dec. 8, 2003, cover, "The Rise of India," observed:

> *This deep source of low-cost, high-IQ, English-speaking brainpower may soon have a more far-reaching impact on the U.S. than China. Manufacturing . . . accounts for just 14% of U.S. output and 11% of jobs. India's forte is services—which make up 60% of the U.S. economy and employ two-thirds of its workers. And Indian knowledge workers are*

*making their way up the New Economy food chain, mastering tasks requiring analysis, marketing acumen, and creativity. This means India is penetrating America's economic core.*

India's proficiency in software and computer science is proving to be its entrée into the full spectrum of industries. Companies like Infosys, Tata Consulting Services, Wipro, HCL, and Satyam got their global starts as low-cost software-writing job shops for foreign corporations. Leveraging the nation's enormous pool of engineers and scientists, such companies have expanded into consulting, business process outsourcing, and R&D services. By undercutting companies such as IBM Services, Accenture, and EDS by 30% to 40%, Indian IT companies already have transformed the pricing and structure of the global $650 billion IT services industry. Now they are becoming vital links in the innovation chain from autos and aerospace to pharmaceuticals. Using 3-D computer simulations, engineers can remotely test the chemical reactions of new compounds and tweak designs of virtual prototypes of engines, aircraft wings, and even entire automated factory assembly lines. India's strength in embedded software, meanwhile, is growing more valuable as more functions of cars, consumer electronics, and machine tools converge onto silicon wafers.

The next step, many experts predict, is for India to parlay its software and design industries into a foothold as the world's next major manufacturing base. Multinationals such as Nokia, Hyundai, BMW, and Jabil Circuits (a leading electronics contract manufacturer) are building sprawling industrial parks that will help establish India's component industry. India also boasts manufacturers that are globally competitive at small-batch production of sophisticated, engineering-intensive products, such as medical equipment, power generators, and precision auto parts. India's decrepit infrastructure, bureaucratic red tape, and rigid labor laws that make it hard to lay off workers have retarded industrial development. If India solves these bottlenecks, however, it could challenge China with an entirely different manufacturing model.

## Business Culture

Despite nearly three decades of economic reform, five years of World Trade Organization (WTO) membership, and all of the physical trappings of modern capitalism, China's business culture remains remarkably nontransparent and tethered to the state. True, the share of economic output by state-owned companies has shrunk to around 30% in the past two decades. Ownership by government ministries is concentrated in utilities, transportation, and heavy industry, not unlike Britain or France a few decades ago.

But the state still permeates China's business scene. Beijing directly controls the nation's four largest banks, which hold 80% of private deposits, decides which companies can list their shares (almost all are state enterprises), and directs low-cost loans to favored corporations with the express aim of nurturing national champions. Beijing also maps five-year plans to develop key industries such as cars, semiconductors, steel, and telecom. The Communist Party appoints all key executives of big corporations like China Telecom and CNOOC. Intervention in industry at the local level varies from province to province and town to town, but remains pervasive. Virtually all major consumer appliance manufacturers, for example, are partially owned by local government bodies. And true financial and management control is murky in countless factories that appear to be private. No media, including Internet sites, are free of government oversight nor are labor unions or even significant business associations. As a result, business success in China still requires careful nurturing of *guanxi*, or connections, with Communist Party officials and power brokers.

Still, China Inc. bears little resemblance to the centrally planned economy of old. Beijing may set broad parameters for an industry, but allows freewheeling competition within sectors. Ventures controlled by General Motors, Volkswagen, Honda, and other foreign car makers rule China's burgeoning auto market, which has hundreds of assemblers. Motorola, Nokia, and Samsung slug it out in the cell-phone arena with hundreds of hard-charging domestic upstarts. The consumer electronics sector is such a free-for-all that margins for even the leading Chinese

TV, air-conditioner, and DVD player brands are razor thin. The central government has been unable to control the breakneck expansion of myriad steel and chemical makers. This competitive jungle keeps prices low and forces survivors to continually invest in new technology. Beijing's inability to enforce national laws protecting intellectual property, unfortunately, has retarded China's progress in innovation.

China Inc.'s biggest handicap is management. Most big companies are run by executives who rose to their positions through party connections or by steadily climbing the ladder. Private companies are run by entrepreneurs with little formal business training. MBA graduates from Chinese and foreign universities have tended to flock to foreign corporations. Even though China has brilliant business leaders and enrollment in business programs is growing rapidly, the acute lack of management depth and poor governance standards limits the ability of Chinese companies to expand globally.

India's business culture couldn't be more different. Even though its banking system and major industries are in private hands, austere rules and suffocating bureaucracy prevented entrepreneurs from investing aggressively until the 1990s. Onerous restrictions on bank lending and foreign investment—a legacy of the Nehru-era obsession with self-reliance—limited access to outside capital. National and local government agencies ignored physical infrastructure and did little to help industry with subsidies. To this day, India's roads, power grid, and airports are woefully inadequate.

Business success in India, therefore, has been all about learning to manage with scarcity and physical constraints. Fortunately, India has a wealth of top-notch, globally minded managerial talent groomed in the outstanding Indian Institutes of Management, Western business schools, U.S. corporations, and Silicon Valley start-ups. American business visitors to China often feel like they never really comprehend their counterparts. In India, they often are struck by the executives' fluency in the latest financial, marketing, technology, and management concepts and lingo. India also has an enormous pool of gifted, English-speaking scientists and engineers who thrive in cyberspace. The result is a tech-savvy business elite ideally suited to the fast, flat, and virtual New Economy entrepreneurial culture of the U.S.

India's constraints have forced entrepreneurs to devise creative business models for delivering high-quality goods and services at extremely low prices to what management guru C. K. Prahalad dubs the "bottom of the pyramid"—the vast majority of the world's population living in relative poverty. Indian companies are mastering the art of making money by selling everything from $50 air flights and $200 loans to eye and cardiac surgery at a fraction of U.S. costs. The focus on technology, services, and consumer goods for the masses has been a theme of *BusinessWeek*'s India coverage. As Indian companies perfect such models at home and gain critical mass, they could soon begin to change the competitive landscape of industries globally.

## Social Challenges

Since setting out on their own paths following World War II—China as a communist state, India as a democracy newly independent of Britain—leaders of both nations have faced a similarly daunting dilemma: How to feed and employ immense, rapidly growing, poorly educated, multiethnic, impoverished populations?

Both nations have made tremendous gains, but excruciating pressures remain. By unofficial estimates, 200 million Chinese and Indians lack full-time employment, even as tens of millions of youth pour into their workforces each year. In 2005 alone, China witnessed 57,000 labor strikes. In India, frustrated low-income voters who are not enjoying the fruits of growth could derail free-market reforms needed to push the economy forward. So China and India both require strong, sustained growth to keep living standards from deteriorating. They also must now come to grips with the negative fallout of rapid industrialization, such as serious pollution, and deforestation. Both nations face potential health crises. By 2010, for example, China could have as many as 10 million AIDS victims and India 20 million. Because neither has adequate public health systems, a flu pandemic could kill millions.

China without doubt has done the better job in terms of human development, despite the disastrous Great Leap Forward from 1958 to 1962 and the Cultural Revolution from 1966 to 1976. The decades of rapid growth since have lifted hundreds of millions out of poverty. The literacy rate has risen from 60% to 85% and is at 96% among people between the ages of 12 and 40. But China lags the records of neighbors like South Korea and Taiwan. Only 40% of youth enroll in high school and 13% in university. As Beijing pushes more of the financial burden of education onto local governments, quality is suffering, especially in the poor interior areas.

China also faces a demographic time bomb. Due in part to its one-child policy, China has one of the world's most rapidly aging populations. By 2015, its working-age population will quickly begin to decline. In 20 years, an estimated 300 million Chinese will be 60 or older. Because China is phasing out cradle-to-grave worker benefits, only one in six has a pension. Just 5% have guaranteed medical benefits. Erecting a social safety net is one of China's most urgent tasks, one that could consume vast future wealth.

India faces the mind-boggling challenge of managing a population expected to reach 1.7 billion by mid-century. In terms of sheer economic potential, though, its demographic profile is better than China's. Nearly 500 million people are 19 or younger, so India's workforce and consumer class will keep growing for decades. India also has begun to make impressive social gains. The number of Indians living on $1 a day dropped from 300 million to around 200 million since 1993. But that's still one-fifth of the population. School enrollment for those aged 6 to 14 has risen from 75% to 90% since 2000. Still, only one-quarter make it past eighth grade, and only 7% graduate from high school. Very few make it to university—and there the picture is mixed. India's elite institutes of technology, management, science, and statistics produce world-class graduates. Quality at the tens of thousands of private and public second-tier colleges and institutes is spotty.

How well China and India manage their social, financial, and political challenges will determine whether they achieve their full economic potential. There no doubt will be booms, busts, and calamities along the way. But while the momentum may slow, the long-term direction appears set. China and India are destined to become the chief drivers of global growth and will force immense adjustments on industries, societies, and economies in rich nations and poor.

The following chapters will offer a flavor of *Business Week*'s journalistic journey to comprehend the many dimensions in which China and India will change our world. We hope they also provide an insightful and engaging guide to both the opportunities and challenges facing business leaders as they engage these rising 21st-century superpowers.

# 2

# The Rise of Chindia

CHINA AND INDIA EACH ARE STARTING to exert powerful influence in virtually every dimension of global business. In the coming decades, they will likely be the biggest forces reshaping the world economy. The following articles lay out the many implications of the rise of these two emerging economic superpowers.

"A New World Economy," the opening article in *Business Week*'s special issue, argues that China and India could have as much impact as America's ascent in the 19th century. In part, that is because the economic takeoffs of both of these immensely populated nations are occurring simultaneously. What's more, they complement each other's strengths.

The lead article summarizes the impact China and India are exerting as consumer markets, manufacturers, investors, sources of skilled labor, drivers of global technology trends, and partners in corporate innovation. It also analyzes the fundamental differences between the two nations' economic models. China's model is characterized by massive mobilization of capital and labor, foreign investment, strength in large-scale manufacturing, and heavy state intervention. India's model is characterized by strength in engineering and services, private capital markets, business models that focus on high-quality goods and services at low costs, and small-batch precision manufacturing. The article also touches on the debate over which economy is in a better position to achieve high growth over the long term. Until now, China has attained dramatically higher growth. But some experts believe India's superior capital efficiency, higher population growth, and younger workforce mean growth is more sustainable and will enable India to surpass China in economic growth in the coming decades.

To attain their enormous potential, however, China and India must overcome tremendous challenges. As their economic and political roles grow bigger, these domestic problems also pose risks for the entire world. "Crouching Tigers, Hidden Dragons" cites the key obstacles as domestic political strife, environmental degradation, health crises, regional wars, and the need to continuously create enough jobs to employ tens of millions of new workers annually. Two leading economists—Hai Wen of Beijing's China Center for Economic Research and William T. Wilson of Keystone Business Intelligence India—offer their views on why both nations are headed for decades more of high growth.

---

# A New World Economy

*The balance of power will shift to the East as China and India evolve*

It may not top the must-see list of many tourists. But to appreciate Shanghai's ambitious view of its future, there is no better place than the Urban Planning Exhibition Hall, a glass-and-metal structure across from People's Square. The highlight is a scale model bigger than a basketball court of the entire metropolis—every skyscraper, house, lane, factory, dock, and patch of green space—in the year 2020.

There are white plastic showpiece towers designed by architects such as I. M. Pei and Sir Norman Foster. There are immense new industrial parks for autos and petrochemicals, along with new subway lines, airport runways, ribbons of expressway, and an elaborate riverfront development, site of the 2010 World Expo. Nine futuristic planned communities for 800,000 residents each, with generous parks, retail districts, man-made lakes, and nearby college campuses, rise in the suburbs. The message is clear. Shanghai already is looking well past its industrial age to its expected emergence as a global mecca of knowledge workers. "In an information economy, it is very important to have urban space with a better natural and social environment," explains Architectural Society of Shanghai President Zheng Shiling, a key city advisor.

It is easy to dismiss such dreams as bubble-economy hubris, until you take into account the audacious goals Shanghai already has achieved. Since 1990, when the city still seemed caught in a socialist time warp, Shanghai has erected enough high-rises to fill Manhattan. The once-rundown Pudong district boasts a space-age skyline, some of the world's biggest industrial zones, dozens of research centers, and a bullet train. This is the story of China, where an extraordinary ability to mobilize workers and capital has tripled per capita income in a generation, and has eased 300 million out of poverty. Leaders now are frenetically laying the groundwork for decades of new growth.

## Invaluable Role

Now hop a plane to India. It is hard to tell this is the world's other emerging superpower. Jolting sights of extreme poverty abound even in the business capitals. A lack of subways and a dearth of expressways result in nightmarish traffic.

But visit the office towers and research and development centers sprouting everywhere, and you see the miracle. Here, Indians are playing invaluable roles in the global innovation chain. Motorola, Hewlett-Packard, Cisco Systems, and other tech giants now rely on their Indian teams to devise software platforms and dazzling multimedia features for next-generation devices. Google principal scientist Krishna Bharat is setting up a Bangalore lab complete with colorful furniture, exercise balls, and a Yamaha organ—like Google's Mountain View (Calif.) headquarters—to work on core search-engine technology. Indian engineering houses use 3-D computer simulations to tweak designs of everything from car engines and forklifts to aircraft wings for such clients as General Motors Corp. and Boeing Co. Financial and market-research experts at outfits like B2K, OfficeTiger, and Iris crunch the latest disclosures of blue-chip companies for Wall Street. By 2010 such outsourcing work is expected to quadruple, to $56 billion a year.

Even more exhilarating is the pace of innovation, as tech hubs like Bangalore spawn companies producing their own chip designs, software, and pharmaceuticals. "I find Bangalore to be one of the most exciting places in the world," says Dan Scheinman, Cisco Systems Inc.'s senior vice-president for corporate development. "It is Silicon Valley in 1999." Beyond Bangalore, Indian companies are showing a flair for producing high-quality goods and services at ridiculously low prices, from $50 air flights and crystal-clear 2-cents-a-minute cell-phone service to $2,200 cars and cardiac operations by top surgeons at a fraction of U.S. costs. Some analysts see the beginnings of hypercompetitive multinationals. "Once they learn to sell at Indian prices with world quality, they can compete anywhere," predicts University of Michigan management guru C. K. Prahalad. Adds A.T. Kearney high-tech consultant John Ciacchella: "I don't think U.S. companies realize India is building next-generation service companies."

## Simultaneous Takeoffs

China and India. Rarely has the economic ascent of two still relatively poor nations been watched with such a mixture of awe, opportunism, and trepidation. The postwar era witnessed economic miracles in Japan and South Korea. But neither was populous enough to power worldwide growth or change the game in a complete spectrum of industries. China and India, by contrast, possess the weight and dynamism to transform the 21st-century global economy. The closest parallel to their emergence is the saga of 19th-century America, a huge continental economy with a young, driven workforce that grabbed the lead in agriculture, apparel, and the high technologies of the era, such as steam engines, the telegraph, and electric lights.

But in a way, even America's rise falls short in comparison to what's happening now. Never has the world seen the simultaneous, sustained takeoffs of two nations that together account for one-third of the planet's population. For the past two decades, China has been growing at an astounding 9.5% a year, and India by 6%. Given their young populations, high savings, and the sheer amount of catching up they still have to do, most economists figure China and India possess the fundamentals to keep growing in the 7% to 8% range for decades.

Barring cataclysm, within three decades India should have vaulted over Germany as the world's third-biggest economy. By mid-century, China should have overtaken the U.S. as No. 1. By then, China and India could account for half of global output. Indeed, the troika of China, India, and the U.S.—the only industrialized nation with significant population growth—by most projections will dwarf every other economy.

What makes the two giants especially powerful is that they complement each other's strengths. An accelerating trend is that technical and managerial skills in both China and India are becoming more important than cheap assembly labor. China will stay dominant in mass manufacturing and is one of the few nations building multibillion-dollar electronics and heavy industrial plants. India is a rising power in software, design, services, and precision industry. This raises a provocative question: What if the two nations merge into one giant "Chindia"? Rival political and economic ambitions make that unlikely. But if their industries truly collaborate, "they would take over the world tech industry," predicts Forrester Research Inc. analyst Navi Radjou.

In a practical sense, the yin and yang of these immense workforces already are converging. True, annual trade between the two economies is just $14 billion. But thanks to the Internet and plunging telecom costs, multinationals are having their goods built in China with software and circuitry designed in India. As interactive design technology makes it easier to perfect virtual 3-D prototypes of everything from telecom routers to turbine generators on PCs, the distance between India's low-cost laboratories and China's low-cost factories shrinks by the month. Managers in the vanguard of globalization's new wave say the impact will be nothing less than explosive. "In a few years you'll see most companies unleashing this massive productivity surge," predicts Infosys Technologies CEO Nandan M. Nilekani.

To globalization's skeptics, however, what's good for Corporate America translates into layoffs and lower pay for workers. Little wonder the West is suffering from future shock. Each new Chinese corporate takeover bid or revelation of a major Indian outsourcing deal elicits howls of protest by U.S. politicians. Washington think tanks are publishing thick white papers charting China's rapid progress in microelectronics, nanotech, and aerospace—and painting dark scenarios about what it means for America's global leadership.

Such alarmism is understandable. But the U.S. and other established powers will have to learn to make room for China and India. For in almost every dimension—as consumer markets, investors, producers, and users of energy and commodities—they will be 21st-century heavyweights. The growing economic might will carry into geopolitics as well. China and India are more assertively pressing their interests in the Middle East and Africa, and China's military will likely challenge U.S. dominance in the Pacific.

One implication is that the balance of power in many technologies will likely move from West to East. An obvious reason is that China and India graduate a combined half a million engineers and scientists a year, versus 70,000 in the U.S. In life sciences, projects the McKinsey Global Institute, the total number of young researchers in both nations will rise by 35%, to 1.6 million by 2008. The U.S. supply will drop by 11%, to 760,000. As most Western scientists will tell you, China and India already are making important contributions in medicine and materials that will help everyone. Because these nations can throw more brains at technical problems at a fraction of the cost, their contributions to innovation will grow.

## Consumers Rising

American business isn't just shifting research work because Indian and Chinese brains are young, cheap, and plentiful. In many cases, these engineers combine skills—mastery of the latest software tools, a knack for complex mathematical algorithms, and fluency in new multimedia technologies—that often surpass those of their American counterparts. As Cisco's Scheinman puts it: "We came to India for the costs, we stayed for the quality, and we're now investing for the innovation."

A rising consumer class also will drive innovation. This year, China's passenger car market is expected to reach 3 million, No. 3 in the world. China already has the world's biggest base of cell-phone subscribers—350 million—and that is expected to near 600 million by 2009. In two years, China should overtake the U.S. in homes connected to broadband. Less noticed is that India's consumer market is on the same explosive trajectory as China five years ago. Since 2000, the number of cellular subscribers has rocketed from 5.6 million to 55 million.

What's more, Chinese and Indian consumers and companies now demand the latest technologies and features. Studies show the attitudes and aspirations of today's young Chinese and Indians resemble those of Americans a few decades ago. Surveys of thousands of young adults in both nations by marketing firm Grey Global Group found they are overwhelmingly optimistic about the future, believe success is in their hands, and view products as status symbols. In China, it's fashionable for the upwardly mobile to switch high-end cell phones every three months, says Josh Li, managing director of Grey's Beijing office, because an old model suggests "you are not getting ahead and updated." That means these nations will be huge proving grounds for next-generation multimedia gizmos, networking equipment, and wireless Web services, and will play a greater role in setting global standards. In consumer electronics, "we will see China in a few years going from being a follower to a leader in defining consumer-electronics trends," predicts Philips Semiconductors Executive Vice-President Leon Husson.

For all the huge advantages they now enjoy, India and China cannot assume their role as new superpowers is assured. Today, China and India account for a mere 6% of global gross domestic product—half that of Japan. They must keep growing rapidly just to provide jobs for tens of millions entering the workforce annually, and to keep many millions more from crashing back into poverty. Both nations must confront eco-logical degradation that's as obvious as the smog shrouding Shanghai and Bombay, and face real risks of social strife, war, and financial crisis.

Increasingly, such problems will be the world's problems. Also, with wages rising fast, especially in many skilled areas, the cheap labor edge won't last forever. Both nations will go through many boom and har-rowing bust cycles. And neither country is yet producing companies like Samsung, Nokia, or Toyota that put it all together, developing, making, and marketing world-beating products.

Both countries, however, have survived earlier crises and possess immense untapped potential. In China, serious development only now is reaching the 800 million people in rural areas, where per capita annual income is just $354. In areas outside major cities, wages are as little as 45 cents an hour. "This is why China can have another 20 years of high-speed growth," contends Beijing University economist Hai Wen.

Very impressive. But India's long-term potential may be even higher. Due to its one-child policy, China's working-age population will peak at 1 billion in 2015 and then shrink steadily. China then will have to provide for a graying population that has limited retirement benefits. India has nearly 500 million people under age 19 and higher fertility rates. By mid-century, India is expected to have 1.6 billion people and 220 million more workers than China. That could be a source for insta-bility, but a great advantage for growth if the government can provide education and opportunity for India's masses. New Delhi just now is pushing to open its power, telecom, commercial real estate, and retail sectors to foreigners. These industries could lure big capital inflows. "The pace of institutional changes and industries being liberalized is phenomenal," says Chief Economist William T. Wilson of consultancy Keystone Business Intelligence India. "I believe India has a better model than China, and over time will surpass it in growth."

For its part, China has yet to prove it can go beyond forced-march industrialization. China directs massive investment into public works and factories, a wildly successful formula for rapid growth and job creation. But considering its massive manufacturing output, China is surprisingly weak in innovation. A full 57% of exports are from foreign-invested factories, and China underachieves in software, even with 35 software colleges and plans to graduate 200,000 software engineers a year. It's not for lack of genius. Microsoft Corp.'s 180-engineer R&D lab in Beijing, for example, is one of the world's most productive sources of innovation in computer graphics and language simulation.

While China's big state-run R&D institutes are close to the cutting edge at the theoretical level, they have yet to yield many commercial breakthroughs. "China has a lot of capability," says Microsoft Chief Technology Officer Craig Mundie. "But when you look under the covers, there is not a lot of collaboration with industry." The lack of intellectual property protection, and Beijing's heavy role in building up its own tech companies, make many other multinationals leery of doing serious R&D in China.

China also is hugely wasteful. Its 9.5% growth rate in 2004 is less impressive when you consider that $850 billion—half of GDP—was mainly plowed into already-glutted sectors like crude steel, vehicles, and office buildings. Its factories burn fuel five times less efficiently than in the West, and more than 20% of bank loans are bad. Two-thirds of China's 1,300 listed companies don't earn back their true cost of capital, estimates Beijing National Accounting Institute President Chen Xiaoyue. "We build the roads and industrial parks, but we sacrifice a lot," Chen says.

India, by contrast, has had to develop with scarcity. It gets scant foreign investment and has no room to waste fuel and materials like China. India also has Western legal institutions, a modern stock market, and private banks and corporations. As a result, it is far more capital-efficient. A *BusinessWeek* analysis of Standard & Poor's Compustat data on 346 top listed companies in both nations shows Indian corporations have achieved higher returns on equity and invested capital in the past five years in industries from autos to food products. The average Indian company posted a 16.7% return on capital in 2004, versus 12.8% in China.

## Small Batch Expertise

The burning question is whether India can replicate China's mass manufacturing achievement. India's info-tech services industry, successful as it is, employs fewer than 1 million people. But 200 million Indians subsist on $1 a day or less. Export manufacturing is one of India's best hopes of generating millions of new jobs.

India has sophisticated manufacturing know-how. Tata Steel is among the world's most efficient producers. The country boasts several top precision auto parts companies, such as Bharat Forge Ltd. The world's biggest supplier of chassis parts to major automakers, it employs 1,200 engineers at its heavily automated Pune plant. India's forte is small-batch production of high-value goods requiring lots of engineering, such as power generators for Cummins Inc. and core components for General Electric Co. CAT scanners.

What holds India back are bureaucratic red tape, rigid labor laws, and its inability to build infrastructure fast enough. There are hopeful signs. Nokia Corp. is building a major campus to make cell phones in Madras, and South Korea's Pohang Iron & Steel Co. plans a $12 billion complex by 2016 in Orissa state. But it will take India many years to build the highways, power plants, and airports needed to rival China in mass manufacturing. With Beijing now pushing software and pledging intellectual property rights protection, some Indians fret design work will shift to China to be closer to factories. "The question is whether China can move from manufacturing to services faster than we can solve our infrastructure bottlenecks," says President Aravind Melligeri of Bangalore-based QuEST, whose 700 engineers design gas turbines, aircraft engines, and medical gear for GE and other clients.

However the race plays out, Corporate America has little choice but to be engaged—heavily. Motorola illustrates the value of leveraging both nations to lower costs and speed up development. Most of its hardware is assembled and partly designed in China. Its R&D center in Bangalore devises about 40% of the software in its new phones. The Bangalore team developed the multimedia software and user interfaces in the hot Razr cell phone. Now, they are working on phones that display and send live video, stream movies from the Web, or route incoming calls to voicemail when you are shifting gears in a car. "This is a very, very critical, state-of-the-art resource for Motorola," says Motorola South Asia President Amit Sharma.

Companies like Motorola realize they must succeed in China and India at many levels simultaneously to stay competitive. That requires strategies for winning consumers, recruiting and managing R&D and professional talent, and skillfully sourcing from factories. "Over the next few years, you will see a dramatic gap opening between companies," predicts Jim Hemerling, who runs Boston Consulting Group's Shanghai practice. "It will be between those who get it and are fully mobilized in China and India, and those that are still pondering."

In the coming decades, China and India will disrupt workforces, industries, companies, and markets in ways that we can barely begin to imagine. The upheaval will test America's commitment to the global trade system, and shake its confidence. In the 19th century, Europe went through a similar trauma when it realized a new giant—the U.S.—had arrived. "It is up to America to manage its own expectation of China and India as either a threat or opportunity," says corporate strategist Kenichi Ohmae. "America should be as open-minded as Europe was 100 years ago." How these Asian giants integrate with the rest of the world will largely shape the 21st-century global economy.

## Crouching Tigers, Hidden Dragons

The economic momentum isn't unstoppable. Plenty of forces can still throw the Chinese and Indian economies far off course. The economic fundamentals of both nations, with their enormous populations of young workers and consumers, point to strong growth for decades under almost every forecast. But it is instructive to remember that financial crashes, coups, political strife, and plain bad management have derailed many other miracle economies from Southeast Asia to Latin America. And the same huge populations that can translate into economic power for China and India also could prove to be a double-edged sword if social, political, and environmental challenges are not deftly managed. Indeed, growth doesn't have to slow all that much to pose serious social problems. Both China and India need annual growth of at least 8% just to provide jobs for the tens of millions joining the workforce each year. Fear of worker unrest is a big reason Beijing has kept stoking its boom with massive lending and growth in the money supply, despite economists' warnings that it is setting the stage for a nasty bust. If India grows only 6.5% a year, which seems a respectable rate, its jobless rate would still jump, resulting in another 70 million unemployed by 2012, forecasts India's Planning Commission.

Slower growth also could keep China and India from fulfilling the widespread predictions that they will become superpowers. For example, in forecasting that India will rank just behind the U.S. as the world's No. 3 economy by mid-century, with a gross domestic product of $30 trillion, Goldman, Sachs & Co. assumes 8.5% average annual growth. But what if India grows at less than 6%, its average for the past 20 years? By 2050, it would have only a $7.3 trillion economy—smaller than Taiwan's even then and just 2.6% of global GDP, notes Stephen Howes, the World Bank's former chief India economist. Worse, India's masses would remain extremely poor. "If you don't grow fast enough, will you have social forces that bring everything to a stalemate?" asks Infosys Technologies Ltd. CEO Nandan M. Nilekani. "That's the worry."

To achieve the high growth predictions, China and India will have to overcome formidable challenges. Some of the biggest:

## Environment

Both countries have paid a steep ecological price for rapid industrial and population growth, with millions of deaths attributed to air and water pollution each year. Air quality in big cities like New Delhi, Chongqing, and Bombay is among the world's worst. And forests are vanishing at alarming rates.

Enforcement of environmental laws in both nations is poor. Many power plants and factories depend on coal and don't invest in clean technologies. China is one of the world's most wasteful users of oil. If it does not act quickly, the long-term costs of health problems linked to the environment and the required cleanup will skyrocket. A growing scarcity of water in both nations could slow industry within two decades.

## Political Backlash

China's Communist Party harshly represses dissent. But virtually each week brings new reports of big protests in cities and villages over corruption, pollution, or worker abuse. They underscore China's lack of democratic institutions and the widening gap between rich and poor. Serious challenges to Communist rule can still erupt, especially if the economy stalls. Judging from history, the process could be tumultuous.

India has a democracy, but it also has extremely unbalanced growth and rampant corruption. The surprise electoral defeat of the ruling Bharatiya Janata Party by a more populist coalition led by Sonia Gandhi's Congress Party in 2004 served as a warning of mass discontent. The new government also is reform-minded, but the pace of economic liberalization has slowed. Further electoral setbacks for reformers are possible if the poor don't see the benefits of growth. Tensions between Hindus and Muslims have eased after bloody riots in 2003 and 2004. But communal violence remains a threat.

## Financial Crisis

Debt and currency crises have derailed many high-flying emerging markets. India needed an International Monetary Fund bailout in 1991. China withstood the 1997 Asian financial crisis mainly because it lacks a convertible currency. Also, Beijing controls the banks. Bailouts and the banks' near-monopoly over China's vast domestic savings have kept them solvent despite mountains of bad loans to state firms.

Soon, however, Beijing will start letting foreign banks compete for deposits and domestic loans. That could put more financial pressure on state banks. China also is starting to loosen its currency controls a bit. China has plenty of foreign reserves now. But if Beijing can't whip its banks into shape, there's a danger that financial market liberalization will go wrong, leading to a crash. India's financial system is in stronger shape, but its public finances remain a mess, with budget deficits at the federal and state level reaching 10% of GDP.

## Health

Perhaps China's biggest worry over the long term is inadequate medical care for its rapidly aging population. In 20 years, China will have an estimated 300 million people age 60 or older. Yet only one in six Chinese workers now has a pension plan, and just 5% have guaranteed medical benefits. What's more, many retirees will not be able to rely on children for support. Beijing promises to build a broader safety net, but adequate health care and pensions could consume a huge portion of GDP and deplete China's economic strength in the future.

Both nations also could face full-blown crises with AIDS, tuberculosis, avian flu, and other infectious diseases, and their health systems have been slow to mobilize. At least 5 million Indian adults are infected with HIV, one of the world's highest rates outside sub-Saharan Africa. India's National Intelligence Council predicts the number could pass 20 million in 2010. The U.N. estimates the number of Chinese with HIV could hit 10 million in five years. Some 200,000 Chinese also die annually of TB. And a serious flu epidemic could kill millions. "Many investors don't appreciate the economic damage a serious outbreak would cause in our crowded cities," says Subroto Bagchi, chief operating officer of Bangalore info-tech services firm MindTree Consulting Ltd.

## War

India and neighboring Pakistan have fought three times since their independence in 1947—and have had many border skirmishes over Kashmir. Now, both nations possess nuclear weapons, so a war could be catastrophic. New Delhi and Islamabad have recently eased tensions and begun peace talks. But the rise to power of a radical Islamic regime in Pakistan, or election of a stridently Hindu nationalist government in India, could easily reignite tensions. China's biggest flash point remains Taiwan. Beijing has cooled its fiery rhetoric lately, but it still vows to invade should the island declare independence. Any war in the Taiwan Strait would likely involve the U.S. and possibly Japan—China's two biggest trade partners— and paralyze shipping in and out of China's southern ports. It also would likely result in long-term Sino–U.S. tensions that would spill into trade.

It's too much to expect for any developing nation to avoid military, financial, environmental, and health crises for decades. But the test for a great power is how well it manages a great crisis.

---

## Why India May Be Destined to Overtake China

It has only been a few years since Asia bulls have been touting the arrival of the Chinese Century, citing that nation's enormous potential. Now, get ready for predictions of the India Century. That, in fact, was the title of a recent white paper by the Chicago-based consultancy Keystone-India, founded by a group of top economists from Ernst & Young who believe that India is on track to surpass China in growth. "We believe this is India's moment," declares Keystone Chief Economist William T. Wilson.

Hold on, you are probably saying. China has a two decade–long track record of 9.5% average annual growth, exports 10 times as much as India, and dwarfs India as a magnet for foreign investment. By contrast, India has achieved an annual growth rate of 7% or higher only seven times in the past two decades. And largely because of its unruly politics and stifling bureaucracy, it wasn't long ago that economists bemoaned the "Hindu growth rate," implying the nation is simply culturally incapable of achieving high growth.

Even under Keystone's projections, India wouldn't match China's current hypergrowth rates for at least another 15 years. And even by

2050, China's economy would be bigger measured in U.S. dollars. But longer term, Keystone contends India will be in a stronger position. It projects that China's average annual growth will peak at 8.8% over the next five years, and then gradually trend downward to under 7% in the 2020s and around 4% by the 2040s. India's annual growth is projected to rise to around 7.3% by 2010 and stay over 7% until the mid-2030s, and still be in the 6% range until 2050. What's more, Wilson contends that Keystone's forecasts are conservative.

Why is Keystone so bullish? Some of the key reasons:

## Demographics

The biggest reason India has more long-term growth potential is simply that its population is younger and is growing more quickly than China's. Currently, China has 300 million more people than India. But because of its very low birth rate, largely due to the one-child policy, China's population is expected to peak at around 1.45 billion by 2030. India's population is expected to increase by 350 million by 2030, more new people than the U.S., Western Europe, and China combined. India will have 200 million more people than China by mid-century. What's more, China's population is aging rapidly. As a result, the number of working-age Chinese is projected to peak in 2020 and start declining steadily thereafter, while India's workforce will keep growing for at least four more decades. However, India's fertility rate also is declining, meaning future families will have fewer children to support and more to spend on consumption. Development experts call this combination of a growing workforce and declining fertility a "demographic dividend," which helped power explosive economic growth in East Asia's Tiger economies from the 1960s through the early 1990s.

## Capital Efficiency

The big driver of China's economic growth has been massive investment, equal to 40% to 45% of gross domestic product a year, an extraordinarily high rate on world standards—and twice the percentage of India's. In 2004, investment in China was equal to half of its $1.5 trillion in GDP. In that context, China's 9.5% growth rate that year shouldn't be too surprising. "It is staggering how much investment was needed to power Chinese growth in recent years," Wilson notes. "Any nation investing half of GDP in fixed-capital income looks a lot like pre-crisis Asia." India, however, gets much more bang for the rupee. It has achieved 6% average growth with an investment rate half that of China's, around 22% to 23% a year.

## Investment Growth

Many signs point to big increases in investment in India, Wilson says. In fact, he estimates investment in India could reach 35% of GDP within a decade, which would enable it to match China's 9% plus growth. One reason is that the savings rate in India rose from 23.5% of GDP in 2001 to 28.1% in 2004. And because of its growing workforce and the decline in family size, India's savings rate should continue to rise to a projected 37% in 20 years. Since investment is highly correlated to domestic savings, that should translate into higher investment and economic growth. Meanwhile, the rapidly aging population of China means that its savings rate also is likely to drop in the future, as it has in most other nations with graying workforces.

Second, India thus far has gotten by with minimal foreign investment. Keystone notes that in the past four years alone, China has drawn $200 billion more in foreign investment. However, India is planning to open up many long-protected sectors that have great allure to foreign investors—and that could draw huge inflows of money. They include telecom, where Indian demand now is growing even faster than China's, commercial real estate, and department stores. Although some of the reforms have stalled recently due to domestic political opposition, Wilson believes the government will prevail. "If you look at the institutional changes and the number of industries that have liberalized over the past five years, the pace has been phenomenal," he says. Wilson predicts India's real estate sector will draw a huge influx of money from foreign hedge funds, and liberalization of retail will be "the real big bang" for the economy.

## New Entrepreneurs

Indian industry so far has been led by many of the big business families and conglomerates that dominated when India was still a quasi-socialist, heavily regulated economy. They generally have done a good job of taking advantage of new opportunities offered by liberalization since the early 1990s. But the more dynamic companies in India are smaller ones that are led by new generations of entrepreneurs who take greater risks or are more connected to the global economy. These new companies also have more creative managers, argues Debashis Ghosh, another Keystone partner who worked at Ernst & Young. Keystone focuses on researching mid-sized Indian companies with $10 million to $100 million in annual sales. "The bigger companies are still led by old-school types who used to depend on access to government and got huge when there was nobody else in the game. Because they had scale, foreigners had to deal with them," says Ghosh. "Now, though, the top talent from the Indian Institutes of Technology and the Indian Institutes of Management are flowing into the mid-sized sector. That is like getting a management team of all Wharton and Massachusetts Institute of Technology grads." As a result, he contends that the Indian companies of the future are more dynamic than those of China, where management tends to be weak.

## Higher Productivity

India has averaged respectable productivity growth of 2.5% a year over the past two decades. But that can grow sharply, thanks to liberalization of many industries, a literacy rate that has risen from 18% in 1951 to 65% now, and India's rising openness to foreign trade, which has jumped from 15% of GDP in 1991 to 26% now.

## Manufacturing Surge

China dwarfs India as a manufacturing power, especially for export. And it will be a long time before India, with its inadequate infrastructure and components supply base, will be a serious export rival. But in recent years, India's domestic manufacturing industry has been growing strongly. What's more, a number of Indian companies are especially strong in high-end manufacturing, such as auto parts, power generators, and medical equipment, that requires a lot of engineering. In terms of quality and efficiency, several Indian auto parts companies are on par with the U.S. "If you look at engineering work across the board, in industries from pharmaceuticals to telecom, what India is doing is an order of magnitude beyond what China is doing," says Keystone's Ghosh.

Anyone who visits both countries today may find it hard to imagine India overtaking China in economic performance. But when you look at the fundamental drivers—growth in the workforce, fixed investment, and productivity—over the long run the prospect looks a lot more plausible.

# What's Next for China's Miracle?

*Economist Hai Wen on the challenges ahead in maintaining the current momentum in coming years, from exports to health care*

An economics-degree holder from the University of California, Davis, Hai Wen is a leading authority on China's reform and development trends. He serves as senior deputy director of the China Center for Economic Research, a Beijing think tank, and is a professor of economics at Beijing University. He discussed China's economy with Pete Engardio at the center's offices, based in a beautifully restored complex of red-lacquered Qing Dynasty–era buildings with sloping tiled roofs at the Beijing University campus.

**Q: What should China do about its currency?**
**A:** The government has a choice. It can choose high inflation, or it can adjust the yuan. I think sometimes the government is too cautious. The current government will make a choice between a slowdown and inflation. They don't want either.

**Q: Will China's current account continue to soar?**
**A:** I don't think this trend will continue at the same speed. In recent years, especially last year, the capital inflows increased very fast. This will not continue. Also I believe the trade surplus will gradually reduce as China's demand for foreign goods goes up and trade barriers drop.

Another source of foreign reserves is foreign direct investment [FDI]. I believe FDI will continue but also will slow down. The reason FDI is so high is that China has opened some fields that weren't open before, like finance, telecom, and other services. This will continue for 5 to 10 years, but the [pace of growth] will slow down.

Reserves also are high because we have to prepare for the free exchange of the yuan. Once you open up the foreign currency market, there will be an initial shock—and it won't be completely rational.

**Q: Where is China's next export push?**
**A:** I think China will start to export cars very soon, because the market now is in overcapacity. Twenty-seven provinces produce cars, and almost all of the foreign manufacturers are here. Demand will begin to slow, but supply is growing fast. Where will those cars go? To the international market.

Right now prices are high, because prices are set by the state, and there are high taxes.

I spoke with the head of Volkswagen a while back. He said if you reduce taxes, our cars already are competitive with international prices. If the government gives a tax rebate, it will be very easy to export.

Exporting is not an explicitly stated goal, but this is the reality. Just like what happened when color TVs were in oversupply. When China becomes very competitive, it will be in economy cars. So the U.S. and Japan will have to upgrade to more luxury cars. What were mid-priced cars 10 or 15 years ago are now becoming economy cars. A car will be more like a bicycle in 15 years.

**Q: What is China's long-term growth potential?**
**A:** China's labor cost advantage will stay for a long time, if you look at how far it has to go to catch up in terms of per capita GDP with the West. This is why China can have another 20 years of high-speed economic growth.

Another reason high growth can last for decades is the large size of the country and the imbalances that remain. Japan and Korea had small populations, so very quickly their standard of living went up. It was easier to make everyone rich. But on the other hand, they lost competitiveness in wages in just two decades.

**Q: Why is China less capital-efficient than India?**
**A:** One reason is that we still have a planned economy. Much investment is still not really rational. Second, India is at a different stage. India is maybe like China 10 or 15 years ago. In the early stages of opening up, efficiency is higher because capital goes to the most efficient, most productive sectors. But later, the returns gradually slow down. The first dollar is usually the most productive, and the second is less productive.

**Q: Can Chinese companies compete globally?**
**A:** The problem with competing globally is that our companies are too small and too diversified. They are small because of our underdeveloped financial markets. So it is very hard for them to grow up. They could grow very fast by issuing stock or bonds, not just on the domestic market.

On the other hand, they overdiversify. Why? From the company point of view, they still believe in the idea of shared risk. They think in terms of the early Japanese or Korean model, although less than they did before the Asian financial crisis. Also, Chinese companies want self-sufficiency. They want real estate and financial businesses.

These companies should merge. But many are run by first-generation businessmen. Everyone wants to be the head of big companies.

**Q: How would you characterize China's privatization strategy?**
A: We are first going to the stock market. State companies start with the government owning 100%. At the beginning stage, this goes down to maybe 60%, then maybe 40%. Then, the idea is for government to sell all the shares. The state is reducing its shareholding.

Then, the state can use this money to put into pension funds. We need a lot of social security for retired people. Some of this can come from stocks. It is a good idea, but the problem is that when you sell, the stock market collapses. Now the stock market is terrible. This also hurts state-owned enterprises, because their share holdings are dropping more sharply. So it hurts the company.

**Q: What problems does China's aging population present?**
A: Housing isn't a problem, because we're different from the U.S. Older people have a place to live. Also their income is enough to buy food. They have at least enough for the cost of living.

But the most worrisome problem is health care. If people are not covered, they can't afford health care. So the solution is either to provide less medical care or expand coverage. I believe coverage will be limited.

# 3

# The New Global Paradigm

THE RISE OF CHINA AND INDIA is beginning to transform global commerce, industries, and workplaces in many profound ways. China's impact is more visible. Its ballooning trade surplus with the U.S. is a major political issue. "Made in China" is emblazoned on practically everything sold in a Wal-Mart or Home Depot, and factory closures in the U.S. South and Midwest hit entire communities as production shifts to China.

India's impact, however, has been more subtle. The hidden hands of India's armies of highly skilled engineers, analysts, and back-office workers are found in the circuitry designs of semiconductors, the software that powers cell phones and auto navigation systems, the architectural specifications for building a power plant, and the financial statements issued by credit card, insurance, and mutual fund companies. Because India is helping transform international services, design, and analysis, its influence on the economic lives of citizens in the industrialized world may be even more important than that of China.

*BusinessWeek*'s landmark covers "The New Global Job Shift" and "The Rise of India" unveiled how India is transforming services, R&D, and back-office processing work. India's assets include its huge pool of low-cost, highly skilled, English-speaking engineers, scientists, call-center operators, accountants, financial analysts, medical technicians, and other professionals. Indian skilled workers can perform numerous jobs remotely, thanks to the rapid advances in the Internet, interactive design software, and cheap, high-speed telecom connections. These articles stimulated national debate in the U.S. about offshore outsourcing by being among the first to explore the implications for the American workplace.

What accounts for China's and India's strength in these realms? "The China Price" argues that much more than cheap labor, currency manipulation, and unfair trade practices are behind the mainland's growing domination of manufacturing. Just as important are China's massive investments in infrastructure and modern, large-scale manufacturing capacity. Other key factors are the heavy role of multinationals, China's immense components and materials supply base, its huge consumer market, intense domestic competition, and a highly responsive and flexible entrepreneurial mindset. "A Tale of Two Furniture Makers" dissects the factors that give China a big cost advantage over furniture factories in the U.S. South. "Sucking the Life out of Hoover" shows how downsizing by Hoover's factory in Ohio, which could not compete with lower prices of Chinese-produced vacuum cleaners, affected the lives of former workers. "Dipping a Yankee Toe in China" explains the forces that drove one small U.S. manufacturer to shift to China.

Accompanying articles offer an on-the-ground look at big back-office operations and multinational R&D centers in India and the Philippines. In an interview, CEO Nandan Nilekani of India's Infosys Technologies offers his take on how globalization and outsourcing may impact the U.S. economy.

---

# The New Global Job Shift

*The next round of globalization is sending upscale jobs offshore. They include basic research, chip design, engineering—even financial analysis. Can America lose these jobs and still prosper? Who wins? Who loses?*

The sense of resignation inside Bank of America (BofA) was clear from the e-mail dispatch. "The handwriting is on the wall," writes a veteran information-technology specialist who says he has been warned not to talk to the press. In 2000, the Charlotte (N.C.)-based bank needed IT talent so badly it had to outbid rivals. But by 2003, his entire 15-engineer team was told their jobs "wouldn't last through September." BofA had slashed 3,700 of its 25,000 tech and back-office jobs, and an additional 1,000 cuts were imminent.

Corporate downsizings, of course, are part of the ebb and flow of business. These layoffs, though, aren't just happening because demand has dried up. Ex-BofA managers and contractors say one-third of those jobs are headed to India, where work that costs $100 an hour in the U.S. gets done for $20. Many former BofA workers are returning to college to learn new software skills. Some are getting real estate licenses. BofA acknowledged it will outsource up to 1,100 jobs to Indian companies in 2003, but it insists not all India-bound jobs are leading to layoffs.

Cut to India. In dazzling new technology parks rising on the dusty outskirts of the major cities, no one's talking about job losses. Inside Infosys Technologies Ltd.'s impeccably landscaped 22-hectare campus in Bangalore, 250 engineers develop IT applications for BofA. Elsewhere, Infosys staffers process home loans for Greenpoint Mortgage of Novato, Calif. Near Bangalore's airport, at the offices of Wipro Ltd., five radiologists interpret 30 CT scans a day for Massachusetts General Hospital. Not far away, 26-year-old engineer Dharin Shah talks excitedly about his $10,000-a-year job designing third-generation mobile-phone chips, as sun pours through a skylight at the Texas Instruments Inc. research center. Five years ago, an engineer like Shah would have made a beeline for Silicon Valley. Now, he says, "the sky is the limit here."

About 1,600 km north, on an old flour mill site outside New Delhi, all four floors of Wipro Spectramind Ltd.'s sandstone-and-glass building are buzzing at midnight with 2,500 young college-educated men and women. They are processing claims for a major U.S. insurance company and providing help-desk support for a big U.S. Internet service provider—all at a cost up to 60% lower than in the U.S. Seven Wipro Spectramind staff with Ph.D.s in molecular biology sift through scientific research for Western pharmaceutical companies. Behind glass-framed doors, Wipro voice coaches drill staff on how to speak American English. U.S. customers like a familiar accent on the other end of the line.

Cut again to Manila, Shanghai, Budapest, or San Jose, Costa Rica. These cities—and dozens more across the developing world—have become the new back offices for Corporate America, Japan Inc., and Europe GmbH. Never heard of Balazs Zimay? He's a Budapest architect—and just might help design your future dream house. The name SGV & Co. probably means nothing to you. But this Manila firm's accountants may crunch the numbers the next time Ernst & Young International audits your company. Even Bulgaria, Romania, and South Africa, which have a lot of educated people but remain economic backwaters, are tapping the global market for services.

It's globalization's next wave—and one of the biggest trends reshaping the global economy. The first wave started two decades ago with the exodus of jobs making shoes, cheap electronics, and toys to developing countries. After that, simple service work, like processing credit card receipts, and mind-numbing digital toil, like writing software code, began fleeing high-cost countries.

Now, all kinds of knowledge work can be done almost anywhere. "You will see an explosion of work going overseas," says Forrester Research Inc. analyst John C. McCarthy. He goes so far as to predict at least 3.3 million white-collar jobs and $136 billion in wages will shift from the U.S. to low-cost countries by 2015. Europe is joining the trend too. British banks like HSBC Securities Inc. have huge back offices in China and India; French companies are using call centers in Mauritius; and German multinationals from Siemens to roller-bearings maker INA-Schaeffler are hiring in Russia, the Baltics, and Eastern Europe.

The driving forces are digitization, the Internet, and high-speed data networks that girdle the globe. These days, tasks such as drawing up detailed architectural blueprints, slicing and dicing a company's financial disclosures, or designing a revolutionary microprocessor can easily be performed overseas. That's why Intel Inc. and Texas Instruments Inc. are furiously hiring Indian and Chinese engineers, many with graduate degrees, to design chip circuits. Dutch consumer-electronics giant Philips has shifted research and development on most televisions, cell phones, and audio products to Shanghai. In a 2003 PowerPoint presentation, Microsoft Corp. Senior Vice-President Brian Valentine—the No. 2 exec in the company's Windows unit—urged managers to "pick something to move offshore today." In India, said the briefing, you can get "quality work at 50% to 60% of the cost. That's two heads for the price of one."

Even Wall Street jobs paying $80,000 and up are getting easier to transfer. Brokerages like Lehman Brothers Inc. and Bear, Stearns & Co., for example, are starting to use Indian financial analysts for number-crunching work. "A basic business tenet is that things go to the areas where there is the best cost of production," says Ann Livermore, head of services at Hewlett-Packard Co., which has 3,300 software engineers in India. "Now you're going to see the same trends in services that happened in manufacturing."

The rise of a globally integrated knowledge economy is a blessing for developing nations. What it means for the U.S. skilled labor force is less clear. At the least, many white-collar workers may be headed for a tough readjustment. The unprecedented hiring binge in Asia, Eastern Europe, and Latin America comes at a time when companies from Wall Street to Silicon Valley are downsizing at home. In Silicon Valley, employment in the IT sector dropped by 20% from early 2001 to early 2003, according to the nonprofit group Joint Venture Silicon Valley.

Should the West panic? It's too early to tell. Obviously, the bursting of the tech bubble and Wall Street's woes are chiefly behind the layoffs. Also, any impact of offshore hiring is hard to measure, since so far a tiny portion of U.S. white-collar work has jumped overseas. For security and practical reasons, corporations are likely to keep crucial R&D and the bulk of back-office operations close to home. Many jobs can't go anywhere because they require face-to-face contact with customers. Americans will continue to deliver medical care, negotiate deals, audit local companies, and wage legal battles. Talented, innovative people will adjust as they always have.

Indeed, a case can be made that the U.S. will see a net gain from this shift—as with previous globalization waves. In the 1990s, Corporate America had to import hundreds of thousands of immigrants to ease engineering shortages. Now, by sending routine service and engineering tasks to nations with a surplus of educated workers, the U.S. labor force and capital can be redeployed to higher-value industries and cutting-edge R&D. "Silicon Valley doesn't need to have all the tech development in the world," says Doug Henton, president of Collaborative Economics in Mountview, Calif. "We need very-good-paying jobs. Any R&D that is routine can probably go." Silicon Valley types already talk about the next wave of U.S. innovation coming from the fusion of software, nanotech, and life sciences.

Globalization should also keep services prices in check, just as it did with clothes, appliances, and home tools when manufacturing went offshore. Companies will be able to keep shaving overhead costs and improving efficiency. "Our comparative advantage may shift to other fields," says City University of New York economist Robert E. Lipsey, a trade specialist. "And if productivity is high, then the U.S. will maintain a high standard of living." By spurring economic development in nations such as India, meanwhile, U.S. companies will have bigger foreign markets for their goods and services.

For companies adept at managing a global workforce, the benefits can be huge. Sure, entrusting administration and R&D to far-flung foreigners is risky. But Corporate America already has become comfortable hiring outside companies to handle everything from product design and tech support to employee benefits. Letting such work cross national boundaries isn't a radical leap. Now, American Express, Dell Computer, Eastman Kodak, and other companies can offer round-the-clock customer care while keeping costs in check. What's more, immigrant Asian engineers in the U.S. labs of Texas Instruments, IBM, and Intel for decades have played a big, hidden role in American tech breakthroughs. The difference now is that Indian and Chinese engineers are managing R&D teams in their home countries. General Electric Co., for example, employs some 6,000 scientists and engineers in 10 foreign countries. GE Medical Services integrates magnet, flat-panel, and diagnostic imaging technologies from labs in China, Israel, Hungary, France, and India in everything from its new X-ray devices to $1 million CT scanners. "The real advantage is that we can tap the world's best talent," says GE Medical Global Supply Chain Vice-President Dee Miller.

That's the good side of the coming realignment. There are hazards as well. During previous go-global drives, many companies ended up repatriating manufacturing and design work because they felt they were losing control of core businesses or found them too hard to coordinate. In a 2002 Gartner Inc. survey of 900 big U.S. companies that outsource IT work offshore, a majority complained of difficulty communicating and meeting deadlines. As a result, predicts Gartner Inc. Research Director Frances Karamouzis, many newcomers will stumble in the first few years as they begin using offshore service workers.

A thornier question: What happens if all those displaced white-collar workers can't find greener pastures? Sure, tech specialists, payroll administrators, and Wall Street analysts will land new jobs. But will they be able to make the same money as before? It's possible that lower salaries for skilled work will outweigh the gains in corporate efficiency. "If foreign countries specialize in high-skilled areas where we have an advantage, we could be worse off," says Harvard University economist Robert Z. Lawrence, a prominent free-trade advocate. "I still have faith that globalization will make us better off, but it's no more than faith."

If the worries prove valid, that could reshape the globalization debate. Until now, the adverse impact of free trade has been confined largely to blue-collar workers. But if more politically powerful middle-class Americans take a hit as white-collar jobs move offshore, the opposition to free trade could broaden.

When it comes to developing nations, however, it's hard to see a downside. Especially for those countries loaded with college grads who speak Western languages, outsourced white-collar work will likely contribute to economic development even more than new factories making sneakers or mobile phones. By 2008 in India, IT work and other service exports will generate $57 billion in revenues, employ 4 million people, and account for 7% of gross domestic product, predicts a joint study by McKinsey & Co. and NASSCOM, an Indian software association.

What makes this trend so viable is the explosion of college graduates in low-wage nations. In the Philippines, a country of 75 million that churns out 380,000 college grads each year, there's an oversupply of accountants trained in U.S. accounting standards. India already has a staggering 520,000 IT engineers, with starting salaries of around $5,000. U.S. schools produce only 35,000 mechanical engineers a year; China graduates twice as many. "There is a tremendous pool of well-trained people in China," says Johan A. van Splunter, Philips' Asia chief executive.

William H. Gates III, for one, is dipping into that pool. Although Microsoft started later than many rivals, it is moving quickly to catch up. In November 2002, Chairman Gates announced his company will invest $400 million in India over three years. That's on top of the $750 million it's spending over three years on R&D and outsourcing in China. At the company's Beijing research lab, one-third of the 180 programmers have Ph.D.s from U.S. universities. The group helped develop the "digital ink" that makes handwriting show up on Microsoft's new tablet PCs and submitted four scientific papers on computer graphics at 2002's prestigious Siggraph conference in San Antonio. Hyderabad, India, meanwhile, is key to Microsoft's push into business software.

This is no sweatshop work. Just two years out of college, Gaurav Daga, 22, is India project manager for software that lets programs running on Unix-based computers interact smoothly with Windows applications. Daga's $11,000 salary is a princely sum in a nation with a per capita annual income of $500, where a two-bedroom flat goes for $125 a month. Microsoft is adding 10 Indians a month to its 150-engineer center and indirectly employs hundreds more as IT contractors. "It's definitely a cultural change to use foreign workers," says Sivaramakichenane Somasegar, Microsoft's vice-president for Windows engineering. "But if I can save a dollar, hallelujah."

Corporations are letting foreign operations handle internal finances as well. Procter & Gamble Co.'s 650 Manila employees, most of whom have business and finance degrees, help prepare P&G's tax returns around the world. "All the processing can be done here, with just final submission done to local tax authorities" in the U.S. and other countries, says Arun Khanna, P&G's Manila-based Asia accounting director.

Virtually every sector of the financial industry is undergoing a similar revolution. Processing insurance claims, selling stocks, and analyzing companies can all be done in Asia for one-third to half of the cost in the U.S. or Europe. Wall Street investment banks and brokerages, under mounting pressure to offer independent research to investors, are buying equity analysis, industry reports, and summaries of financial disclosures from outfits such as Smart Analyst Inc. and OfficeTiger that employ financial analysts in India. By mining databases over the Web, offshore staff can scrutinize an individual's credit history, access corporate public financial disclosures, and troll oceans of economic statistics. "Everybody these days is drawing on the same electronic reservoir of data," says Ravi Aron, who teaches management at the Wharton School at the University of Pennsylvania.

Architectural work is going global too. Fluor Corp. of Aliso Viejo, Calif., employs 1,200 engineers and drafters in the Philippines, Poland, and India to turn layouts of giant industrial facilities into detailed specs and blueprints. For a multibillion-dollar petrochemical plant Fluor is designing in Saudi Arabia, a job requiring 50,000 separate construction plans, 200 young Filipino engineers earning less than $3,000 a year collaborate in real time via Web portals with elite U.S. and British engineers making up to $90,000. The principal Filipino engineer on plumbing design, 35-year-old Art Aycardo, pulls down $1,100 a month—enough to buy a Mitsubishi Lancer, send his three children to private school, and take his wife on a recent U.S. trip. Fluor CEO Alan Boeckmann makes no apologies. At a recent meeting in Houston, employees asked point-blank why he is sending high-paying jobs to Manila. His response: The Manila operation knocks up to 15% off Fluor's project prices. "We have developed this into a core competitive advantage," Boeckmann says.

It's not just a game for big players: San Francisco architect David N. Marlatt farms out work on Southern California homes selling for $300,000 to $1 million. He fires off two-dimensional layouts to architect Zimay's PC in Budapest. Two days later, Marlatt gets back blueprints and 3-D computer models that he delivers to the contractor. Zimay charges $18 an hour, versus the up to $65 Marlatt would pay in America. "In the U.S., it is hard to find people to do this modeling," Zimay says. "But in Hungary, there are too many architects."

So far, white-collar globalization probably hasn't made a measurable dent in U.S. salaries. Still, it would be a mistake to dismiss the trend. Consider America's 10 million-strong IT workforce. In 2000, senior software engineers were offered up to $130,000 a year, says Matt Milano, New York sales manager for placement firm Atlantis Partners. The same job in 2003 paid up to $100,000. Entry-level computer help-desk staffers would fetch about $55,000 then. Now they get as little as $35,000. "Several times a day, clients tell me they are sending this work offshore," says Milano. Companies that used to pay such IT service providers as IBM, Accenture, and Electronic Data Services $200 an hour now pay as little as $70, says Vinnie Mirchandani, CEO of IT outsourcing consultant Jetstream Group. One reason, besides the tech crash itself, is that Indian providers like Wipro, Infosys, and Tata charge as little as $20. That's why Accenture and EDS, which had few staff in India in 2000, now have several thousand each.

Outsourcing experts say the big job migration has just begun. "This trend is just starting to crystallize now because every chief information officer's top agenda item is to cut budget," says Gartner's Karamouzis. Globalization trailblazers, such as GE, AmEx, and Citibank, have spent a decade going through the learning curve and now are ramping up fast. More cautious companies—insurers, utilities, and the like—are entering the fray. Karamouzis expects 40% of America's top 1,000 companies will at least have an overseas pilot project under way within two years. The really big offshore push won't be until 2010 or so, she predicts, when global white-collar sourcing practices are standardized.

If big layoffs result at home, corporations and Washington may have to brace for a backlash. Already, New Jersey legislators are pushing a bill that would block the state from outsourcing public jobs overseas. At Boeing Co., an anxious union is trying to ward off more job shifts to the aircraft maker's new 350-person R&D center in Moscow.

The truth is, the rise of the global knowledge industry is so recent that most economists haven't begun to fathom the implications. For developing nations, the big beneficiaries will be those offering the speediest and cheapest telecom links, investor-friendly policies, and ample college grads. In the West, it's far less clear who will be the big winners and losers. But we'll soon find out.

---

# The Rise of India

*Growth is only just starting, but the country's brainpower is already reshaping Corporate America*

As you pull into General Electric's John F. Welch Technology Centre, a uniformed guard waves you through an iron gate. Once inside, you leave the dusty, traffic-clogged streets of Bangalore and enter a leafy campus of low buildings that gleam in the sun. Bright hallways lined with plants and abstract art—"it encourages creativity," explains a manager—lead through laboratories where physicists, chemists, metallurgists, and computer engineers huddle over gurgling beakers, electron microscopes, and spectrophotometers. Except for the female engineers wearing saris and the soothing Hindi pop music wafting through the open-air dining pavilion, this could be GE's giant research-and-development facility in the upstate New York town of Niskayuna.

It's more like Niskayuna than you might think. The center's 1,800 engineers—a quarter of them have Ph.D.s—are engaged in fundamental research for most of GE's 13 divisions. In one lab, they tweak the aerodynamic designs of turbine-engine blades. In another, they're scrutinizing the molecular structure of materials to be used in DVDs for short-term use in which the movie is automatically erased after a few days. In another, technicians have rigged up a working model of a GE plastics plant in Spain and devised a way to boost output there by 20%. Patents? From the time the center opened in 2000, engineers here had filed for 95 in the U.S. by late 2003.

Pretty impressive for a place that just a few years ago was a fallow plot of land. Even more impressive, the Bangalore operation has become vital to the future of one of America's biggest, most profitable companies. "The game here really isn't about saving costs but to speed innovation and generate growth for the company," explains Bolivian-born Managing Director Guillermo Wille, one of the center's few non-Indians.

The Welch Centre is at the vanguard of one of the biggest mind-melds in history. Plenty of Americans know of India's inexpensive software writers and have figured out that the nice clerk who booked their air ticket is in Delhi. But these are just superficial signs of India's capabilities. Quietly but with breathtaking speed, India and its millions of world-class engineering, business, and medical graduates are becoming enmeshed in America's New Economy in ways most of us barely imagine. "India has always had brilliant, educated people," says tech-trend forecaster Paul Saffo of the Institute for the Future in Menlo Park, Calif. "Now Indians are taking the lead in colonizing cyberspace."

This techno takeoff is wonderful for India—but terrifying for many Americans. In fact, India's emergence is fast turning into the latest Rorschach test on globalization. Many see India's digital workers as bearers of new prosperity to a deserving nation and vital partners of Corporate America. Others see them as shock troops in the final assault on good-paying jobs. Howard Rubin, executive vice-president of Meta Group Inc., a Stamford (Conn.) information-technology consultant, notes that big U.S. companies are shedding 500 to 2,000 IT staffers at a time. "These people won't get reabsorbed into the workforce until they get the right skills," he says. Even Indian execs see the problem. "What happened in manufacturing is happening in services," says Azim H. Premji, chairman of IT supplier Wipro Ltd. "That raises a lot of social issues for the U.S."

No wonder India is at the center of a brewing storm in America, where politicians are starting to view offshore outsourcing as the root of the jobless recovery in tech and services. An outcry in Indiana in 2003 prompted the state to cancel a $15 million IT contract with India's Tata Consulting. The telecom workers' union is up in arms, and Congress is probing whether the security of financial and medical records is at risk. As hiring explodes in India, the jobless rate among U.S. software engineers had more than doubled, to 4.6%, by late 2003. The rate was 6.7% for electrical engineers and 7.7% for network administrators. In all, the Bureau of Labor Statistics reported that 234,000 IT professionals were unemployed in 2003.

The biggest cause of job losses, of course, was the U.S. economic downturn. Still, there's little denying that the offshore shift was a factor. By some estimates, there are more IT engineers in Bangalore (150,000) than in Silicon Valley (120,000). Meta figures at least one-third of new IT development work for big U.S. companies is done overseas, with India the biggest site. And India could start grabbing jobs from other sectors. A.T. Kearney Inc. predicts that 500,000 financial-services jobs will go offshore by 2008. Indiana notwithstanding, U.S. governments are increasingly using India to manage everything from accounting to their food-stamp programs. Even the U.S. Postal Service is taking work there. Auto engineering and drug research is next.

## More Science in Schools

Tech luminary Andrew S. Grove, CEO of Intel Corp., warns that "it's a very valid question" to ask whether America could eventually lose its overwhelming dominance in IT, just as it did in electronics manufacturing. Plunging global telecom costs, lower engineering wages abroad, and new interactive-design software are driving revolutionary change, Grove said at a software conference in October 2003. "From a technical and productivity standpoint, the engineer sitting 6,000 miles away might as well be in the next cubicle and on the local area network." To maintain America's edge, he said, Washington and U.S. industry must double software productivity through more R&D investment and science education.

But there's also a far more positive view—that harnessing Indian brainpower will greatly boost American tech and services leadership by filling a big projected shortfall in skilled labor as baby boomers retire. That's especially possible with smarter U.S. policy. Companies from GE Medical Systems to Cummins to Microsoft to enterprise-software firm PeopleSoft that are hiring in India say they aren't laying off any U.S. engineers. Instead, by augmenting their U.S. R&D teams with the 260,000 engineers pumped out by Indian schools each year, they can afford to throw many more brains at a task and speed up product launches, develop more prototypes, and upgrade quality. A top electrical or chemical engineering grad from Indian Institutes of Technology (IITs) earns about $10,000 a year—roughly one-eighth of U.S. starting pay. Says Rajat Gupta, an IIT-Delhi grad and senior partner at consulting firm McKinsey & Co.: "Offshoring work will spur innovation, job creation, and dramatic increases in productivity that will be passed on to the consumer."

Whether you regard the trend as disruptive or beneficial, one thing is clear. Corporate America no longer feels it can afford to ignore India. "There's just no place left to squeeze" costs in the U.S., says Chris Disher, a Booz Allen Hamilton Inc. outsourcing specialist. "That's why every CEO is looking at India, and every board is asking about it." neoIT, a consultant advising U.S. clients on how to set up shop in India, says it has been deluged by big companies that have been slow to move offshore. "It is getting to a state where companies are literally desperate," says Bangalore-based neoIT managing partner Avinash Vashistha.

As a result of this shift, few aspects of U.S. business remain untouched. The hidden hands of skilled Indians are present in the interactive Web sites of companies such as Lehman Brothers and Boeing display ads in your Yellow Pages, and the electronic circuitry powering your Apple Computer iPod. While Wall Street sleeps, Indian analysts digest the latest financial disclosures of U.S. companies and file reports in time for the next trading day. Indian staff troll the private medical and financial records of U.S. consumers to help determine if they are good risks for insurance policies, mortgages, or credit cards from American Express Co. and J.P. Morgan Chase & Co.

By 2008, forecasts McKinsey, IT services and back-office work in India will swell fivefold, to a $57 billion annual export industry employing 4 million people and accounting for 7% of India's gross domestic product. That growth is inspiring more of the best and brightest to stay home rather than migrate. "We work in world-class companies, we're growing, and it's exciting," says Anandraj Sengupta, 24, an IIT grad and young star at GE's Welch Centre, where he has filed for two patents. "The opportunities exist here in India."

If India can turn into a fast-growth economy, it will be the first developing nation that used its brainpower, not natural resources or the raw muscle of factory labor, as the catalyst. And this huge country desperately needs China-style growth. For all its R&D labs, India remains visibly Third World. IT service exports employ less than 1% of the workforce. Per capita income is just $460, and 300 million Indians subsist on $1 a day or less. Lethargic courts can take 20 years to resolve contract disputes. And what pass for highways in Bombay are choked, crumbling roads lined with slums, garbage heaps, and homeless migrants sleeping on bare pavement. More than a third of India's 1 billion citizens are illiterate, and just 60% of homes have electricity. Most bureaucracies are bloated, corrupt, and dysfunctional. The government's 10% budget deficit is alarming. Tensions between Hindus and Muslims always seem poised to explode, and the risk of war with nuclear-armed Pakistan is ever-present.

So it's little wonder that, compared to China with its modern infrastructure and disciplined workforce, India is far behind in exports and as a magnet for foreign investment. While China began reforming in 1979, India only started to emerge from self-imposed economic isolation after a harrowing financial crisis in 1991. China has seen annual growth often exceeding 10%, far better than India's decade-long average of 6%.

## In the Valley's Marrow

Still, this deep source of low-cost, high-IQ, English-speaking brain-power may soon have a more far-reaching impact on the U.S. than China. Manufacturing—China's strength—accounts for just 14% of U.S. output and 11% of jobs. India's forte is services—which make up 60% of the U.S. economy and employ two-thirds of its workers. And Indian knowledge workers are making their way up the New Economy food chain, mastering tasks requiring analysis, marketing acumen, and creativity.

This means India is penetrating America's economic core. The 900 engineers at Texas Instruments Inc.'s Bangalore chip-design operation boast 225 patents. Intel Inc.'s Bangalore campus is leading worldwide research for the company's 32-bit microprocessors for servers and wireless chips. "These are corporate crown jewels," says Intel India President Ketan Sampat. India is even getting hard-wired into Silicon Valley. Venture capitalists say anywhere from one-third to three-quarters of the software, chip, and e-commerce start-ups they now back have Indian R&D teams from the get-go. "We can barely imagine investing in a company without at least asking what their plans are for India," says Sequoia Capital partner Michael Moritz, who nurtured Google, Flextronics, and Agile Software. "India has seeped into the marrow of the Valley."

It's seeping into the marrow of Main Street too. In 2003, the tax returns of some 20,000 Americans were prepared by $500-a-month CPAs such as Sandhya Iyer, 24, in the Bombay office of Bangalore's MphasiS. After reading scanned seed and fertilizer invoices, soybean sales receipts, W2 forms, and investment records from a farmer in Kansas, Iyer fills in the farmer's 82-page return. "He needs to amortize these," she types next to an entry for new machinery and a barn. A U.S. CPA reviews and signs the finished return. In 2004, up to 200,000 U.S. returns were expected to be done in India, says CCH Inc. in Riverwoods, Ill., a supplier of accounting software. And it's not only Big Four firms that are outsourcing. "We are seeing lots of firms with 30 to 200 CPAs—even single practitioners," says CCH Sales Vice-President Mike Sabbatis.

The gains in efficiency could be tremendous. Indeed, India is accelerating a sweeping reengineering of Corporate America. Companies are shifting bill payment, human resources, and other functions to new, paperless centers in India. To be sure, many corporations have run into myriad headaches, ranging from poor communications to inconsistent quality. Dell Inc. recently said it is moving computer support for corporate clients back to the U.S. Still, a raft of studies by Deloitte Research, Gartner, Booz Allen, and other consultants find that companies shifting work to India have cut costs by 40% to 60%. Companies can offer customer support and use pricey computer gear 24/7. U.S. banks can process mortgage applications in three hours rather than three days. Predicts Nandan M. Nilekani, managing director of Bangalore-based Infosys Technologies Ltd.: "Just like China drove down costs in manufacturing and Wal-Mart in retail," he says, "India will drive down costs in services."

But deflation will also mean plenty of short-term pain for U.S. companies and workers who never imagined they'd face foreign rivals. Consider America's $240 billion IT-services industry. Indian players led by Infosys, Tata, and Wipro got their big breaks during the Y2K scare, when U.S. outfits needed all the software help they could get. Indians still have less than 3% of the market. But by undercutting giants such as Accenture, IBM, and Electronic Data Systems by a third or more for software and consulting, they've altered the industry's pricing. "The Indian labor card is unbeatable," says Chief Technology Officer John Parkinson of consultant Capgemini Ernst & Young. "We don't know how to use technology to make up the difference."

## Wrenching Change

Many U.S. white-collar workers are also in for wrenching change. A study by McKinsey Global Institute, which believes offshore outsourcing is good, also notes that only 36% of Americans displaced in the previous two decades found jobs at the same or higher pay. The incomes of a quarter of them dropped 30% or more. Given the higher demands of employers, who want technicians adept at innovation and management, it could take years before today's IT workers land solidly on their feet.

India's IT workers, in contrast, sense an enormous opportunity. The country has long possessed some basics of a strong market-driven economy: private corporations, democratic government, Western accounting standards, an active stock market, widespread English use, and schools strong in computer science and math. But its bureaucracy suffocated industry with onerous controls and taxes, and the best scientific and business minds went to the U.S., where the 1.8 million Indian expatriates rank among the most successful immigrant groups.

Now, many talented Indians feel a sense of optimism India hasn't experienced in decades. "IT is driving India's boom, and we in the younger generation can really deliver the country from poverty," says Rhythm Tyagi, 22, a master's degree student at the new Indian Institute of Information Technology in Bangalore. The campus is completely wired for Wi-Fi and boasts classrooms with videoconferencing to beam sessions to 300 other colleges.

That confidence is finally spurring the government to tackle many of the problems that have plagued India for so long. Since 2001, Delhi has been furiously building a network of highways. Modern airports are next. Deregulation of the power sector should lead to new capacity. Free education for girls to age 14 is a national priority. "One by one, the government is solving the bottlenecks," says Deepak Parekh, a financier who heads the quasi-governmental Infrastructure Development Finance Co.

## Future Vision

India also is working to assure that it will be able to meet future demand for knowledge workers at home and abroad. India produces 3.1 million college graduates a year, but that's expected to double by 2010. The number of engineering colleges is slated to grow 50%, to nearly 1,600, by 2007. Of course, not all are good enough to produce the world-class grads of elite schools like the IITs, which accepted just 3,500 of 178,000 applicants in 2002. So there's a growing movement to boost faculty salaries and reach more students nationwide through broadcasts. India's rich diaspora population is chipping in too. Prominent Indian Americans helped found the new Indian School of Business, a tie-up with Wharton School and Northwestern University's Kellogg Graduate School of Management that lured most of its faculty from the U.S. Meanwhile, the six IIT campuses are tapping alumni for donations and research links with Stanford, Purdue, and other top science universities. "Our mission is to become one of the leading science institutions in the world," says director Ashok Mishra of IIT-Bombay, which raised $16 million from alumni between 1998 and 2003.

If India manages growth well, its huge population could prove an asset. By 2020, 47% of Indians will be between 15 and 59, compared with 35% now. The working-age populations of the U.S. and China are projected to shrink. So India is destined to have the world's largest population of workers and consumers. That's a big reason why Goldman, Sachs & Co. thinks India will be able to sustain 7.5% annually. Skeptics fear U.S. companies are going too far, too fast in linking up with this giant. But having watched the success of the likes of GE Capital International Services, many execs feel they have no choice. Inside GECIS's Bangalore center—one of four in India—Gauri Puri, a 28-year-old dentist, is studying an insurance claim for a root-canal operation to see if it's covered in a certain U.S. patient's dental plan. Two floors above, members of a 550-strong analytics team are immersed in spreadsheets filled with a boggling array of data as they devise statistical models to help GE sales staff understand the needs, strengths, and weaknesses of customers and rivals. Other staff prepare data for GE annual reports, write enterprise resource-planning software, and process $35 billion worth of global invoices. Said then-GE Capital India President Pramod Bhasin in 2003: "We are mission-critical to GE." The 700 business processes done in India save the company $340 million a year, he says. GECIS has since been spun off as a new company, Genpact.

Indian finance whizzes are a godsend to Wall Street, too, where brokerages are under pressure to produce more independent research. Many are turning to outfits such as OfficeTiger in the southern city of

Madras. The company employs 1,200 people who write research reports and do financial analysis for eight Wall Street firms. Morgan Stanley, J.P. Morgan, Goldman Sachs, and other big investment banks are hiring their own armies of analysts and back-office staff. Many are piling into Mindspace, a sparkling new 140-acre city-within-a-city abutting Bombay's urban squalor. Some 3 million square feet are already leased to Western finance firms. Morgan Stanley fills several floors of a new building.

For Silicon Valley start-ups, Indian engineers let them stretch R&D budgets. PortalPlayer Inc., a Santa Clara (Calif.) maker of multimedia chips and embedded software for portable devices such as music players, has hired 100 engineers in India and the U.S. who update each other daily at 9 a.m. and 10 p.m. J. A. Chowdary, CEO of PortalPlayer's Hyderabad subsidiary Pinexe, says the company has shaved up to six months off the development cycle—and cut R&D costs by 40%. Impressed, venture capitalists have pumped $82 million into PortalPlayer.

## More Bang for the Buck

Old Economy companies are benefiting too. Engine maker Cummins is using its new R&D center in Pune to develop the sophisticated computer models needed to design upgrades and prototypes electronically. Says International Vice-President Steven M. Chapman: "We'll be able to introduce five or six new engines a year instead of two" on the same $250 million R&D budget—without a single U.S. layoff.

The nagging fear in the U.S., though, is that such assurances will ring hollow over time. In other industries, the shift of low-cost production work to East Asia was followed by engineering. Now, South Korea and Taiwan are global leaders in notebook PCs, wireless phones, memory chips, and digital displays. As companies rely more on IT engineers in India and elsewhere, the argument goes, the U.S. could cede control of other core technologies. "If we continue to offshore high-skilled professional jobs, the U.S. risks surrendering its leading role in innovation," warns John W. Steadman, incoming U.S. president of Institute of Electrical & Electronics Engineers Inc. That could also happen if many foreigners—who account for 60% of U.S. science grads and who have been key to U.S. tech success—no longer go to America to launch their best ideas.

Throughout U.S. history, workers have been pushed off farms and out of textile mills and steel plants. In the end, the workforce has managed to move up to better-paying, higher-quality jobs. That could well happen again. There will still be a crying need for U.S. engineers, for example. But what's called for are engineers who can work closely with customers, manage research teams, and creatively improve business processes. Displaced technicians who lack such skills will need retraining; those entering school will need broader educations.

Adapting to the India effect will be traumatic, but there's no sign Corporate America is turning back. Yet the India challenge also presents an enormous opportunity for the U.S. If America can handle the transition right, the end result could be a brain gain that accelerates productivity and innovation. India and the U.S., nations that barely interacted 15 years ago, could turn out to be the ideal economic partners for the new century.

## The Way, Way Back Office

Drop by the Manila offices of Source 1 Asia at two or three in the morning, and you might think you've stumbled into some late-night college cram session. Some 750 men and women in their early twenties, jazzed on cappuccino and junk food, are pulling all-nighters in front of their computers. The walls of the cavernous room are painted hot pink, purple, and lime green. But it's not Calculus 101 that has these Filipinos burning the midnight oil. They're busy handling credit card queries from ChevronTexaco Corp. customers and walking users through the intricacies of Microsoft Corp. software.

Say "call center" to most Americans, and they think of tedious, low-paid, dead-end jobs fielding complaints about phone bills or bank statements. But in the Philippines, call centers are viewed as a gateway to exciting careers working on behalf of the best service companies in the world. Some 10,000 Filipinos, almost all with college degrees, staff 45 such centers around the clock, seven days a week. Companies like American Express, Eastman Kodak, Intel, Microsoft, and Dell Computer are flocking to the Philippines, lured by the country's low wages, generous tax breaks, and ample supply of English speakers. The call-center staff "are a very, very talented pool of people," says Arun Khanna, Procter & Gamble's Manila-based accounting director. "They're committed, and comfortable with being trained and taking on responsibility."

Philip Sy is a typical call-center worker. After graduating in 1998 from the University of the Philippines with a degree in German and Italian, Sy took a $250-a-month job at Source 1 providing assistance to people installing software on their computers. Now 28, Sy is a Source 1 operations manager overseeing 150 people and earning $13,000 a year, a small fortune in a country where 40% of the population lives on less than a dollar a day. "Considering the career growth opportunities, a job here is pretty desirable," says Sy, practicing yo-yo tricks as he wanders the floor monitoring calls. Another Source 1 employee, Karen Betita, 25, is the daughter of a diplomat and has a college degree in communications. She says she views the job as a good starting place for a marketing career.

Because they are able to hire some of the country's best talent, call centers in the Philippines are moving far beyond telemarketing. At the offices of Tampa (Fla.)-based Sykes Enterprises in the heart of Manila's Makati financial district, some of the 2,200 agents troubleshoot for control systems for oil rigs made by a U.S. manufacturer. "The salary difference between a qualified engineer in the U.S. and here is colossal—at least 10 times," says Michael Henderson, Asia managing director at Sykes. Others advise customers interested in life insurance and mutual funds offered by a major U.S. financial services company that Source 1 says it cannot identify. To get the licenses needed to market U.S. securities, Sykes flies Filipino staff to the U.S. and

Hong Kong to take tests given by the National Association of Securities Dealers. Others at Sykes provide online support for users of Microsoft's Internet-access service, MSN 8.0, and help buyers figure out how to operate Kodak digital cameras. Says 24-year-old Sykes employee Michelle Abreu: "I see myself working in the industry for a long time."

It's that kind of attitude—and the fact that good jobs are scarce in the Philippines—that helps keep turnover at call centers under 10% a year, compared with upwards of 70% in the U.S. Indeed, Nathan Shapiro, Source 1's director of Asian operations, says he has just one headache: The Filipino employees are too polite, leading to longer, costly phone chats. "We have to teach them to be more rude," says Shapiro. That may be the one area in which U.S. service providers can't be beaten.

---

# For India's Tech Grads, There's No Place Like Home

*Who needs Silicon Valley when Bangalore offers fulfilling work and an upwardly mobile lifestyle?*

Time was, the career path for any Indian whiz kid with ambition and a degree in electrical engineering from one of the country's top technology institutes was clear. These young engineers headed straight for Silicon Valley, Boston, or Austin, Tex., to work at a premier U.S. semiconductor company. Then, after years in the lab, the most talented—and lucky—among them might befriend an Indian venture capitalist and start up a new chip company.

No longer. These days, India's best and brightest tech minds need move no farther than Bangalore, where they can do cutting-edge work for the rapidly expanding labs of Intel, Texas Instruments, Hewlett-Packard, and other tech giants. India has some 7,500 chip designers working for 65 companies, and their ranks are swelling by 20% a year. Their pay, starting at $8,000 to $10,000 annually, may be a pittance compared with what's available in Silicon Valley. But in India, it's enough to enjoy a comfortable, fulfilling life.

Ask Dharin Shah. Tall, rail-thin, and with intense dark eyes, 26-year-old Shah sees his $10,000-a-year job at Texas Instruments Inc. as the fulfillment of a childhood dream. The son of a Gujarat government bank employee, Shah graduated near the top of his class at Bangalore's prestigious Indian Institute of Science, where he earned a master's in instrumentation engineering. Today, Shah is making a name for himself as a member of a 15-engineer team designing custom chips for next-generation cell phones and telecom routers and switches, a core TI business. "He has depth, innovates, and solves problems that sometimes even senior folks in Dallas [TI's headquarters] miss," says his project manager, R. Harinath.

His position and his salary place Shah well within India's upwardly mobile middle class. With a moped and an apartment in a decent building, "I don't feel the need" to move to the U.S., says Shah. On weekends, he indulges his passions for cycling and bird-watching in the lush woods near Bangalore and volunteers as a mathematics and science teacher at a home for girls from poor families. "The opportunity is here in India, and I need to contribute to society," he says.

These days, India has legions of talented engineers who, like Shah, are willing to forsake the glamour and financial gratification of Silicon Valley to stay close to home. That's a big reason why Indian cities such as Bangalore seem destined to emerge as some of the hottest innovation zones of the 21st century. And chip companies aren't the only ones recruiting Indian talent. Microsoft Corp., for example, is hiring 10 software engineers like Gaurav Daga every month. Daga, 22, develops software for Microsoft from a teak-paneled, air-conditioned office in Hyderabad—a far cry from the dilapidated industrial area in Madras where his father works as a metals trader. "Microsoft was my first, second, and third choice" for a job, Daga says.

The shift is chipping away at India's conservative mindset. While some parents object to their daughters entering the male-dominated engineering world, for example, others embrace the opportunity it gives them. Sindhu Kumar, 25, one of only 20 women in her college engineering class of 400, is already a project leader at Wipro Technologies, fast emerging as one of the world's top contract engineering houses for Western electronics companies. Her current task: speeding up and improving the print quality of Hewlett-Packard Co.'s inkjet printers. Kumar's opportunities far exceed those available to her father, an engineer who could only land a job as a civil servant in Uttar Pradesh. Soon, she plans to buy a car for her parents "to give something back to them, finally, for all the support they gave me."

Almost without exception, India's young engineers want to give something back—both to their families and to their country. "There's a lot of idealism among these young Indians," says Rukmini Bhaya Nair, a professor of humanities at the Indian Institute of Technology in New Delhi. They're "the new magicians for India." If engineers and young professionals like Shah and Kumar continue to work their magic, the biggest payback may well be the development of their country.

## The China Price

*They are the three scariest words in U.S. industry. Cut your price at least 30% or lose your customers. Nearly every manufacturer is vulnerable—from furniture to networking gear. The result: A massive shift in economic power is under way.*

From the rich walnut paneling and carved arches to the molded Italian Renaissance patterns on the ceiling, the circa 1925 council chamber room of Akron's municipal hall evokes a time when America's manufacturing heartland was at the peak of its power. But when the U.S.–China Economic & Security Review Commission, a congressionally appointed panel, convened there on Sept. 23, 2004, it was not to discuss power but decline. One after another, economists, union officials, and small manufacturers took the microphone to describe the devastation Chinese competitors are inflicting on U.S. industries, from kitchenware and car tires to electronic circuit boards.

These aren't stories of mundane sunset industries equipped with antiquated technology. David W. Johnson, CEO of 92-year-old Summitville Tiles Inc. in Summitville, Ohio, described how imports forced him to shut a state-of-the-art, $120 million tile-making plant four football fields long, sending his company into Chapter 11 bankruptcy protection. Now, a tenfold surge in high-quality Chinese imports at "below our manufacturing costs" threatens to polish Summitville Tiles off. Makers of precision machine tools and plastic molds—essential supports of America's industrial architecture—told how their business has shrunk as home-appliance makers have shifted manufacturing from Ohio to China. Despite buying the best computer-controlled gear, Douglas S. Bartlett reported that at his Cary (Ill.)-based Bartlett Manufacturing Co., a maker of high-end circuit boards for aerospace and automotive customers, sales are half the late-1990s level and the workforce is one-third smaller. He waved a board Bartlett makes for a U.S. Navy submarine-detection device. His buyer says he can get the same board overseas for 40% less. "From experience I can only assume this is the Chinese price," Bartlett said. "We have faced competition in the past. What is dramatically different about China is that they are about half the price."

## Where the Jobs Went

"The China price." They are the three scariest words in U.S. industry. In general, it means 30% to 50% less than what you can possibly make something for in the U.S. In the worst cases, it means below your cost of materials. Makers of apparel, footware, electric appliances, and plastics products, which have been shutting U.S. factories for decades, know well the futility of trying to match the China price. It has been a big factor in the loss of 2.7 million manufacturing jobs since 2000. Meanwhile, America's deficit with China keeps soaring to new records. It passed $150 billion in 2004. Now, manufacturers and workers who never thought they had to worry about the China price are confronting the new math of the mainland. These companies had once held their own against imports, mostly because their businesses required advanced skills, heavy investment, and proximity to customers. Many of these companies are in the small-to-midsized sector, which makes up 37% of U.S. manufacturing. The China price is even being felt in high tech. Chinese exports of advanced networking gear, still at a low level, are already affecting prices. And there's talk by some that China could eventually become a major car exporter.

Multinationals have accelerated the mainland's industrialization by shifting production there, and midsized companies that can are following suit. The alternative is to stay at home and fight—and probably lose. Ohio State University business professor Oded Shenkar, author of the book *The Chinese Century*, hears many war stories from local companies. He gives it to them straight: "If you still make anything labor intensive, get out now rather than bleed to death. Shaving 5% here and there won't work." Chinese producers can make the same adjustments, he notes, so "you need an entirely new business model to compete."

America has survived import waves before, from Japan, South Korea, and Mexico. And it has lived with China for two decades. But something very different is happening. The assumption has long been that the U.S. and other industrialized nations will keep leading in knowledge-intensive industries while developing nations focus on lower-skill sectors. That's now open to debate. "What is stunning about China is that for the first time we have a huge, poor country that can compete both with very low wages and in high tech," says Harvard University economist Richard B. Freeman. "Combine the two, and America has a problem."

How much of a problem? That's in fierce dispute. On one side, the benefits of the relationship with China are enormous. After years of struggling to crack the mainland market, U.S. multinationals from General Motors to Procter & Gamble and Motorola are finally reaping rich profits. They're making cell phones, shampoo, autos, and PCs in China and selling them to its middle class of some 100 million people, a group that should more than double in size by 2010. "Our commercial success in China is important to our competitiveness worldwide," says Motorola China Chairman Gene Delaney.

By outsourcing components and hardware from China, U.S. companies have sharply boosted their return on capital. China's trade barriers continue to come down, part of its agreement to enter the World Trade Organization in 2001. Big new opportunities will emerge for U.S. insurers, banks, and retailers. China's surging demand for raw materials and commodities has driven prices up worldwide, creating a windfall for U.S. steelmakers, miners, and lumber companies. The cheap cost of Chinese goods has kept inflation low in the U.S. and fueled a consumer boom that helped America weather a recession and kept global growth on track.

But there's a huge cost to the China relationship too. Foremost is the question of America's huge trade deficit, of which China is the largest and fastest-growing part. While U.S. consumers binge on Chinese-made goods, the U.S. balance-of-payments deficit is nearing a record 6% of gross domestic product. The trade shortfall—coupled with the U.S. budget deficit—is driving the dollar ever downward, raising fears that cracks will appear in the global financial system. And by keeping its currency pegged to the greenback at a level analysts see as undervalued, China amplifies the problem.

## America's Eroding Base

The deficit with China will keep widening under most projections. That raises the issue: Will America's industrial base erode to a dangerous level? So far the hardest-hit industries have been those that were destined to migrate to low-cost nations anyway. But China is ramping up rapidly in more advanced industries where America remains competitive, adding state-of-the-art capacity in cars, specialty steel, petrochemicals, and microchips. These plants are aimed at meeting insatiable demand in China. But the danger is that if China's growth stalls, the resulting glut will turn into another export wave and disrupt whole new strata of American industry. "As producers in China end up with significant unused capacity, they will try to be much more creative in how they deploy it," says Jim Hemerling, a senior vice-president at Boston Consulting Group's Shanghai office.

That's why China is an even thornier trade issue for the U.S. than Japan was in the 1980s. It's clear some Chinese exporters cheat, from intellectual-property theft and dumping to securing unfair subsidies. Many Chinese factories also cheat workers out of overtime pay. Washington can get much more aggressive in fighting violations of trade law. But broader protectionism is a nonstarter. On a practical level the U.S. is now so dependent on Chinese suppliers that resurrecting trade barriers would just raise costs and diminish the real benefits that China trade confers. Also, unlike Japan 20 years ago, China is a much more open economy. It continues to lower tariffs and even runs a slight trade deficit with the whole world—which makes America's deficit with China all the more glaring. Hiking the value of the yuan 30% might help. But that's unlikely. For one thing, Beijing fears what such a shift would do to jobs—and the value of its $515 billion in foreign reserves. The real solution is for the U.S. to reduce its twin deficits on its own—but that's more America's issue than China's.

Meanwhile, U.S. companies are no longer investing in much new capacity at home, and the ranks of U.S. engineers are thinning. In contrast, China is emerging as the most competitive manufacturing platform ever. Chief among its formidable assets is its cheap labor, from $120-a-month production workers to $2,000-a-month chip designers. Even in sophisticated electronics industries, where direct labor is less than 10% of costs, China's low wages are reflected in the entire supply chain—components, office workers, cargo handling, you name it.

China is also propelled by an enormous domestic market that brings economies of scale, feverish local rivalry that keeps prices low, an army of engineers that is growing by 350,000 annually, young workers and managers willing to put in 12-hour days and work weekends, an unparalleled component and material base in electronics and light industry, and an entrepreneurial zeal to do whatever it takes to please big retailers such as Wal-Mart Stores, Target, Best Buy, and J.C. Penney. "The reason practically all home furnishings are now made in China factories is that they simply are better suppliers," says Janet E. Fox, vice-president for international procurement at J.C. Penney Co. "American manufacturers aren't even in the same game."

Fox's point is important. China's competitive advantages are built on much more than unfair trade practices. Some 70% of exports now come from private companies and foreign ventures mainly owned by Taiwanese, Hong Kong, Japanese, and U.S. companies that have brought access to foreign markets, advanced technology, and managerial know-how. Aside from cheap land and tax breaks in some areas, private Chinese manufacturers get minimal government help. "The Chinese government cannot afford to offer financial support to the export economy," says business professor Gu Kejian of People's University in Beijing. And as capital floods in and modern plants are built in China, efficiencies improve dramatically. The productivity of private industry in China has grown an astounding 17% annually for five years, according to the U.S. Conference Board.

China needs U.S. imports, though not as much as imagined when Beijing agreed to join the WTO. U.S. exports to China have risen 25% to 35% annually in the past two years. But China's exports still outstrip its imports from the U.S. by 5 to 1. The U.S. sells about $2.4 billion worth of aircraft a year, and its semiconductor exports tripled in three years. Otherwise the U.S. looks like a developing nation. It runs surpluses in commodities such as oil seeds, grains, iron, wood pulp, and raw animal hides.

Meanwhile, the Chinese keep expanding their export base. Chinese competition arrives so fast that it's nearly impossible to adjust through the usual strategies, such as automating or squeezing suppliers. The Japanese, South Koreans, and Europeans often took "four or five years to develop their place in the market," says Robert B. Cassidy, a former U.S. Trade Representative official who helped negotiate China's entry into the WTO and now works for Washington law firm Collier Shannon Scott, which wages dumping cases on behalf of U.S. clients. "China overwhelms a market so quickly you don't see it coming."

## "Shock and Awe"

Georgetown Steel Co. is a case in point. The Georgetown (S.C.) maker of wire rods used in everything from bridge cables to ball bearings had battled Asian and Mexican imports for years. In 2004, it shut its 600-worker plant, citing a tenfold leap in Chinese imports, to 252,000 tons, from 2001 to 2003. International Steel Group Inc. has since bought the facility after U.S. antidumping duties on imports and a rise in global demand helped hike domestic prices. The Gardiner (Mass.) plant of Seaman Paper Co., a maker of crepe and decorative paper, is highly automated. Yet Chinese imports have grabbed a third of the market. Big U.S. retailers buy Chinese-made 81-foot streamers for as little as 9 cents each. That's below Seaman's cost of materials. "We thought we could offset Chinese labor cost by automating, but we just couldn't," says Seaman President George Jones III.

In bedroom furniture, 59 U.S. plants employing 15,500 workers have closed between January 2001 and the fall of 2004 as Chinese imports rocketed 221%, to $1.4 billion—half of the U.S. market. Prices have plunged 30%. Dumping certainly seems to be one factor. At its Galax (Va.) factory, Vaughan-Bassett Furniture Co. displays a Chinese knock-off of one of its dressers that wholesales for $105—below the world market cost for the wood. But the main competition comes from Chinese megaplants that sell directly to U.S. retailers and can get a new design into mass production in two months. The new Chinese factories of suppliers such as Lacquer Craft Furniture, Markor, and Shing Mark, some of them Taiwanese-owned, employ thousands and are so big they seem meant to build Boeing 747s, making most U.S. factories look like cottage industries. "The first wave is shock and awe," says John D. Bassett III, CEO of Vaughan-Bassett, even though it has boosted productivity by 250% at its 600-worker Galax plant since 1995 by investing in computer-controlled wood drying, cutting, and carving gear. "American industry has never encountered [such] competition."

As component industries and design work follow assembly lines to China, key elements of the U.S. industrial base are beginning to erode. American plastic-molding and machine-tool industries have shrunk dramatically in the past five years. Take Incoe Corp. in Troy, Mich., a maker of steel components for plastic-injection machines. "When the economy turned soft, we anticipated the business would come back," says

Incoe CFO Robert Hoff. "But it didn't. We saw our customer base either close or migrate to China." The U.S. printed-circuit-board (PCB) industry has seen sales go from $11 billion to under $5 billion since 2001. In that time, PCB exports from China have more than doubled, to around $3.4 billion in 2004, says market researcher Global Sources Ltd. Most U.S. production of key electronics materials, such as copper-clad laminates, has fled too. "The whole industry is hollowing out," says Joseph C. Fehsenfeld, CEO of Midwest Printed Circuit Services Inc. in Round Lake Beach, Ill.

The migration of electronics to China began when the Taiwanese shifted plants and suppliers across the Taiwan Strait in the late 1990s. As recently as 2000, though, the U.S. exported $45 billion in computer hardware. By 2004, that number has slid to $28 billion as the industry headed en masse for China, which is even more competitive than Taiwan. "All electronics hardware manufacturing is going to China," says Michael E. Marks, former CEO of Flextronics Corp., a contract manufacturer that employs 41,000 in China. Flextronics and other companies are hiring Chinese engineers to design the products assembled there. "There is a myth that the U.S. would remain the knowledge economy and China the sweatshop," says BCG's Hemerling. "Increasingly, this is no longer the case."

A visit to Flextronics' campus in the Pearl River Delta town of Doumen vividly illustrates Marks's point. The site employs 18,000 workers making cell phones, X-box game consoles, PCs, and other hardware in 13 factories sprawled over 149 acres. The bamboo scaffolding is about to come down on an additional 720,000-square-foot factory nearing completion. Almost every chemical, component, plastic, machine tool, and packing material Flextronics needs is available from thousands of suppliers within a two-hour drive of the site. That alone makes most components 20% cheaper in China than in the U.S., says campus General Manager Tim Dinwiddie. Plus, China will soon eliminate remaining tariffs on imported chips. In the past five years, electronic manufacturing-services companies such as Flextronics have cut their U.S. production from $37 billion to $27 billion while doubling their China output to $31 billion. That's likely to double again by 2007.

## "Gravitational Pull"

China is even making its presence felt in the U.S. market for networking gear, a bastion of American comparative advantage. On Nov. 15, 2004, struggling 3Com Corp. in Marlborough, Mass., launched a data-communications switching system for corporate networks of 10,000 users or more. It claims twice the performance of Cisco Systems Inc.'s comparable switch. At $183,000, 3Com's list price is 25% less. Its secret? 3Com is settling for lower margins and taking advantage of a 1,200-engineer joint venture with China telecom giant Huawei Technologies Co. This is the first high-end piece of networking gear sold by a U.S. company that is designed and manufactured in China. For the price of one U.S. engineer, the joint venture can throw four engineers into the task of making customized products for a client. Even if 3Com does not succeed, similar tie-ups are expected, which could drive down prices of high-end gear sold in the U.S. Says 3Com President Bruce Claflin: "We want to change the pricing structure of this industry." 3Com hopes this is the start of a whole line of networking gear designed and made in China for the global market. Without referring to China, Cisco CEO John T. Chambers says: "We are starting to see a stream of good, very price-competitive competitors, particularly from Asia."

The next step for China is critical mass in core industries. Outside Beijing, Semiconductor Manufacturing International Corp. has just opened a chip plant fabricating 12-inch silicon wafers that experts say is just two generations behind Intel Corp. A foundry that makes chips on a contract basis, this plant won't compete directly with U.S. chipmakers. But with four more 12-inch wafer plants due in 2006 and many more fabs in the pipeline, the U.S. Semiconductor Industry Association warns that a "gravitational pull" could suck capital, talent, and leading-edge research-and-development and design functions from the U.S.

Digital technologies aren't the only areas where the Chinese have huge ambitions. In the past decade, U.S. petrochemical makers have invested in little new capacity. But at a three-mile-long site in Nanjing, 12,000 workers are erecting a $2.7 billion network of pipes and towers for China's Sinopec and Germany's BASF that by next year will be among the world's biggest, most modern complexes for ethylene, the basic ingredient in plastics. An even bigger complex is going up in Shanghai. "The Chinese understand everything that *scale* means," says Fluor Corp. Group President Robert McNamara, who lives part-time in Shanghai and whose company has design contracts at both complexes. "When they target an industry to dominate, they don't mitigate."

Can China dominate everything? Of course not. America remains the world's biggest manufacturer, still producing more than half of what it consumes. Industries requiring huge R&D budgets and capital investment, such as aerospace, pharmaceuticals, and cars, still have strong bases in the U.S. "I don't see China becoming a major car exporter in the foreseeable future," says former GM China Chairman Philip F. Murtaugh. "There is no economic rationale." Murtaugh cites high production costs and quality issues at Chinese car plants, as well as just-in-time delivery needs in the West, as impediments.

## Burning Rubber

Don't tell that to Miao Wei, president of Dongfeng Motor Corp. On Nov. 7, 2004, Dongfeng and Honda Motor Co. announced that their joint venture will invest $340 million to boost output of Honda CR-Vs and Civics fivefold, to 120,000. The plant aims to achieve world standards by employing Honda's flexible manufacturing system. "Honda will sell some of the Chinese-built cars in Europe," says Miao. Nissan Motor Co. is also talking about exporting with Dongfeng.

China's carmakers are developing the suppliers that one day could sustain exports. Auto-parts maker Wanxiang Group in Hangzhou started as a tiny township-owned farm-machinery shop in 1969. Now it's a $2.4 billion conglomerate that supplies the Chinese assembly plants of GM, Ford Motor, Volkswagen, and others and also exports 30% of its output. China has agreed to drop the rule that its auto plants buy at least 40% of parts locally. Wanxiang is getting ready: It is opening a $42 million plant loaded with U.S. and European testing gear. And since 1995, Wanxiang has bought 10 U.S. auto-parts makers. "Our goal is to acquire technology, management, and most important, to get access to overseas markets," says Chairman Lu Guanqiu.

Some U.S. manufacturers hope China will run out of steam. Factories in Guangdong and Fujian are starting to face serious labor shortages for the first time. Red-hot demand has meant skyrocketing costs for China's producers, most of which rely on imported goods such as steel, plastics, and components. Energy shortages have forced manufacturers to shut factories several times a week. In almost any industry one can think of, vicious price wars are biting into already razor-sharp margins. "There are so many small companies competing that they crowd out all profit," says Beijing University economist Zhang Weiying. Indeed, given the low emphasis on profits and the unsophisticated accounting of many Chinese companies, often their pricing isn't based on a full understanding of costs. Having gotten as far as they can on cheap production costs, Chinese manufacturers must develop their own technologies and innovative products to move ahead—areas in which they've made slow progress so far.

The juggernaut will slow, but only slightly. While salaries for top Chinese designers are rising fast, they are still a fifth to a tenth of those in Silicon Valley. If China's wages rise 8% annually for the next five years, says a Boston Consulting Group study, the average factory hand will still earn just $1.30 an hour by then. If China allowed the yuan to appreciate by around 10% in the next year, productivity gains would more than offset the higher costs, figures China expert Nicholas R. Lardy of the Institute for International Economics. "I don't think revaluation will have a significant impact," he says.

And Chinese producers are hardly standing still. In a recent survey of Chinese and U.S. manufacturers by *Industry Week* and Cleveland-based Manufacturing Performance Institute, 54% of Chinese companies cited innovation as one of their top objectives, while only 26% of U.S. respondents did. Chinese companies spend more on worker training and enterprise-management software. And 91% of U.S. plants are more than a decade old, versus 54% in China. Shanghai-based TV maker SVA Group, for example, has opened China's first plant to make flat panels, a venture with Japan's NEC Corp. That is enabling SVA to secure a U.S. beachhead by selling liquid-crystal display and plasma TV sets through channels such as the online sites of Costco Wholesale and Target. Starting price: $1,600—30% below similar models by Royal Philips Electronics and Panasonic.

More innovation. Better goods. Lower prices. Newer plants. America will surely continue to benefit from China's expansion. But unless it can deal with the industrial challenge, it will suffer a loss of economic power and influence. Can America afford the China price? It's the question U.S. workers, execs, and policymakers urgently need to ask.

## A Tale of Two Furniture Makers

Doug Bassett poses a seemingly simple question: How can a factory in China sell a five-piece set of bedroom furniture for one-third the $599 wholesale price his company charges? Same boxy, "traditional American" style that Galax (Va.)-based Vaughan-Bassett Furniture Co. has turned out for decades. Same North American oak and veneers.

Sure, wages and benefits in China are 20 times less than what Vaughan-Bassett pays its 600 workers, many of them middle-aged, who make 9,500 bedroom sets a month in an 85-year-old brick factory nestled alongside a river and rugged hills near the Blue Ridge Parkway. But while assembly and finishing still require lots of hand labor, Vaughan-Bassett boasts the most advanced computer-controlled wood-processing equipment on the market. "Nobody in China has this," shouts Bassett, vice-president for sales, as he strides past a long $1.8 million "optimizing" line that detects knots in wood and cuts 70,000 board feet per day into six different sizes. And two $500,000 computer-controlled machines can carve 100 bedposts in the time it would take a single craftsperson working by hand to finish one piece.

Bassett's conclusion: Chinese rivals are selling below cost and benefiting from an undervalued currency and government subsidies. He and his father, CEO John D. Bassett III, 67, and older brother Wyatt, 38, have spearheaded an antidumping case that prompted the U.S. Commerce Dept. on Nov. 12, 2004, to slap margins averaging 8.64% on 115 Chinese exporters of bedroom furniture. But whether this trade action will do much to revive the U.S. furniture industry is in doubt. Since January 2001, imports of bedroom furniture from China have leapt more than threefold, to an estimated $2 billion in 2004. Over that time, some 65 U.S. furniture factories shut down. And many of China's biggest furniture makers, such as Lacquer Craft, Fine Furniture, and Starcorp, are dramatically increasing the size and sophistication of their production facilities.

Indeed, step into the factory of Lacquer Craft Manufacturing Co. near the southern Chinese city of Dongguan, and one wonders how furniture can still be affordably made in America. Most of Lacquer Craft's more upmarket pieces, which often involve more intricate workmanship, don't compete directly with Vaughan-Bassett's. But the plant is indicative of the kind of modern facility being built by fast-growing Chinese suppliers such as Markor, Art Heritage, Fine Furniture, and Starcorp. In Dongguan, 4,500 workers in their twenties turn out some 50,000 pieces of stylish furniture each month, including dining and living room furniture as well as bedroom sets, in a light-drenched facility that is so cavernous it looks like it could serve as an airport terminal. A new 4 million-square-foot Lacquer Craft factory in Shanghai is even bigger, with six production lines. And that is just the first phase in Shanghai. Economies of scale alone give Chinese plants a big cost edge over smaller U.S. factories when they are running at full capacity, says Lacquer Craft Executive Vice-President Mohamad Amini, a California native with years of experience in U.S. furniture plants. Like many of China's best furniture makers, Lacquer Craft is owned by a Taiwanese investor.

Wood processing isn't quite as automated in Galax. But Chinese wages average just 60 cents an hour, including benefits. And because many Chinese factories don't pay overtime, the actual hourly rate can be much lower. This compares to around $16 in Virginia. As a result, labor still comes to only 6% to 8% of total production costs in China, versus 22% at Vaughan-Bassett. The lower labor cost offsets the higher costs of shipping furniture to the U.S., Amini says. What's more, Lacquer Craft can afford hundreds more workers for intricate detail work—carving, veneers, finishing—that is prohibitively expensive in the U.S. This work also enables Lacquer Craft to sell higher-priced furniture. As a result, the added cost of shipping the furniture from China—which can add roughly another $150 per set depending on where it goes in the U.S.—becomes a smaller share of the total price by the time it ends up in a retail showroom. Amini also contends that the price advantage of China's currency, which economists believe is undervalued against the U.S. dollar by anywhere from 10% to 40%, is exaggerated: The biggest cost of the furniture is wood. Because Lacquer Craft imports most of its wood and veneers from the U.S., it must pay in dollars, rather than cheap Chinese yuan.

The key competitive edge of China-based manufacturers such as Lacquer Craft, Amini contends, is their business model. U.S. makers such as Vaughan-Bassett mainly design their own pieces and then go out and market them to retailers. Most of Lacquer Craft's furniture is based on designs and specifications provided by its U.S. customers, which include big furniture retailers such as Haverty and department stores like Macy's and J.C. Penney Co. that now offer their own brands in order to boost profit margins. Lacquer Craft's factories can turn a design into a prototype in two weeks and get the new pieces into mass production and onto ships in two months. Says a J.C. Penney purchasing manager: "We could never find a U.S. manufacturer willing to do that." Many other big U.S. furniture retailers echo the same sentiment that American furniture makers, who over the past decade have taken over greater and greater shares of the U.S. furniture market from mom-and-pop stores and small regional players, are too unresponsive to their needs. The Bassetts strongly disagree. "We have made to customers' designs in the past," Wyatt contends. "But I don't know of any retailer that has asked us to do this for years."

Still, Vaughan-Bassett is starting to change its strategy. In recent years it has expanded beyond its traditional lines into dining and youth furniture and higher-end bedroom sets. It slashed wholesale prices on its basic line. Early in 2004, Vaughan-Bassett shut one factory. Its total workforce is down by about one-third since 2000, while sales have shrunk by about 10%, to $149 million. But now, business is starting to grow again. And production at the remaining Galax plant has leapt by 250% since 1995 with only a 30% increase in the workforce at that facility, thanks to automation and more efficient manufacturing practices, Doug Bassett estimates.

But the dumping-suit victory won't bring much relief. Not only were the margins too low to offset the huge price advantage of key Chinese rivals, but also there are new rising players in China that clearly seem to be dumping, the Bassetts argue. At the company's Galax conference room, Doug Bassett points to an oak dresser that Vaughan-Bassett whole-sales for $275. Next to it is a look-alike dresser by Dalian Huafeng Furniture Co., based in the northern Chinese port city of Dalian. Its U.S. wholesale price before shipping: $105. That's below the $117.15 Vaughan-Bassett says it pays for materials. "So they must be losing money even if their labor costs, overhead, and profits are zero," he says.

What's more, Huafeng is ramping up quickly, with stated plans of having 14 million square feet of factory, warehousing, and showroom space. According to a 2003 article in a Chinese newspaper, the *Liaoning Daily*, that Vaughan-Bassett submitted as evidence in a Nov. 9, 2004, U.S. international Trade Commission hearing, company founder He Yungeng said: "The reason why we built such a huge industrial zone for our U.S. export is to force the U.S. furniture manufacturers to close so as to make way for Chinese products." The Chinese company adamantly denies selling at below fair-market price. "We never dump or sell products below production costs," says Dalian Huafeng international trade manager Xu Jing.

Vaughan Bassett is pressing ahead in its bid to get the U.S. Commerce Department to start a new dumping investigation of Huafeng and other manufacturers. Both in court and through their investments, the Bassetts have made strides toward assuring that their factory doesn't become another icon of America's industrial decline. But they have many more fights ahead.

# Sucking the Life out of Hoover

*As rivals abroad continue to underprice it by huge margins, one factory worker tries to cope with her fading prospects for a job in Ohio*

Melissa Knight, 28, has been a single mother for the last four-and-a-half years. Now, she's unemployed too. She was laid off from Maytag's Hoover floor-care factory in North Canton, Ohio, in June 2005. She had been cut loose for several weeks in 2003 and again in 2004, but both times she got recalled as inventories were worked off.

Knight might be back at the plant. But she doesn't know if the job will last long. "I'm afraid to get my hopes up," she says.

Over the last several years, Knight was a "Jill of all trades" at the factory. She drove a forklift, worked on the assembly line, and built electric motors and seals—"whatever they needed." This was her second factory job.

## "Wish It Was Me"

Previously, she had worked at a nonunion metals-casting shop nearby. That job paid only $7.50 an hour. At Hoover she was making more than $15 an hour. Plus, she got benefits that she thought were wonderful—among the best offered in north central Ohio—even after she and other hourly co-workers had their wages frozen and began paying health-care premiums and expenses under a concessionary labor pact in late 2003.

Knight and her daughter, Madison, live in a house she rents from an aunt who still works for Hoover. Her home is literally two houses away from the factory, so Knight is reminded constantly about what she has lost. "I watch the people walk in everyday and wish it was me," she says. "It's sad."

## Made in China

Why did Knight lose her job? Maytag has been getting killed by competitors who make their vacuum cleaners in China and have been able to underprice Hoover models by incredible margins.

You can get a Chinese-made upright vacuum cleaner for well under $100 at Wal-Mart, Target, or Sears. Hoovers generally start at upward of $200. Not surprisingly, Hoover has lost market share, though it still was No. 1 in upright cleaners in 2004.

Maytag's response was to get concessions from the plant's union, the International Brotherhood of Electrical Workers, and to trim its workforce in North Canton, where Hoover began in 1908. Then it started shifting production itself, outsourcing the work to its own *maquiladora* in Mexico, as well as outside shops in Asia, including China.

## More Layoffs?

With 320 workers dismissed in the first half of 2005, the headcount at that time was under 900, according to the union—a far cry from the 2,200 employed in 2000.

Today, the factory primarily makes steam vacuums, which still warrant higher prices. But cheap imports are beginning to steal market share from Hoover in this line as well.

Management told the union in July 2005 the company will transfer more work to its border factories in Juarez, Mexico, and El Paso, Tex. The union figures that will mean a total of 150 more layoffs.

## What's Ahead?

Local 1985 President James A. Repace worries that the plant could be shut down entirely in 2008 when the current contract runs out. One reason: Maytag says despite employee concessions and white-collar layoffs, it's the second-highest-cost plant in the company, because of its relatively well-paid and senior workforce.

Another unknown is what Maytag's new owner will do with the entire Hoover subsidiary. In August 2005, Whirlpool acquired Maytag for $2.7 billion, acing Ripplewood Holdings' offer of $2.1 billion.

## Getting By

But Whirlpool may not save Hoover, either. The Benton Harbor (Mich.) company jettisoned its own floor-care business years ago. Some former Hoover employees have found new work, mostly in the service sector. But even those jobs aren't plentiful. Ohio's unemployment rate, at 6.1% in June 2005, was the sixth worst in the U.S.

Knight is getting by on unemployment compensation, which comes to just half of her old pay. Because she can now be home with her daughter, she no longer has to pay for day care, so the cut in income doesn't seem that deep. She also gets a pretty good deal on rent since her aunt owns the house. And Knight had just finished paying off her 2000 Ford Focus before she got laid off.

Still, she has cut back on expenses. "I minimize, and I watch what I spend," she says. "I make sure my daughter's got clothes on her back and food on the table. That's about it. I can't live on unemployment forever."

## "I Love Factory Work"

She also looks for new work, but had no prospects until Maytag started recalling workers. Her old employer in the casting business has said she could return—at $7.50 an hour. That would be no better than subsisting on unemployment, she points out.

She would like to get another well-paying job in manufacturing. "I love factory work," she says. "I'm not a desk person. I like people, but I don't like to have to deal with them all the time."

In her view, plenty of parties share responsibility for her plight. She blames Maytag management for not running a better company and President George Bush and others in Washington for allowing or even encouraging a flood of cheap products from China and elsewhere.

She would like the government to put duties on these goods, making them priced more like products made in the U.S. And she blames her fellow citizens. "The American economy wants cheaper things, and we want everything today," she says. Knight doesn't spare herself when it comes to doling out blame. She admits: "I'm guilty of this too."

# Dipping a Yankee Toe in China

John Bank runs a successful small manufacturing company in Chicago—but he feels compelled to stake out a future in Asia. Here's why.

Back in 2001, John Bank was just another owner of another small American manufacturer. Today, he's CEO of a Chicago-based multinational with two joint ventures in China. The change makes him both excited and anxious.

Bank serves as chairman and chief executive of Phoenix Electric Manufacturing, started in 1938. The privately held company makes components for small variable-speed electric motors used in power tools, treadmills, kitchen appliances, golf carts, and automobiles. Its customers include General Electric and Emerson Electric. A lawyer who wanted to do something more entrepreneurial, Bank bought Phoenix in 1991 following the unexpected death of its CEO.

## Helpful Rivals

The company then had $3 million in annual sales and 30 employees. Today, Phoenix Electric boasts nearly $20 million in sales and roughly 100 U.S. employees in a couple of sites in and around Chicago. It also just started operations in China, its first foray outside of the U.S. Bank had begun planning to move into China in 2001, when he made his first visit to Suzhou, near Shanghai.

As a small-business owner, how did he even know where to go in China? His big customers weren't much help. The contacts he had at Emerson, for instance, couldn't lead him to the right folks in China. Instead, Bank availed himself of his network of competitors and suppliers for leads, as well as fellow members of the Young Presidents Organization (YPO). He also used the Internet to vet potential joint-venture partners.

His smartest move was to rely on a Japanese competitor—which manufactures similar products in China—to help him make contacts. "The 21st century is creating strange bedfellows," Bank says.

## Picking and Choosing

Within months, he formed a 50-50 joint venture with that Japanese outfit, in an economic zone in an industrial park in Suzhou. The metal-stamping factory produces components sold to motormakers in China, primarily for export to the U.S.

Then, in 2004, he set up a second joint venture, to make molded plastic parts outside of Hong Kong with a Chinese supplier he had met through one of his YPO pals. To get those two partnerships, he probably inquired into 20 businesses. "At the beginning, it's all a lovefest. Then you find the quality is bad, or they don't deliver," he says. "There have been a lot of dead ends."

Today, China accounts for less than 10% of Phoenix Electric's annual sales. Bank employs 100 people combined at the two factories. He has not cut his U.S. payroll as a result of his new Chinese facilities, but employment is likely to grow in the Middle Kingdom and stay stagnant in the U.S.

## "Under Assault"

Bank says he himself has invested less than $1 million in China, relying on his partners for more capital. He has also cut down on his investment risks by shipping old machines from his Chicago factories to China, where, because the Chinese don't need to worry about the latest in labor-saving technology, they're good enough. Bank has traveled to China six times now.

Why did he make the move? "The American motor business itself is under assault from foreign competition—the Chinese especially. Our customer base is moving over there, and our customer base is losing business to Chinese motor manufacturers. So we wanted to have a manufacturing presence to supply our customer base and to supply potential Chinese customers."

It's almost impossible to compete head-on with Chinese manufacturers, Bank says, so he has had to join them. Wages are just too low in

China. His factory workers typically get 50 cents to $1 an hour, for a nine-hour day, six days a week, with no overtime pay or paid breaks. In the U.S., his workers get $10 an hour, plus benefits.

## Skinny Margins

Despite the financial advantages of working in China, "It's not a miracle," Bank says. "It's an opportunity. It's not a ticket to riches."

The risks are also great, he points out. "As a small company, you can't afford to make mistakes. Your capital is coming right out of your pocket. If you make a mistake, it could mean the very survival of your business."

The competition is fierce, according to Bank. "The profit margins are razor thin. There's overcapacity in almost every single industry in China, and the barriers to entry are almost nonexistent. You have guys who will open up garage shops with used equipment. The Chinese are geniuses at using old, discarded equipment."

## Extortion Threat

Efficiency, however, is a different matter. The bureaucracy remains cumbersome, and infrastructure lacking. Quality often comes only as an afterthought. Around the Chinese New Year, many workers go back to their ancestral villages, and the economy more or less shuts down. Afterward, many simply don't come back.

Provincial authorities often try to shake down foreign companies, says Bank. His advice: "As a small company, you've got to stick to the economic development zones, because that's where the Chinese government will take care of you and protect you from the vagaries of the provincial governments. Once you're out in the provinces, all bets are off."

There's also a huge risk of Chinese knocking off your products and stealing your intellectual property. "But you can't be afraid to go into China because of that," he says.

## Next Wave

He doesn't think the China juggernaut can be stopped. "Chinese manufacturers continue to move further and further downstream," he says. "First it was component parts. Now it's finished goods. It's not that Maytag goes and buys motors from China. It's that the entire refrigerator is made in China and shipped directly to a Sears or Wal-Mart."

And it won't end with manufacturing, he believes. "The next phase is going to be more R&D and engineering over there." And companies ignore China at their own peril, he says. "You've got to have some sort of China strategy, no matter what your company size is. If not, you're withering on the vine."

---

# India: An Agent of Change

*That's how Infosys CEO Nandan Nilekani sees the country's impact on the U.S. economy, through globalization and outsourcing*

While many U.S. tech companies are stuck in the slow-demand doldrums, India's Infosys Technologies is soaring. The reason: Infosys and its Indian brethren are rewriting the rules of global competition in the software and tech-services industries with their use of highly skilled but low-cost Indian talent.

In 2005, Infosys Chief Executive Nandan Nilekani visited with *BusinessWeek* writers and editors, including Senior Writer Steve Hamm after accompanying Indian Prime Minister Manmohan Singh. Edited excerpts of the interview follow:

**Q: What was the significance of the group of Indian CEOs traveling with Prime Minister Singh to Washington?**

**A:** From an India point of view, it's the recognition that economic diplomacy is part of the whole thing. This is the first time that a bunch of CEOs have traveled as part of the Prime Minister's delegation to any country. It shows how far India has come in terms of recognizing the role of business and entrepreneurs.

They treated us like part of the team. It shows how much more relaxed people are about business and government. The mindsets have changed dramatically.

**Q:  How is India's role changing in the world economy?**

**A:**  Look at the last 10 years. A lot of American companies came to India to increase their markets, but they ended up doing outsourcing instead. The markets hadn't yet opened up. General Electric came in 1989, and they were ahead of their time. But they found this huge storehouse of human capital and the whole outsourcing story happened.

Now, because the economy has opened up, and there's more wealth, it's also becoming a huge market. To give you a recent example: When the Paris Air Show was held, all the Indian carriers put together ordered 200 planes. This is mind-boggling to anybody from India. We don't know where they'll land. They'll probably just circle in the air. (Laughs)

The point is, who would have thought this country would become such a huge market? Suddenly, people are beginning to realize there's a huge market opening up.

**Q:  What's the political dimension?**

**A:**  One of the big agendas in the U.S. is the spreading of democratic values. India is a player in that game. It has shown you can run a practicing democracy in an underdeveloped part of the world.

You can have free and fair elections. You can have different races and religious groups coexisting more or less peacefully. As spreading democratic values becomes a high U.S. priority, India's a partner in that game. You have a role model in that part of the world who shows it's doable.

**Q:  There was a lot of concern last year about a backlash against India over outsourcing. You just spent three days in Washington, D.C. Is that still part of the discussion?**

**A:**  In the run-up to the [presidential] elections, it was an issue. But last week it wasn't on anybody's radar screen. Maybe I was meeting a bunch of free-traders. When I look back, it peaked in the primaries. [Senator John]

Edwards was coming from the left. [John] Kerry had to react to it. But after the primaries, it cooled off. A lot of it was posturing.

**Q: Do you expect any particular category of American worker to be harmed as a result of more outsourcing of manufacturing and service jobs?**
A: If you have a more interconnected world, if you have more of the world economy being services, and if more of the services can be delivered remotely over a wire, it has its ramifications. We can't wish that away.

But the strength of the U.S. has been its extraordinary focus on productivity. And, ultimately, productivity is doing more things with less people. Here, you have an economy that makes and destroys millions of jobs a year.

Outsourcing is more visible. A guy in Detroit loses his job, and somebody in India gets it. When you put a face to it, it's more emotional.

**Q: If the entry-level service jobs are going to India, how do you get a training ground for U.S. citizens to develop higher-level skills here?**
A: It's a valid question. I don't have a clear answer. Maybe you should ask: Is it stuff you retain at the firm level or is it stuff you retain at the country level?

If I'm a global company, as long as I retain the intellectual property in my firm, then it doesn't matter so much if it's in Des Moines or Delhi. Look at what's happening on the business process outsourcing level today—a lot of it is really captive units. It's offshoring but not outsourcing. J.P. Morgan or Goldman Sachs will have their own employees there. It's in the firm, but across the border.

The reality is that in the next 20 years, if India continues to grow at 6%, it will be one of the big drivers of global economic growth. It's all related.

**Q: Can you picture the future of the U.S. economy? How might it change as a result of the rise of India and China?**
A: There's a potential to unleash a huge productivity surge in the way companies are run. Partly, it's because digitization and the advent of IP technology have made everything so simple. And then there's the labor pool, and so on. Also, you're designing things to make them more customer-facing and customer-empowering.

There's also a huge amount of process efficiencies that aren't in large corporations yet. It hasn't been looked at. So in a few years you'll see most companies unleashing this massive productivity surge. When the dust settles, the firms will look very differently. They'll be global.

Then it becomes a faith issue. Is it good or bad? Either you believe productivity improvements will ultimately be good for everybody, or you believe the whole thing is going to fall apart. Obviously, India and China will become a much bigger part of global GDP.

In 1830, India and China were probably half the world GDP. We both missed the industrial boat. And we're seeing a new boat, the information-led boat. Some of it is just catch-up.

**Q: What kind of corporate models are being created in India? How will they change the game elsewhere in the world?**
**A:** Clearly, the kind of things you can do will scale up and become more sophisticated. Instead of 100,000 guys doing IT, you'll have 500,000 guys doing it. That's the scale part. You'll also do programming, consulting, and design. You'll have a breadth of services.

The question is about innovation. At the end of the day, the U.S. is the world's most dynamic innovation engine. You have the whole innovation ecosystem. You have the world's great universities. You have the venture capital, the capital markets.

You have the fantastically bright people. It's the adaptability of the society that's its strength. It's absorbing the changes.

For other countries, creating the innovation engine is a much longer play. It's happening. But it will take a while.

We're one of the agents of the change—the productivity surge. It's the big enchilada. Part of it is technology. Part of it is process globalization, so you leverage global resources and redesign things. Part of it is much more customer involvement—which the Web has enabled.

The other thing is that once you're trying to use technology and process globalization, you start to take a hard look at how you run your company inside. You find fat and nonvaluation. You clean it up. You do all of these things simultaneously, and the productivity boost will be spectacular.

**Q: Do you see India causing this disruption of global business models?**
**A:** In the IT stuff, the disruption is happening to our competitors. In the other stuff, it's happening, but not at the level it's happening in IT. As these large global corporations embark on this large productivity surge caused by these four or five factors, since we've done this in our business, we're uniquely positioned to partner with them in driving that productivity surge.

That's the impact we can have. In a sense, we're a paradigm of the global company you want to be. We're the model of what we're preaching to others.

**Q: You were asked in the past, what can America do to get back these jobs it's losing to India. You said nothing, we can do it better and cheaper, right?**
**A:** It's the wrong question. By the same argument you should not allow Bank of America to buy Fleet Bank, because it's eliminating 15,000 jobs. You should stop automatic checkout counters because it's taking away jobs.

The reality is that technology productivity has created more job loss than anything else. We don't stop it. We accept that as part of evolution. Now you should think of this as one more dimension of how the world is going to change. I don't think it's stoppable.

**Q: You said India is becoming a big market, yet Infosys itself doesn't do much business in India. Is that going to change?**
**A:** We're the dominant player in the banking industry. We're looking at other sectors. Right now, the big markets in India will be driven by consumption stuff—cell phones and planes. We don't really have [a] play in that. Indian companies have a lot of employees, so eventually we'll have a role in making them more efficient.

The same stuff and know-how that's allowing Indian firms to make the rest of the world become more competitive is going to start playing out in India. It's happening. Today we have an airline called Jet Airways. I've met some executives from the Western airlines who say Jet Airways has the best customer services of anybody. I was pleasantly shocked to hear that. We're going to see more and more of that.

Telecom is the big success story. We have tremendous growth and the lowest prices in the world.

There's a delay between technology and social adaption. We're seeing that lag period. But in the next 10 to 20 years, technology will play as important a role in domestic productivity growth and social change as it has played in the West.

**Q: Things are happening much faster in China, where they build infrastructure so rapidly.**
**A:** It's going to happen, but not the way it happens in China. In China, a bunch of guys get in a room and decide to build a 16-lane highway from Shanghai to Beijing, and it's going to happen.

There's no way that will happen in India. It's too chaotic and argumentative. But what's going to happen is these 200 planes will be ordered, they won't land. They'll be circling. Everybody will get [very angry]. Finally, there will be such public outcry that the airports will get built. It's a different model. But it's a model.

In India, we have a 6% growth rate. That's going to happen. The question is: How do we take it to 8% or 9%? The right things are better infrastructure, common economic market, reducing hurdles to business.

The real question is: Will the government stuff happen to take it from 6% to 9%? You need that because you have 10 million people coming to the workforce every year. If you don't grow fast enough, will you have social forces that stalemate everything? That's the worry.

4

# The New Corporate Model

CHINA AND INDIA BOTH HAVE BIG corporations that are starting to become familiar names abroad, such as Huawei, CNOOC, Wipro, and Infosys. But what do we know exactly about these new breeds of multinationals? How do their business strategies, goals, management structures, and corporate cultures differ from those of the West, Europe, Japan, and the rest of East Asia? Do they represent new, unique business models? Do Chinese and Indian corporations have sound strategies and enough management depth to succeed beyond their borders and emerge as 21st-century global giants?

India's corporate scene has been largely shaped by the pressures on private entrepreneurs to succeed in an environment of scarce resources, an impoverished mass market, and minimal government help. As the article "Asking the Right Questions" shows, one distinguishing feature of successful Indian companies such as Bharti Telecom, Tata Motor, and ICICI Bank is their ability to deliver high-quality goods and services at very low prices to the masses. Some analysts believe that if Indian companies succeed with this approach at home, they can transform industries worldwide. "Taking a Page from Toyota's Playbook" looks at how one major Indian information technology company has been able to become a world player in tech services and business process outsourcing. "Ratan Tata: No One's Doubting Now" profiles one of India's most innovative and globally minded conglomerates, the Tata Group.

China's corporate culture, by contrast, remains an enigma to foreigners. With few exceptions, China's leading corporations are state-private hybrids with nontransparent finances and decision-making processes. Still, China is starting to produce a number of corporations with professional managements that have global aspirations. "The State's Long Apron Strings" explains the complex interaction between the state and corporate management at major Chinese companies. "China's Power Brands" examines the successes and challenges of a number of ambitious consumer product companies that aim to go global. "TCL Multimedia's Global Agenda" and " 'Survival of the Fittest' at China Netcom" assess the strategies of two other Chinese companies with big ambitions. Meanwhile, China also is starting to produce truly private firms that finally are developing into important regional corporations. "China's Free Range Cash Cow" profiles one of them, Mengniu Dairy.

Finally, "Who's Got Performance?" analyzes whether Chinese or Indian companies are better managed. An analysis of Standard Poor's Compustat data on return on equity and return on investment for 340 publicly listed companies from both countries suggests corporate India is in better shape.

---

## Asking the Right Questions

The main hall of the Sciences Technology Museum in Shanghai was packed. More than 150 top executives of multinational companies had arrived at the invitation of IBM Chief Sam Palmisano to participate in IBM's Business Leadership Forum, a high-level conference held on a different continent every May for the past three years. On the dais, Palmisano introduced the day's speaker: Sunil Mittal, chairman and CEO of India's premier mobile-services provider, Bharti Tele-Ventures Ltd. This company, said Palmisano, "is on a rocket to the moon."

Why would IBM's chief be in China lauding an Indian telco that few outside India had even heard of a short time ago? It's not just because Bharti did a 10-year $750 million IT-outsourcing deal with IBM. It's also because Bharti—one of the world's fastest-growing telcos and the most capital-efficient—is one of the many Indian companies proving to be visionary in their fields. We're not talking about the champions of Bangalore, innovative as they are. These trendsetters range from telco newcomers such as Bharti to established giants like the $18 billion Tata Group and even former state-run players like ICICI Bank. All are rethinking the way they manage assets, distribute products, and use technologies to create new services. India's "rapid, incremental innovations," in the words of John Hagel III, a business-strategy consultant and author of a book on India and China, *The Only Sustainable Edge*, can provide lessons to companies everywhere.

What characterizes the best of the Indian outfits? They've learned to question the basic concepts of their industries, an attitude born of collective experience. For decades after achieving independence in 1947, India imposed severe restrictions on the capital private companies could tap, the technologies they could import, and the foreign exchange they could hold. So the best ones learned how to devise ingenious, low-cost solutions to their problems and even reimagine industries such as software services.

Since Indian industry was unshackled from state strictures in 1991, it has accelerated the process of innovation to stress affordability and quality. Bharti is the largest mobile operator in India, with 12 million subscribers and a 22% market share. It earned a net profit of $330 million on sales of $1.8 billion for the fiscal year ending Mar. 31, 2005. CEO Mittal, 48, likes to tell investors that Bharti charges just 2 cents a minute for phone calls on its Airtel service—and pockets 1 cent of that.

Mittal realized that the Western model for mobile-phone businesses—building and maintaining huge, expensive cellular networks—wasn't for Bharti, which wanted to keep costs down in any way possible while providing reliable service. So in February 2004, Bharti became the largest telco in the world to try something truly radical. It outsourced its entire cellular network to its three existing equipment suppliers: Ericsson, Nokia, and Siemens—a $725 million, three-year deal. The move to "deep outsourcing" was revolutionary. Networks are as crucial to telecom players as engines are to automakers. But it worked, and the effect on Bharti was profound. With executives no longer focused on managing the network, Bharti has turned its attention to marketing and customer service. In one year it added 6 million subscribers—one-fourth of India's annual subscriber growth and by far the fastest sign-up rate in India's history. "It's a big transformation, and it's becoming a global model," says Erik Oldmark, who runs marketing strategy worldwide for Ericsson. Bharti then took its model one step further by outsourcing its call-center operations.

## Cars on Demand

Bharti was able to tap outside expertise to remake its business. The $18 billion Tata Group relies on outside know-how as well—but in this case, it's the traditional skills of India's working class. Tata, a conglomerate, has long made sturdy trucks. But in 2001, Chairman Ratan Tata plunged into the passenger-car business despite much skepticism. The result was India's first indigenously designed, developed, and produced car—the $6,600 Indica. Tata used all of India's low-cost engineering skills to develop the car, at 60% of the usual cost of launching a new model. Now he has put his team to work on his dream project: a car that will sell for only $2,200. "I wanted to change the rules of the game," Tata says. "I wanted to change the way business is done."

The "people's car" will use a combination of steel and composite plastic for its body, put together with industrial adhesive along with nuts and bolts. But what's the business changer? Tata will attempt to do away with the traditional model of manufacturing solely in a factory and distributing exclusively through established dealers. The plan is to make the basic components of the car in Tata plants—and then to send the car off the company's assembly line much like a bicycle, in a knocked-down kit form. These will be shipped across the country to Tata-trained franchisees. Some of them will be Tata Motors car dealers. But other franchisees may be any of India's thousands of roadside garages.

The mechanics will keep the kits in their garages and assemble them on demand for customers—then service them as needed. "It will give an opportunity to young, capable people to create an enterprise," says Tata. But the move will also save an estimated 20% of an auto's production, experts say. "Tata's plan makes the car a commodity," says Kumar Bhattacharyya, director of Warwick Manufacturing Group at the University of Warwick in Britain.

If Ratan Tata's plan works, he will have stripped away a layer of distribution and manufacturing costs. Other Indian companies are tackling different kinds of distribution costs—and blowing away traditional assumptions in the process. In the case of Indian Tobacco Co. (ITC), managers are aggressively seeking ways to eliminate the exploitative middlemen who buy, transport, and market Indian farmers' produce.

Calcutta-based ITC is best known as a hotelier and as India's largest producer of cigarettes. But it also sells fertilizer to farmers and buys their grain to make processed foods. For years, ITC conducted its business with farmers through a maze of intermediaries, from brokers to traders. So ITC's head of international business, S. Sivakumar, thought of using e-commerce as a way to break the unhealthy hold of traders over the supply chain. In the initial experiment—begun in the central Indian state of Madhya Pradesh—Sivakumar set up computer kiosks in 20 villages and hired a well-known local farmer to run each kiosk. He and other farmers would access the company's intranet—dubbed e-chaupal, for electronic "town square"—twice a day to check ITC's own offer price for produce, as well as prices in the closest village market, in the state capital, in New Delhi, and on the Chicago commodities exchange. The site relayed daily weather conditions and educated users about new farming techniques worldwide. In the evening, the local children took free lessons on the computer. In return, the farmers would usually give ITC first dibs on their crops, thus eliminating the middlemen.

## Rising Incomes

How well the model works can be seen in the life of farmers such as 38-year-old Gulab Singh Varma. His two-room house is well-appointed by the standards of Bhaukhedi, the village of 3,000 where he lives in Sehore district, Madhya Pradesh. In pride of place, next to a bright-red velvet sofa, is the e-chaupal computer, complete with speakers, printer, a satellite connection, and two sets of solar-powered batteries.

Before e-chaupal was set up, he says, farmers would spend three days traveling to the nearest market to sell their produce and never got a fair price. Then they would buy fertilizer and pesticides at premium rates and return home feeling cheated. "Now it takes a few hours to make a sale in the local market," Varma says, "because we know the prices a day ahead of time, and we negotiate with the local market on the Web site." Selling produce to ITC, thanks to the direct connection, nets the farmers 5% to 15% more than in the traditional marketplace. ITC is now building large, rural Wal-Mart-like supermarkets where farmers come to sell their produce and buy everything they need, from tractors to cell phones. "Since e-chaupal began, the farmers' incomes have increased by 25% to 30%," estimates Varma.

Through 2010, when ITC hopes to reach its goal of 100,000 villages participating in e-chaupal, the company will spend $100 million a year on developing this network. None of the competition, including U.S. rival Cargill Corp., can match this head start. Consultant Hagel worries that Western companies are "far too complacent about the changes and won't have the capabilities to respond" to such business models.

Will Western multinationals find themselves confronting model Indian companies outside India as well? For now, Indian companies are venturing overseas more slowly and cheaply than their state-backed Chinese counterparts. The Indians are making $1 million to $100 million acquisitions to learn about foreign markets or to tap capabilities for their own operations.

But that doesn't mean there won't be surprises. "Companies out of India and China will be disruptive business models, coming at you in ways you can't anticipate," says Jayant Sinha, author of a recent McKinsey & Co. study of globalizing companies from the developing world. Already, India's ICICI Bank, with $42 billion in assets, is adapting the outsourcing model to finance. It has turned itself into a low-cost consumer bank by building its own high-tech back office and is expanding in rural India by setting up automated teller machines in villages.

Now, ICICI is using that technological edge abroad, opening up a wholly owned bank subsidiary in Canada. By operating its low-cost back end in India, the bank is passing on those benefits to locals who bank through the Internet in the form of interest some 35 to 75 basis points higher than what's available at other Canadian banks. The product has been so popular that the bank already has 22,000 customers, with 1,500 new ones signing up every week. Indian companies like ICICI can successfully take their models overseas because they are firmly anchored to their home market. A home market that is constantly being reinvented.

## Taking a Page from Toyota's Playbook

*Wipro and other Indian info-tech companies are boosting efficiency by emulating the Japanese carmaker*

In 2004, executives of Wipro Ltd. got a glimpse inside a Toyota assembly plant. During a guided tour of the factory that produces Corollas near their headquarters in Bangalore, India, Wipro execs hoped to pick up fresh ideas for their businesses of developing software and handling clients' back-office operations.

There were plenty of lessons to learn, but for Sambuddha Deb, Wipro's chief quality officer, one stands out. Deb began to take a shortcut when the safety path painted on the factory floor made a sharp turn. The Japanese manager walking behind him reached out, took his shoulders, and gently guided him back onto the path. The message—all the little rules count. "They had that sort of discipline. It's second nature to them," marvels Deb.

Before the Toyota tour, Wipro had been struggling to get on track in back-office services. That might sound odd: With $1.7 billion in revenues, 42,000 employees, and a U.S.-traded stock that has advanced 230% in two years, Wipro is the embodiment of India's info-tech revolution. It's not only a leader in software development but also a pioneer in business process outsourcing, where it does everything for clients from running accounting operations to processing mortgage applications. In that business, the company was respected for its low prices and dependability, but the work was too labor-intensive. Wipro wasn't doing enough to improve the way it did its clients' business.

That's one reason Wipro decided to use Toyota as a model for overhauling operations. Its aim is to make business processes as simple, smooth, and replicable as the way Corollas slip off that Bangalore assembly line every 5.3 minutes. In an unprecedented move, Wipro took on the tricky task of translating Toyota's vaunted principles for manufacturing into the realm of services. "What we do is apply people, technology, and processes to solve a business problem," says T. K. Kurien, the head of Wipro's 13,600-person business process outsourcing unit.

Today, Wipro's paperwork processing operations in Bangalore, Pune, and Chennai bear an uncanny resemblance to a Toyota plant. Day and night, thousands of eager young men and women line up at long rows of tables modeled on an assembly line. Signs hanging over each aisle describe what process is being handled there—accounts receivable, travel and entertainment, and so on. Team leaders such as P. V. Priya, who oversees medical claims in Bangalore, set goals with their colleagues at the beginning of each shift. Just like in a Toyota factory, electronic displays mounted on the walls will shift from green to red if things bog down.

## Running a 21st-Century Company

This infatuation with Toyota-like efficiency now permeates India's tech-services industry. The Indian companies see a kindred spirit in the Japanese automaker. Like them, Toyota was forced to claw its way into a global business with low prices and a passion for quality. Such commitment is the key to becoming the back office for hundreds of

Western companies, hastening the transfer of many thousands of jobs offshore. "If the Indians get this right, in addition to their low labor rates, they can become deadly competition," says Jeffrey K. Liker, a business professor at the University of Michigan and author of *The Toyota Way*, about Toyota's lean manufacturing techniques.

Think of any job that can be done remotely, by computer or telephone, and you're looking at a job that can be done by an Indian. Business process outsourcing, or BPO, includes handling clients' call centers, accounting, human resources, and the like. Top Indian services companies don't just perform these jobs well. They demonstrate how a 21st-century company ought to run. They have globalized workforces, super-efficient operations, and slavish devotion to customer service.

This emerging industry is helping India along the path to building a world-class economy. Already it supplies relatively well-paying jobs for upwards of 300,000. A 23-year-old can make $7,000—enough to afford a motorbike, or even a Corolla, to commute in style on Bangalore's jam-packed streets. The Indian BPO industry grew 40%, to $5.8 billion, in 2004 and is expected to hit $64 billion and employ 3 million people in 2012, according to a NASSCOM/KPMG study.

## Continuous Improvement

India will only get there if it has more to offer than cheap labor. Any developing nation has that. So Wipro and other Indian tech leaders, including Tata Consultancy Services Ltd. and Infosys Technologies, are upgrading their services. They're automating processes to skip manual steps and using analytical software to mine data about their clients' customers.

The goal for Wipro is to become the Toyota of business services. Toyota preaches continuous improvement, respect for employees, learning, and embracing change. "It's the soft stuff that makes a big impact on the hard numbers," says Kurien, a cheerful 45-year-old. There is plenty of hard-edged analysis, as well. To embrace Toyota's methods, Kurien assigned teams to examine business processes, break them into discrete components, and come up with streamlined services to sell to clients.

Almost immediately, Kurien spotted a surprising problem—cubicles. They're normal for programmers but interrupted the flow for business process employees. So he came up with the idea of positioning people side by side at long tables and running processes up the line step by step. Wipro also adopted *Toyota's kaizen* system of soliciting employee suggestions for incremental improvements, and made *The Toyota Way* required reading. The company even did time-and-motion studies. One discovery: It took an average of nine minutes for employees to regain optimal performance after water and bathroom breaks. The water coolers were quickly moved closer to people's desks.

The initial response to all this "was a roaring disaster," admits Kurien. Some staffers felt like cogs in a machine, and they dragged their heels. Nandini Swamynathan, 34, who runs an employee-benefits help desk, was OK with Kurien's plans. Her staff felt differently. "The factory idea concerned people," she says. After hearing from his middle managers, Kurien did a reboot. He set up classes to explain the concepts and show how the methods would make their lives easier.

The results are coming in. Since the program started, the group has improved productivity by 43% and reduced the percentage of transactions that had to be redone from 18% to 2%. Customers are reaping rewards, too. Look at E-OPS, a Miami start-up. On June 14, 2005, it announced the country's first round-the-clock paperless mortgage-processing service. E-OPS had just six employees on Day One, and they focused solely on marketing. "It's amazing that you can run a national company with just a handful of employees, and Wipro does the rest," says E-OPS Chief Executive Joseph Machado.

Indeed, Wipro's paperwork-handling operations run with factorylike efficiency. There are two shifts—8:30 a.m. to 6 p.m. and 6 p.m. to 3 a.m. When each shift starts, the teams, which are organized by process categories, gather with their team leaders for 10 minutes to discuss the day's goals and divide up tasks accordingly. Then they scatter to their desks.

During a recent visit by *BusinessWeek* to an office in Bangalore, we followed the journey of a single invoice through accounts payable. The first stop was the "imaging" room, where C. Venkatesh fed documents into scanners and attached electronic copies to workflow software, which manages each step of the process. Then H. V. Shivaram typed data from the invoice into the accounting software program, M. Rassal checked the math, Srikanth Vittal Murthy posted the charges in the general ledger, D. S. Varadharajan authorized payment, and B. Ravi Sekhar arranged for a check to be cut. Finally, V. Karunakaran printed and mailed it. If the process had hit a bottleneck, a digital display on the wall would have turned red. That would have prompted managers to swarm to the center of the room, confer, and fix the problem on the spot.

Wipro's employees seem sincerely excited about their jobs—work that would likely be considered sheer drudgery by U.S. college grads. Take 28-year-old Priya, who has worked for Wipro for nearly seven years. She has already submitted a handful of *kaizen* and is thrilled at how quickly her bosses respond. "Even though it's something small, it feels good. You're being considered," she says. Empowerment on the job is spilling over into her private life. She's the first woman in her family to go to college and recently told her parents that while they are free to arrange her marriage, they must pick a man who will not interfere with her career.

Kurien and his lieutenants do plenty to boost morale. It's stuff that would seem corny in the U.S. Employees who submit suggestions to *kaizen* boxes near their desks get little rewards—pens, caps, or shirts. Every week, the bosses wheel out a cake for a top performer. Murthy, a 25-year-old accountant on the accounts payable team who aims to be Wipro's chief financial officer some day, was surprised with one. He had led an effort to improve the handling of Indian government import approvals, cutting the time it took to process them from nearly 30 days to a maximum of 15 days. He got a cake with his name written on it in honey. "I was surprised management knew what I was doing," he says. Now, he says, "I want to do more projects."

Kurien feels he has a long way to go. "On a scale of 1 to 10, we're still at 4," he says. He recently started work in procurement and logistics.

The next likely targets are engineering services and health-care claims processing, which are two of the industries that Wipro focused on for software services. His idea is to weave business process services into the company's tech offerings to give clients an ever-widening menu to pick from. A customer who hires Wipro to write new features into its accounting software program may also hire Kurien's crew to run the new process itself.

With every new initiative, he has to hire and train a fresh team and come up with novel techniques for turning messy, manual processes into highly automated and efficient ones. Think of it this way. He's creating a mirror world to the way business is done today in the West—but the reflection has to be sharper than the original image. If Kurien succeeds, a few years from now management gurus may be trumpeting the Wipro Way.

## Ratan Tata: No One's Doubting Now

*He has transformed Tata from an overgrown conglomerate into an agile global force*

The entrance to Bombay's Birla Matushree Auditorium is festooned with blue and red bunting. Outside, scores of people mill about, waiters serve free coffee and soda, and a long queue waits to get into the hall. Suddenly a flurry of excitement sweeps the crowd. What's the attraction? No, it's not an appearance by the latest Bollywood starlet. It's a tall, graying man in a conservative suit: Ratan N. Tata, 67-year-old chairman of Tata Group, arriving to lead the annual meeting of Tata Motors, the group's largest company. "When Ratan Tata is there, you don't have to worry about anything," says longtime shareowner Pravin D. Shah as the chairman strides by.

Tata, India's largest conglomerate, has certainly achieved the kind of results that set shareholders' hearts aflutter. The group's revenues rose 30% from 2002 to 2003, to $12.8 billion, and profits grew 60%, to $1.2 billion. Stock prices of the group's biggest publicly traded companies, Tata Motors and Tata Steel, have tripled in that period. Tata raised $1.2 billion by selling 13% of Tata Consultancy Services (TCS), Asia's largest software-services player and pioneer of the outsourcing business that has fueled India's fast-growing economy. The initial public offering boosted the group's international profile as Ratan Tata gears up to make Tata a global player. "TCS exemplifies our dual thrust: It is a dominant player within the country, but it will also focus our growth outside India," he says.

It's a sweet moment for the gentlemanly Tata. Since 1991, when he took over as chairman at the behest of his uncle J. R. D. Tata, he has faced plenty of opposition as he dragged the group out of the cozy—but stifling—embrace of socialist India and streamlined the overgrown conglomerate. J. R. D. Tata had been a darling of the Indian Establishment, but many observers were skeptical about his untested nephew. Ratan Tata's plan—sketched out a decade before he became chairman, back when he ran the group's business-development arm—was to build a more focused company without abandoning the best of Tata's manufacturing tradition.

It took the better part of a decade, but Tata's vision is paying off. Today, the group has interests from autos and steel to software and telecom and is prospering as India's economy booms. "The group is now well positioned to benefit from India's rapid growth and evolution as a global sourcing base," says Amit Chandra, a managing director at investment bank DSP Merrill Lynch Ltd. in Bombay.

## Household Name

The group has come a long way in its 138-year history. It was founded by Jamsetji Tata, who started a textile-trading business in 1868 in Bombay and then built the country's first steel mill and hydroelectric plant. Since then, Tata products have become interwoven with the fabric of Indian life. Indians season their food with Tata salt, drink Tata tea, drive Tata cars, and use Tata's power, air conditioners, and phone networks. They stay in Tata hotels and wear Tata watches. India's infrastructure is built with Tata's steel, and its companies and government agencies run Tata's software.

Ratan Tata isn't satisfied: He wants the world—not just India—to embrace Tata products. So in recent years he has been in global expansion mode. In 2000, Tata Tea Ltd. paid $435 million for Britain's Tetley Tea, a company three times its size, to gain a ready-made international brand. In 2004, Tata bought Daewoo's commercial truck operation for $102 million, with the idea of using Daewoo technology for his truck-making operation and establishing a springboard into other Asian markets. In Britain, MG Rover Group Ltd. is selling Tata-built Indica compact cars under its own brand name, while Tata trucks ply roads from Malaysia to South Africa. The lodging division is expanding into luxury and business hotels around the world. And TCS is looking to buy software houses in North and South America.

Tata, though, isn't neglecting his home turf. He is using the group's engineering and technological skills to innovate and develop affordable, high-quality products and services for a young, emerging class of Indians with big aspirations but limited means. In June 2004, Tata's Indian Hotels Co. launched indiOne—a chain of $20-a-night self-service hostelries that feature Wi-Fi connections and flat-screen TVs. Tata Motors is preparing to roll out the first prototype of a four-door car expected to sell for just $2,200. Tata says the ventures are meant to be profitable, but he admits he is also motivated by a family tradition of charity and good works. "It's the foundation on which the group was built," says Tata. Investors are watching to see whether such a model can generate the kind of profits they're accustomed to seeing from Tata. "The challenge is to ensure that the group's sense of social obligation doesn't collide with shareholder-value creation," says Ajay Sondhi, managing director of investment bank Kotak Mahindra Capital in Bombay. "But if anyone can pull it off, it is the Tatas."

Tata's riskiest bet may be on telecommunications. In 2002, the group paid $530 million for 46% of the state-owned international telecom monopoly, VSNL. That investment has been something of a lemon. The sector was deregulated soon after, and instead of benefiting from the monopoly, Tata faced a flood of new competitors. Tata has invested $2 billion in licenses and infrastructure for a mobile network, but in its first 18 months it has attracted just 2 million subscribers and remained a distant fifth in the market. Ratan Tata is nonetheless doubling down his bet and plans to invest an additional $3 billion to expand the network, install new technology, and market its service. Investors worried about Tata's slow pace in cellular are lauding the move. "The group was conservative on telecom for too long," says Dinshaw Irani, who heads portfolio management at Bombay brokerage SSKI Investor Services. "The infusion of funds isn't a moment too soon."

## Built-in Social Conscience

The frenetic activity represents a big change of pace for the old-world Tata Group. Although the conglomerate has always been run by a Tata, family members own only a tiny stake in Tata Sons, the holding company that controls the group's ownership in the various enterprises. Instead, Tata Sons is run by a pair of trusts that get dividends from the group's operations. That money is deployed for social services such as education grants and health care for the poor. Very little wends its way back into the pockets of Tata family members.

That management structure—while laudable—combined with India's restrictive socialist governments to hold back the group's growth for years. Tata companies came to be run by genteel consent and permission, rather than by aggressive ownership control. The group degenerated into a bunch of randomly run fiefdoms, with octogenarians on the boards and no modern management systems, checks, or controls. By 1991, when India liberalized its economy, shares in Tata companies languished in Bombay's then high-flying stock market.

That year, the board appointed Ratan Tata chairman even though investors and employees doubted his ability to pull the group forward. A shy and reticent man, Tata's career had been undistinguished, with desultory stints in various divisions. His early ambition was to be an architect. After earning an architecture degree at Cornell

University, he worked for a few months at a Los Angeles architectural firm. But his uncle pressed Ratan to join the family business. "I often wanted to return to the U.S. Sometimes I felt I wasn't getting anywhere," Tata says. "Many times my name was a disadvantage. My elders didn't want to be seen to be favoring me." So Tata was never offered (and never asked for) company benefits such as subsidized loans for refrigerators—precious perks in the socialist, supply-short India of those days.

Shortly after joining the group, Tata spent three years in the steel business, "shoveling limestone in the steel-melting shops, working with the foreman at the blast furnaces," he recalls. Tata loved the shop floor, and the experience gave him a comfort level with the factory workers across the vast Tata empire that he still deeply values. After his stint with steel, Tata put in time at the auto and software divisions, then faced his first real test: He was given charge of Tata Sons' limping consumer-electronics business. Tata got the company back into the black, but the business was ignored by the group, and it was soon shuttered. In 1981, Tata joined the group's business-development arm and started writing his dream plan. It envisioned a restructured Tata in eight core industries, including Old Economy stalwarts such as steel and utilities, as well as the more forward-looking information-technology and biotechnology businesses. Top management ignored the proposal.

When he got the top job, Tata pulled his plan out of the filing cabinet and set about shaking up the pedigreed but plodding conglomerate. He sold off noncore businesses such as cosmetics and cooking oil. He shrank the group to 80 companies from 250 and angered some investors by strengthening Tata Sons' stake in group companies to at least 26%—which gives the group the right to block takeovers—from as little as 1.7% before.

Doubters watched in amazement as the nonconfrontational and aristocratic Tata started to develop battle instincts. After a year of bitter public spats with powerful group chieftains—especially in the steel and hotel businesses—Tata ousted them and installed new management.

Then he tackled Tata Motors. The truckmaker had too many employees and too many suppliers, and costs were climbing while market share was slipping. So Tata halved the number of suppliers, to 600, using the company's clout in the truck market to get better prices from the survivors, and instituted a rigorous quality-control program in Tata's factories. He sold off real estate holdings and other noncore assets and exited joint ventures such as one with DaimlerChrysler to make the E-class Mercedes—a luxury few Indians could afford. Finally, he introduced a voluntary retirement scheme to trim employment by 40%, to 22,000. That generated $250 million in cash, which Tata Motors used to pay down debts that were pushing $1 billion.

## Fast Repairs

Then he fulfilled a long-cherished dream of his uncle's by making a move into passenger cars. In 1991, Tata Motors introduced a station wagon and later a sport-utility vehicle. Then, in 1999, amid much skepticism, he invested $400 million in the Indica, a four-door hatchback that sells for just $5,100. Known as "Ratan's folly," the Indica would have to face off against Suzuki Motor Corp.'s popular compacts. But Tata took a personal interest in the project, often spending weekends at the factory to help with the rollout. Initially, customers groused about a grinding gear shift, poor air-conditioning, and lousy tires. So Tata's engineers swung into action, going to showrooms and talking to customers about their complaints. In six months, many of the problems were fixed, and a new version of the Indica, the V2, was launched. Now the car is the third-biggest seller in India.

Will Tata realize his dream of remaking the group into a global giant? There are hurdles ahead, and Tata doesn't have much time—he is due to retire soon. He won't disclose his succession plan, but the market is abuzz that his half-brother, Noel Tata, 47, who runs the group's small retailing business and hasn't had a high profile, will inherit the mantle. For now, though, the show is all Ratan Tata's, and Indians—and the world—are watching.

---

# The State's Long Apron Strings

*China's multinationals, powerful as they seem, are still beholden
to the Party. That's both a blessing and a burden.*

The age of the Chinese multinational is upon us. Companies few
Westerners had heard of a few years ago now make the headlines
almost every day. TCL Corp., a Chinese consumer-electronics manufacturer, controls the venerable RCA brand. Lenovo Group Ltd., China's
No. 1 computer maker, owns IBM's PC business. Haier, a white-goods
maker, roiled the waters with its ultimately failed bid for Maytag Corp.
CNOOC Ltd. riled Washington before withdrawing its $18.5 billion
offer for Unocal Corp. Add the exploits of Huawei Technologies and
ZTE in telecom gear, the overseas deals of Shanghai Baosteel, and the
expansionist plans of phone company China Netcom, and it's easy to
imagine that the next decade will belong to China's blue chips.

If China's multinationals do emerge as power players, many of them
will have the state to thank for their success. These companies have
implicit or explicit backing from Beijing and can build on China's other
strengths as well—low wages, vast internal markets, and rapid economic
growth. But having the state as either parent or mentor can be a burden, too; rivals often say the support gives them an unfair edge. Ultimately it may be the Chinese companies that transcend their state
origins—or those that are entirely private—that really excel.

A number of Chinese companies have carved out a smallish piece of
their businesses—typically the most profitable chunks—and floated
them either in Hong Kong or New York. But the listed company is usually majority-owned by its parent, which remains in state hands. In an
initial public offering in 2000, oil and gas producer PetroChina Co.
raised $3.1 billion from investors including Warren E. Buffett. But it's
still 90% owned by China National Petroleum Corp., which is 100%
state-owned. Same goes for Unocal's former suitor, CNOOC Ltd. Its
parent, state-owned China National Offshore Oil Corp., holds 70%
of its shares. China Mobile Communications Corp.—again, entirely

state-owned—owns 75% of cellular operator China Mobile (Hong Kong) Ltd., whose depositary receipts trade in New York.

Abroad, though, those state ties can suddenly start looking less advantageous. Chinese companies' government links and their easy access to loans from state banks are likely to dog their foreign adventures again and again. CNOOC, for instance, is generally considered a well-run company and has been traded in Hong Kong since 2001. But U.S. lawmakers focused instead on its government ownership and access to cheap credit. Provincial electrical-appliance maker Sichuan Changhong Electric Co. last year saw its U.S. color-TV sales dwindle to nothing after it got hit with antidumping duties of 25%—not necessarily because it was actually selling its goods below cost but because its government ownership made it appear to have an unfair advantage over privately owned rivals.

Despite the coddling, mainland companies haven't yet matured into true world-beaters. While the governments of Japan and South Korea walled off their home turf from outsiders as they groomed their giants-to-be, China's borders are much more open to foreign competition. That, plus a cutthroat domestic market where thousands of rivals cut prices relentlessly, means Chinese companies often venture abroad not from a position of strength but of weakness. And lessons learned in China don't always translate abroad. "The management tools Chinese companies used to become the world's leading factory are not the same as those they will need to lead global innovation," says Darrell Rigby, a partner at consultant Bains Co. That's one reason Lenovo insisted that IBM execs stay on board after it acquired Big Blue's PC business. Indeed, consultancy McKinsey & Co. says China will need 75,000 executives with international experience in the next five years. Today it has at most 5,000.

China's listed multinationals are trying to look more like their global rivals. They're hiring Western-educated execs, engaging the likes of Bain and McKinsey, and beefing up investor-relations teams. CNOOC Chairman Fu Chengyu has a master's in petroleum engineering from the University of Southern California. China Netcom CEO Edward

Tian, who got a Ph.D. from Texas Tech University, was recruited after he made a fortune taking the software company AsiaInfo Holdings Inc. public on the NASDAQ in 1999.

Dig a little deeper, though, and many of these companies still resemble their state-owned parents. Tian, for instance, had to renounce his U.S. green card before taking the helm at Netcom. And he drives a company-owned Audi A6 with a 2.4-liter engine. Nice ride, but not as nice as the 2.6-liter version given to company directors, who hold the same rank as vice-ministers. Tian says he still finds it daunting trying to manage 100,000 employees while juggling the interests of shareholders and four state-owned parents—the Ministry of Railways, the city of Shanghai, the Chinese Academy of Sciences, and the State Administration of Radio, Film & Television. "I have learned the skill of how to survive in a large state-owned enterprise," he says. "That means 50% business and 50% communications for finding the right political balance." If these companies focused 100% on business, the results could be formidable.

## China's Power Brands

*Bold entrepreneurs are producing the mainland's hot consumer products. But the multinationals are fighting back. Who will the big winners be?*

How do you get rich in China these days? Build a brand. That's what 35-year-old Huang Guangyu has done. The Guangdong native started out at 18, renting a market stall in Beijing and hawking cheap plastic appliances. Today, his GOME Electrical Appliances is China's top consumer-electronics chain, with well over 100 stores, $2 billion in sales, and the kind of high-plateau brand recognition that Circuit City and Best Buy enjoy in the U.S.

And thanks to a backdoor stock listing in Hong Kong, Huang's net worth as of mid-2004 was at least $830 million. Just one hitch, though. China's domestic retail players, including GOME, are already worried about the impact of foreign competition when Beijing opens the entire country to retailers from abroad.

This little tale neatly sums up the story of China's emerging brands today. Tremendous excitement about the brands, but a good dose of fear about their staying power. Global business executives are certainly agog at the prospect that the next stage of China's superfast development will be the establishment of power brands in everything from retailing to white goods to autos and more—brands strong enough both to dominate at home and thrive overseas. "They are definitely going global," says Glen Murphy, the Shanghai-based managing director of ACNielsen in China. "With their resources and production base, they are large enough to reach out to the world."

There are plenty of well-known local names besides GOME. Haier Group, of course, is the granddaddy, a $10 billion maker of refrigerators, washing machines, and more, with global ambitions nurtured by its well-known boss, Zhang Ruimin. Hangzhou Wahaha Group Co., with $1.2 billion in sales, is the top vendor of bottled water. TCL Corp., with $3.4 billion in revenue, is so powerful in TVs and other electronics that it reached a deal to merge its television business with that of France's Thomson in 2003 and took control of Alcatel's cell-phone business in 2004. Lenovo Group Ltd., formerly known as Legend, with $3 billion in revenue, is No. 1 in China's PC market. Li-Ning Co. Ltd., founded by a Chinese athlete, is the top seller of athletic footwear and apparel: It went public in 2004 too. The roster goes on and on.

But China brand watchers wonder, is this impressive enough? They see the capacity overhang in Chinese industry, the tendency to skimp on innovation, the ever-growing presence of multinationals on the mainland, and the continuing popularity of foreign brands on the mainland. Share prices for many of China's consumer brand companies were way off in 2004. Brand awareness of Chinese companies among U.S. and European consumers is, by and large, low. And for every China brands enthusiast, there's a skeptic. "Export their brands successfully?" asks Tom Doctoroff, CEO for Greater China at U.S. ad agency J. Walter Thompson. "Chinese companies are light years away from it."

Then again, so were the Koreans when they set out 20 years ago to join the stable of world-class brand companies—and no one could have predicted that Samsung, LG, and Hyundai would be the up-and-coming global brands they are now. Like the Koreans, the Chinese are certainly going to stumble many times as they build their brands. But with all the furious activity going on in the marketplace, some of these brands will emerge as real winners, both at home and abroad. Unlike the nationalist Japanese, some will hook up with foreign companies to get a boost—and some will even use the brand name of their foreign partner when they market abroad, as TCL will with RCA, Thomson's big brand in the U.S., and the Thomson brand itself, in Europe. China's huge domestic economy gives these contenders the chance to cut their teeth in the most competitive market on earth, and to build up a war chest of revenues for efforts abroad. "Market shares will go up and down. Some Chinese companies will lose. It's a learning process," says Paul Gao, a principal in the Shanghai office of McKinsey & Co. "But there is no doubt that world-class Chinese brands will emerge." The learning process will involve both making better products and selling them more effectively. Ogilvy & Mather Chairman and CEO Shelly Lazarus recently led a conference of more than a dozen Chinese companies at the former estate of agency founder David Ogilvy. Lazarus was impressed both by their lack of knowledge and their hunger. "Most Chinese companies don't yet understand even what we mean by 'positioning' a brand," Lazarus told *BusinessWeek*. "But they are anxious to know. They can't suck it in fast enough. They are going to figure this out. You can see it in their eyes."

## The Competitive Crush

Who will those winners be? China brand watchers pick TCL, Haier, and SVA, a top TV maker. But at this stage in China's tumultuous economy, it's hard to say for sure. Overcapacity has reached 30% in many industries, including televisions, washing machines, and refrigerators, putting tremendous pressure on margins. "Home electronics appliance prices are decreasing 10% to 15% annually," says Chen Kaixun, vice-president of

Hisense Electric Co. Ltd., an appliance maker and rival to Haier. "For the price war, the only thing we can do is decrease our costs." Hisense managed 2% profit growth in the first six months of 2004. The price war also hit Haier hard; its Shanghai-listed arm pulled off only 6% profit growth for the first half, despite sharply rising sales. And it's not just white goods. Auto prices have fallen 7% in 2002 and 2003 and by an estimated 10% in 2004. The television glut is especially severe—and an aggressive export drive has triggered antidumping suits from the U.S. and Europe.

Another menace is the profusion of copycat products that spring up as soon as a brand gains popularity. Products from Tsingtao beer to Li-Ning shoes all compete with knockoffs. Often the only way for the big Chinese and foreign brands to drive the counterfeiters out of business is to slash prices even further—a strategy that runs counter to developing brand equity.

In this punishing environment, the until-now mediocre record of Chinese companies in innovation is a liability. It's rare for Chinese companies to meet the international norm of spending 5% or more of revenues on research and development. This spending gap can give multinationals the edge.

That's what has happened in cell phones. Between 2000 and 2003, local handset brands like Bird, Amoi, Panda, and TCL beat Nokia, Motorola, and other global brands on price and flashy features like TCL's gem-studded phone, a big success with the nouveaux-riches. The locals went from a zero share in handsets a few years ago to almost 50%. "We take our Chinese competitors seriously," says Maurice Tan, marketing manager for Nokia China. "They are like a wolf pack."

Yet the wolf pack has been retreating of late. In the past few years, Motorola, Nokia, and Sony Ericsson have rolled out a raft of phones with fancy new functions, pushed aggressively into new markets, and slashed prices. Nokia, for example, has added Chinese handwriting functions and expanded its relationships with the thousands of small retailers that sell mobile phones across China. Because of the counterattack, TCL has seen its branded handset market share slip from 8% in 2002 to 6.1% in 2004. Sales of its mobile phones at its Shenzhen-listed arm dropped almost by a third in the first half of 2004, while Bird's sales dropped almost 20%. Overall, domestic vendors have seen their handset sales slip from 42% of the market in 2003 to 37% in the first half of 2004. Says Patrick Kung, general manager of Motorola's handset business in North Asia: "The locals did very well in the past three years. But starting this year (2004), their growth rate has stalled big time." And there are still 37 local handset makers slugging it out.

Foreign manufacturers such as Hitachi and Samsung have also won back share in high-end plasma and flat-screen TVs, while Panasonic and LG have recovered some of the sales they lost in microwaves to local brand Galanz. In autos, the Koreans and Japanese are expected to introduce more affordable models in China. "The next several years will be difficult for local carmakers," predicts Yale Zhang, director of emerging-markets vehicle forecasts at CSM Asia Corp. in Shanghai. General Motors, Ford, and Volkswagen already offer budget models for less than $10,000. That could spell trouble for Geely Auto, a new brand that has quickly captured 4% of the market with cars that sell for as little as $3,500. Geely can't match the foreign brands for quality.

The increasing competition in retail will also hurt, at least in the short run. Today, Chinese companies have an edge in developing relationships with the thousands of small stores and kiosks where most Chinese shop. But with the World Trade Organization–mandated opening of all China to foreign retailers at the end of 2004, multinationals such as Wal-Mart Stores Inc. and Carrefour will further expand their franchises, making those ties less important. "As the distribution model changes, it is becoming less and less suited to domestic brands, making it easier for foreign companies to penetrate China," says Qu Honglin, general manager of Local Strategy, a Shanghai brands consultancy.

A final issue that Chinese companies have to struggle with is the depth of management. Many of China's best brands were conceived by heroic entrepreneurs like GOME's Huang or 59-year-old Zong Qinghou. Zong, who spent years laboring in the rice paddies during the Cultural Revolution, is founder of Wahaha, a beverage group that had profits of $196 million last year. (French company Groupe Danone owns 30%.) A hands-on leader, Zong will lead his managers on a tour of street vendors to see how beverages get sold in China's sprawling sidewalk markets. But he scorns market research, and it's not clear how Wahaha would fare without its charismatic founder. That's also true of other Chinese companies, says Local Strategy's Qu.

## Don't Skimp on R&D

These are all formidable problems. Yet for every setback, the Chinese find a way to move forward. Indeed, losing a few rounds in the most competitive market on earth is excellent training. Look at Lenovo. Several years ago the computer maker hatched big plans to branch out into PDAs, mobile phones, and other areas beyond its expertise in laptops, PCs, and servers. The company pushed its global expansion as well. Bad idea. The loss of focus started costing Lenovo—as Dell Inc. stepped up the pressure in China. Lenovo had to lay off 5% of its workforce last spring. But to its credit, the company has refocused its priorities in the China market, and profits have rebounded. Investors need to keep a watch, though. Lenovo is now going into investment banking—not exactly a core competence.

Other companies are realizing they can't skimp on research. Over the next few years, TCL will ramp up R&D from 3% of sales to 5%. Television maker SVA Group spends 6%. "We must invest and develop new products," says Chen Hong, SVA's vice-president in charge of overseas markets. "If we focus on price alone, we don't have a future." SVA sells only flat-screen and plasma televisions in the U.S. and has hired McKinsey to do consumer research to tailor its branded products.

If foreign connections will help, so be it. SVA has a joint venture with NEC to manufacture LCD panels. TCL, by acquiring Thomson-RCA's TV line and Alcatel's cell-phone business, has acquired Western brand names, distribution networks in Europe, and a bundle of Western technology. Strong sales in televisions in China and abroad helped push up TCL's first half earnings by 44% in 2004, despite its serious setback in cell phones at home.

One brand that has seen its global future and acted on it is telecom equipment maker Huawei Technologies Co. It already spends more than 10% of its revenues on research—and is not only competing successfully against outfits like Cisco in telecommunications gear but could emerge as a consumer brand as well. It now makes handsets and set-top boxes for TVs. Its formidable research machine could give it a winning hand.

Other companies are building up better knowledge of foreign markets. Haier has been criticized for not grasping what it takes to succeed globally. "One of the steps that many of the Asian companies have missed is the huge investment that's required to build brand equity," says David L. Swift, executive vice-president of Whirlpool Corp.'s North American region, which competes with Haier. In the U.S., Haier's greatest success is with budget items such as compact refrigerators.

Yet Haier already spends 4% of revenues on research and is creating local product-development teams in Tokyo and the U.S. to differentiate its line and move upmarket. In Japan, for instance, Haier offers washers that use less water, are quieter, and are narrow enough to fit cramped Japanese homes. "In the past, we tried to design our products in Qingdao and sell them to the U.S. and Japan," says 55-year-old CEO Zhang. "They didn't meet overseas consumers' needs and didn't sell well." Today, Haier has 22 factories overseas, including a refrigerator plant in Camden, South Carolina. Revenues from Haier's overseas operations were up 53% to $1.3 billion in the first eight months of 2004.

Back home, many parts of the Chinese market are still up for grabs, thanks to the vastness of the country. Wahaha, for example, has built up its market by avoiding head-on confrontations with PepsiCo Inc. and Coca-Cola Co. and focusing on less-developed markets. It is now a big force in provincial capitals like Kunming, Yunnan. "We have a huge advantage in second-tier markets," boasts Wahaha's Zong, whose brand leads Coke and Pepsi in most of rural China. "In rural China, Wahaha has a majority position," confirms Zhu Huican, an analyst at Beijing market researcher Gung Ho Group.

Other companies are customizing products for the hinterland. Guangdong Kelon Electrical Holdings Co. has developed the budget

Combine brand of refrigerators and air conditioners for less affluent consumers. "We are targeting poor families and farmers," says Kelon Chairman Gu Chujun, a 45-year-old former scientist who patented his own cooling system for his fridges. Kelon's sales were up 49% in 2004, while profits were up 11%.

Chinese companies are also learning how to raid the competition. Li-Ning has hired Wu Xianyong, a former Procter Gamble manager, to run its marketing and branding. Wu made sure that many of the Chinese athletes at the Athens Olympics wore Li-Ning shoes and other equipment. Such product placement gave Li-Ning an Olympic boost in sales in China, where the company has more than 2,000 outlets and the top spot in athletic shoes, with 12.39% market share, according to Sinomonitor International, a Beijing market monitoring firm. "All of us [Chinese consumer goods] companies must thank P&G for our development," says Li-Ning's general manager Zhang Zhiyong. Geely's Nan Yang, a senior vice-president for overseas production, was formerly general manager of Shanghai Volkswagen Automotive Co., the joint venture between Volkswagen and Shanghai Automotive Industry Corp. Nan has overseen Geely's push into parts of the Arab world. The head of Wahaha's Future Cola unit once was the Beijing bottler for Pepsi.

Like Westerners, the Chinese are learning how to advertise on a grand scale. Ad spending in 2003 was $24 billion in China, making it the third-biggest ad market in the world. A big chunk of that spending will be by Chinese companies, and lines such as Li-Ning's "Anything is possible" are known by millions. The ad spending will only increase as the 2008 date of the Beijing Olympics approaches. Lenovo already became the first-ever Chinese company to be an official "top" sponsor of an Olympics—up there with Coca-Cola and Panasonic—when it signed on to back the 2008 games. It's part of "a longtime dream to become an international brand," says marketing boss Alice Li. Sports marketing is a fast-rising category even without the coming Olympics. To keep its brand front-of-mind in China, SVA in 2001 bought Shanghai's soccer team. Meanwhile, the world beckons. SVA has established its foothold in the U.S. Meanwhile, TCL, with the Alcatel deal it just signed, has big plans for Europe. Geely has borrowed from the Koreans' early marketing strategy and entered other developing countries as a first step to overseas expansion, starting with the Middle East. In 2004, Haier announced it is opening an R&D center and factory in fast-growing India.

Some efforts will fail. But with every ad campaign, every marketing battle, every product launch, the Chinese learn more. Does another Chinese juggernaut, like the one that has taken over much of global manufacturing lie ahead? Not now. But give them time, and the best of these brands will prove themselves.

---

## China's Free Range Cash Cow

*Upstart Mengniu Dairy isn't tethered to the state. It's thriving—and the shareholders are contented.*

Executives at China Mengniu Dairy Co. were ecstatic when China's first astronaut, Lieutenant Colonel Yang Liwei, safely touched down on the grasslands of Inner Mongolia at dawn on Oct. 15, 2003. Sure, they were as proud as the rest of China that their country had put a man in space, and seeing him land on their home turf was a bonus. But Mengniu had a special stake in his safe return. Although Yang didn't drink any milk on his flight, Mengniu was the "official provider" of dairy products during his long months of training. So when Yang returned to earth, the company's marketing machine hit warp speed. Within days, Mengniu had blitzed the country with ads featuring men, women, and children in space suits drinking milk.

That kind of marketing savvy has helped Mengniu rocket into the ranks of China's best-known brands since its founding in 1999. According to ACNielsen, it was the country's top seller of milk in 2004, with 22% of the market. Revenues that year jumped 77%, to $871 million, while profits soared 94.3%, to $38.5 million.

The company listed its shares on the Hong Kong Stock Exchange in June 2004, raising $118 million with a roster of leading international investors including Fidelity Investments, Dreyfus, and ING picking up shares. In 2005, Mengniu announced a $67 million joint venture with Arla Foods of Denmark to make powdered milk for distribution in China, Macao, and Hong Kong.

Mengniu has built its business with no government help. And that makes it a model for a new breed of Chinese company. Unlike better-known giants such as CNOOC Ltd. and Lenovo Group, which have sold shares to outsiders but remain tethered to the state, upstarts like Mengniu have learned to fend off growing competition without the state subsidies or easy credit often enjoyed by China's corporate titans. Such companies can pounce on marketing opportunities that their more hidebound and hierarchical rivals are slow to exploit. Mengniu, for example, recently sponsored a musical talent show similar to *American Idol*—something that would never have flown at a state-controlled enterprise.

Nimble upstarts like Mengniu are giving state-owned companies, as well as some foreign interlopers, a run for their money. Others in this group include Internet portals SINA.com, NetEase Services, Sohu.com, and online gaming company Shanda Interactive Entertainment. Privately owned Minsheng Banking Corp. has the lowest level of nonperforming loans among Chinese banks: NPLs accounted for just 1.44% of Minsheng's outstanding loans in June 2005. Wanxiang Group in Hangzhou is the country's largest maker of auto parts. And Geely Automobile Holdings, with its popular subcompacts, has become the country's second-largest purely Chinese carmaker, and the first to export its cars.

China today has nearly 3.5 million such private companies, according to the All-China Federation of Industry & Commerce, a Beijing trade association. Revenues in the private sector skyrocketed from $5 billion in 1989 to $241 billion last year, accounting for 15% of China's gross domestic product.

Consider Mengniu's steady ascent. It was founded by Niu Gensheng in 1999 after he lost his job as vice-president for sales at state-owned Yili

Dairy in a power struggle. (Niu grew up with Yili Dairy, where his father worked for 38 years and he worked for 17 years.) Niu and several Yili colleagues pooled $12,600 of their own money and went head-to-head with their former employer in its home market of Inner Mongolia (*Mengniu* means Mongolian cow), selling sterilized long-life milk in local supermarkets and restaurants. Mengniu began expanding rapidly beyond the northeast, forging close ties with distributors to China's fragmented retail sector. Today the company works with more than 1,000 independent wholesalers from Shanghai to Tibet, offering some 200 products, ranging from long-life milk and liquid yogurt to baby formula and corn-flavored ice cream bars.

## Yogurt with Soft-Drink Buzz

Mengniu's rapid expansion attracted the attention of overseas investors looking for a way to get into China. Global private equity funds Actis China Investment Company and CDH China Fund teamed up with Morgan Stanley to invest in the company after a survey of supermarket owners found that Mengniu was one of their top performers. Niu, though, wasn't interested at first. "Normally it's enterprises who go after the investors, but we said no to them three times before we said yes," he recalls. Once Niu relented, the three foreigners in 2002 ponied up $25 million and another $35 million a year later. They owned 28% of the company before it went public.

Today, Mengniu is known as far more than just milk for astronauts. Suan Suan Milk, a flavored yogurt drink, has seen its sales rise sharply, thanks to Mengniu's sponsorship of a television show called *Super Voice Girl*, a local program loosely based on *American Idol*. "It's a huge hit tying in with the TV program," says Tom Doctoroff, chief executive of J. Walter Thompson Greater China. "They've brought a soft-drink buzz into yogurt targeted at teenage girls."

Mengniu has also put a new focus on quality and innovation in the dairy industry. Inside the company's headquarters, located in fertile countryside 50 kilometers from the Inner Mongolian capital of Hohhot, engineers monitor each production line from two-meter-wide computer screens. In the company laboratory, technicians in white coats work on new yogurt formulas. Inventory in Mengniu's warehouse is moved around by robotic forklifts with virtually no human intervention.

At its experimental farm a few kilometers away, the company offers cows 12 varieties of grass, including Canadian Alfalfa Violet Flower and Brazilian Bamboo. The facility resembles a bovine spa. In addition to the menu of specialty grasses, the cows enjoy soft music in the milking hall and are offered foam mats to recline on. They can groom themselves by rubbing up against a rotating brush on a swivel arm, and when their udders are full they can wander over to China's only robotic milking machine. The thinking is that a contented cow will produce richer milk. And richer milk adds up to richer shareholders—including Niu and his partners. That's the kind of entrepreneurial thinking that's becoming the norm in the new China.

---

# TCL Multimedia's Global Agenda

*CFO Vincent Yan on how Beijing does—and doesn't—support it, the Thomson merger, and the marketplace's "extreme challenges"*

In 2004, TCL International, now known as TCL Multimedia, acquired the TV business from France's Thomson, owner of the venerable RCA brand. Vincent Yan, chief financial officer of TCL Multimedia, recently spoke to *BusinessWeek* Asia Correspondent Frederik Balfour about the merged business and the challenges of going global. Edited excerpts of their conversation follow:

**Q: Now that you have Thomson's distribution in Europe and North America, do you plan to make TCL a global brand?**
**A:** For now our strategy is to utilize the RCA name globally. To build a brand in a mature market is costly; we don't plan to do that. In China, the brand is pretty much TCL.

**Q: Do you plan to move Thomson's Mexican operations to China?**

**A:** No. We have restructured the Mexico factory. Antidumping law discourages or prevents us from selling TVs from here [duties are 25%]. That's because people advising the [U.S.] government are operating with a mindset of 20 years ago, trying to protect the U.S. producers. It's a joke because nobody in the U.S. is producing TVs, except for the one company that raised the issue with the government.

**Q: But aren't there perceptions abroad that you get Chinese government subsidies, hence you can dump?**

**A:** Of course we don't get any government subsidies. [But] how do you define government support? What is indirect support? Would you say Microsoft is not getting any support from the U.S. government when it meets leaders from China? If you say no, then I say TCL doesn't get any support [from the Chinese government].

TCL Corp. [the parent] is one of the biggest companies in Huizhou [the municipality of Huizhou owns 25% of TCL], so of course the government supports TCL's activities. TCL is an important company nationwide and for the local government as well. [The local government] will do whatever it can to help the company grow, such as tax preferences, something it offers to any company investing in the area. But that is by no means a subsidy.

**Q: What direct input does the government have on TCL's activities?**

**A:** The vice-chairman of our company comes from the government, but we are like any limited liability company where shareholders elect the directors.

**Q: What role does the Communist Party play?**

**A:** I'm not a Party member. The head of the Party organization at TCL Group is also our president and CEO, Mr. [Tomson] Li.

**Q: Is it easier for you to get financing because of your links to the local government?**

**A:** TCL Corp. indirectly supports our cash flow, because we can borrow for some of our working capital needs in China, and our parent provides the loan guarantee to the banks. Otherwise Chinese banks wouldn't lend; they recognize us as a Hong Kong company.

**Q: How did you get such broad distribution in China?**
**A:** We started making large-screen TVs in 1993 or 1994 at a price that no one else was offering. The only [ones] available were Sony and Panasonic imports. We reduced costs by offering fewer features. By 1997 we were nationwide.

**Q: How much do you spend on research and development?**
**A:** TCL Group spends 1.5% of sales, which is low compared to what other multinational companies spend. But you have to look at the business structure. We don't offer products that require concentrated R&D.

Samsung [Electronics] offers cutting-edge technology. We don't. Everyone at the company would like to do that, but it's a matter of feasibility, and I don't see that happening now.

**Q: How much management time is spent on making the merger with Thomson work?**
**A:** The merger is not that difficult. We are pretty complementary, Thomson in Europe and North America, while we have little operations there. If you define "merger" as operating as a company, we have already succeeded. If you say the success of a merger should be a company tightly merged together, that's not the case. We are divided by geography, different profit centers; we operate in different modes.

The most difficult part is communication, to understand each other. Any cross-border deal has that. We knew before the merger that the cross-cultural talent pool is kind of small; [it's] difficult to find people who have a fit with the company.

The next issue is management talent, of how to run the company successfully. We don't have enough talent to do all the work. We face extreme challenges from the marketplace, especially in LCD and plasma screens—areas where neither of us is strong.

**Q: When will TTE [the arm formed when TCL bought Thomson's TV interests] become profitable?**

**A:** Sometime in 2007. The original plan was to become profitable by 2005, based on the assumption of no losses in Europe and North America. But the problem is Europe, where the LCD business is growing faster than we expected [this is an area where TCL is not yet strong], and we made a loss that was unexpected. We had about 16% return on capital in 2003, and 9% in 2004, because of Thomson's loss.

**Q: Would you recommend mergers and acquisitions as a way to go global?**

**A:** Not really. It's just one way. There are other ways to expand your business in the world.

**Q: Does TCL try to distance itself from the government to avoid charges that you receive unfair assistance?**

**A:** I don't see a need to do that. Our business partners and suppliers and customers never thought that way, though there are people who say it. My guess is they don't understand why TCL is so competitive, so they find some excuse. We never sell below cost.

---

# "Survival of the Fittest" at China Netcom

*CEO Edward Tian discusses the challenges of running the state-owned telco and the "50% business and 50% politics balance" it entails*

As chief executive of China Netcom, the country's second-largest fixed-line carrier, 42-year-old Edward Tian has learned the delicate art of keeping foreign investors happy while answering to the company's ultimate majority shareholder, the Chinese government. U.S.-educated Tian—he has a Ph.D. in resource management from Texas Tech University—made a fortune in the private sector after the company he founded, AsiaInfo, went public on NASDAQ, before joining one of China's most important state-linked companies in 1999.

He recently spoke with Frederik Balfour, *BusinessWeek's* Asia correspondent, about the challenges of running the company and the future of the Chinese telecom industry. Edited excerpts of their conversation follow:

**Q: How did you get involved with China Netcom?**

**A:** The four state shareholders—the Ministry of Railways, the Shanghai government, the Chinese Academy of Sciences, and the State Administration of Radio, Film & Television—said they wanted an outsider. They said: "You know how to run a business, why don't you do something for your country?" I couldn't say no.

Once I joined, I found myself on a train I couldn't control, going faster and faster—it became part of the Chinese company reforms. Life became very difficult with four state shareholders and regulations and competition from China Telecom. But I majored in ecology, and evolution taught me about the survival of the fittest.

**Q: How did you deal with different stakeholders?**

**A:** Jiang Minhang [son of former President Jiang Zemin] was a shareholder from the Chinese Academy of Sciences. He was a good director and had something in common with me—we both studied in the U.S. But the first year was a disaster. I was a CEO, but they didn't give me a directorship because all directors must be ministerial level.

I had to wine them and dine them and not let them color me as the foreign-educated Chinese guy with money. That was a handicap. I had to give up my U.S. green card to run this company. You have to become part of them, with a company car and driver. I have an Audi A6 2.4 liter class. Every senior official drives these. Directors drive 2.6 liter versions.

**Q: Do you regret having left AsiaInfo?**

**A:** I don't know. I'm often wondering because a friend of mine, a professor, says India is better at promoting entrepreneurs and world-class companies, but the [Chinese] government always controls large companies. The private sector can only go so far. I'm from private enterprise and learned the skills of surviving in a large state-owned enterprise. That's a 50% business and 50% politics balance.

**Q: What made you decide to take a 20% stake in PCCW [a Hong Kong telco] in 2005?**
**A:** We lack innovation and management know-how, which are hard to find in China, where all telecom operators are state-controlled. Hong Kong is very competitive. The people assets are very important. We also have control of Asia Global Crossing [purchased when Global Crossing went bankrupt] and can work with them on that.

Eventually we will form a joint venture with them—PCCW—in Southern China where we aren't strong. [China Netcom only has operations in the north, China Telecom has the south.] We also have a lot of buildings and land, the legacy of a telco, which we can sell to PCCW Property and let it manage them for us. In Beijing we have more than 2,000 buildings, even a five-star hotel. It's stupid. We want to sell that.

**Q: What's your relationship with board member Rupert Murdoch?**
**A:** He became my mentor. Whenever I get frustrated, I read his [biography]. I cannot let him down.

---

# Who's Got Performance?

*Investor alert: India's companies beat China's*

When it comes to economic growth between these two up-and-coming powerhouses, China is outpacing India by a mile. But take a look at how Chinese companies perform relative to Indian businesses and the results look quite different.

A *BusinessWeek* analysis of financial data from Standard & Poor's Compustat shows Indian corporations are getting more bang for their rupee. A look at over 340 publicly listed companies from 1999 through 2003 reveals that Indian businesses have, with a few exceptions, out-performed their Chinese counterparts on return on equity (ROE) and return on invested capital (ROIC).

Indian companies perform better across various industry groups because they face greater market pressures. Despite plenty of government regulation, India is by and large a well-functioning market economy. This leads businesses to focus more on profits and performance. When it comes to free markets, China is a work in progress. China's government has big stakes in most publicly listed companies, so managers must be mindful of government agendas, such as employment, says Joydeep Mukherji, a director, in the Sovereign Ratings Group at Standard & Poor's.

The two countries also differ greatly when it comes to financing. "It's quite difficult to get capital in India," says Marcus Rosgen, regional head of equity research at Citigroup in Hong Kong. In India, firms raise a larger share of capital in equity markets, so private investors play a key role in allocating capital and place an emphasis on return on equity. In China, the financing situation is quite the opposite. A notoriously high savings rate and large sums of foreign direct investment are keeping the cost of financing low for businesses.

The glut of capital in China is fueling excess capacity. A low cost of capital reduces the financial hurdle to start a new business or open a factory. The problem is compounded by the fact that Chinese manufacturing is concentrated in low-end production. The resulting price competition reduces profitability. And since most of China's major banks are state-owned, there is little emphasis on maximizing returns.

Progress is being made in China. There is a noticeable difference in ROE and ROIC between companies listed in the more internationally exposed Hong Kong stock market—the so-called Red Chips—and those listed solely on mainland exchanges. In 2003, the 25 Red Chip stocks had a return on equity of 14.8%, versus 12.9% for mainland listed companies. In terms of ROIC, Red Chips produced an 11.6% return, compared with 9.7% for mainland outfits.

What's more, China is moving faster than India to improve its infrastructure. Unless India quickens the pace to improve energy production and distribution, as well as its transportation systems, the country risks stunting the growth potential of the economy and its own companies.

5

# The New Megamarkets

FOR DECADES, MULTINATIONALS HAVE VIEWED THE immense populations of China and India as vast potential consumer markets. But until recently, they have remained frustratingly out of reach. This is changing fast as wealth spreads to greater portions of their populations and as both governments allow foreign companies greater latitude to operate. As a result, China and India now truly are emerging as the world's most important new megamarkets for everything from cars to cell phones.

China and India share many characteristics as future growth markets. Both have an immense, upwardly mobile, and worldly emerging middle class whose aspirations and outlook on life differ dramatically from those of previous generations. Rapid social changes and greater diversity in lifestyle mean companies must become more sophisticated in tailoring their message and products to different consumer segments. Both nations also have a seemingly insatiable demand for foreign technology. "A Thousand Chinese Desires Bloom" and "India's New Worldly Women" reveal some of the surprising findings of extensive studies into the consumer psychology of young adults in both nations by Grey Global.

The two nations have numerous idiosyncrasies, however, that marketers must understand. As this chapter shows, savvy multinationals are beginning to unlock those secrets. "It's Getting Hotter in the East" concludes that decades of hard work and trial and error are now paying off big for companies such as General Motors, Motorola, Caterpillar, and Procter & Gamble. These companies have learned to cultivate profitable relationships and partnerships, customize products for the Chinese market, quickly exploit new opportunities, nurture local talent, and develop creative business models.

What's more, vast portions of China remain barely tapped. "China: Go West, Westerners" explains how multinationals, drawn by national and local governments, are beginning to invest in heavily populated interior provinces. Case studies of GM, Volkswagen, and Haworth Furniture draw lessons from their successes and missteps on the mainland.

Success in India can be driven by different factors. They include cultivating India as a base for global R&D, outsourced back-office operations, and the manufacture of goods with high engineering content. Success in the domestic mass market, meanwhile, often requires innovative strategies to develop very low-cost but high-quality products with appropriate technologies. "Getting the Best to the Masses" profiles successful strategies various companies have developed to provide goods and services at extremely low prices using technologies that are appropriate for the circumstances of Indian consumers. This chapter also includes a case study of General Electric in India.

In conclusion, "How Cummins Does It" analyzes the different strategies that the U.S. engine maker deploys to succeed in India *and* China, both of which have become crucial growth markets as well as key elements to the U.S. engine maker's game plan to boost its competitiveness in America.

---

## It's Getting Hotter in the East

*After years of frustration for U.S. companies, China starts to pay off*

For more than two decades, Western bosses chased the China dream. They professed to love the scorching Maotai served at those endless government banquets celebrating yet another costly and complex joint venture. Just as they began noticing rising profits from sales of cars or telecom gear, they'd get blindsided by sudden rule changes favoring local players, demands for new technology transfers, or cutthroat pricing from Chinese imitators unconcerned about profits. Some early entrants ended up writing off huge investments. But more often, CEOs groveled before their boards back home, begging for another $100 million to sink into a mainland venture that was always just about to turn the corner. This was China, after all. Everybody had to be in China, right?

Finally, the long march is reaping benefits. Of more than 450 U.S. companies surveyed by the American Chamber of Commerce, 68% today say they are profitable in the mainland, and 70% say their China margins equal or exceed their global averages. Such an answer would have been unthinkable before China entered the World Trade Organization in 2001 and had to open its economy wider to foreign companies. The biggest beneficiaries are the pioneering multinationals— such as Procter & Gamble, Caterpillar, and United Technologies—that arrived in the 1980s, then stuck it out in the worst of times. But now even small and medium-sized U.S. companies are realizing they have to play their China hand or lose out altogether.

If a company stays the course, the results can be remarkable. China contributed 9% of Motorola Inc.'s $31.3 billion in sales last year, and, thanks to smart products and marketing, the Schaumberg (Ill.)-based company is battling with Nokia Corp. for leadership in the world's biggest handset market. Low-cost exports from China and the brainwork done at 16 labs have also helped revive Motorola's fortunes. For many products, "China will become a larger market than the U.S.," says Motorola Asia Pacific Senior Vice-President Simon Leung. "And it helps our global operation from the perspective of costs, quality, and time to market."

The prospects of some companies, in fact, may be brighter in China than at home, where they have entrenched competition or are saddled with high-cost operations. "In China, nobody has home-court advantage," says Jonathan Woetzel, McKinsey & Co.'s Greater China director. "You can play a new game and get a new lease on life." While Hewlett-Packard Co. has been in crisis mode in the U.S., its China sales have risen 20% annually for four years. And booming China is one of the most important markets for slumping General Motors Corp.

China also is a godsend for financially troubled auto-parts giant Delphi Corp., whose sales there grew 30% annually between 1993 and 2004, when they hit $637 million. Delphi has opened a tech center on a still-muddy site in Shanghai's Pudong district where, by 2010, 1,500 engineers will design parts for the explosion of new models rolling off the assembly lines of customers like GM, Volkswagen, and Nissan. "China is our company's hope for a growth machine," says Delphi Asia President Choon T. Chon. As China liberalizes to meet World Trade Organization commitments, new opportunities are opening in fast-growing areas such as finance, retail, and tourism. It's also easier to make acquisitions. "The beauty of China today is that all options are open," says Stuart L. Levenick, group president of Caterpillar Inc., which has recently bought several Chinese construction machinery makers.

This isn't to say China has suddenly become an easy place to do business. Indeed, it remains one of the world's riskiest and most complex markets. Intellectual property is brazenly ripped off and contracts are violated with little recourse. Corruption is rampant. The baffling regulatory environment is a work in progress. Growing capacity gluts and fierce competition from Chinese companies—some aided with cheap state loans—still can keep prices and margins low. Then there is the sheer pace of change, making it necessary to constantly adapt to stay ahead.

## Local Talent

Still, many multinationals that invested the time, effort, and resources have begun to learn the lessons needed. Among them, obviously, are that *guanxi*, or connections, and investing early do matter, as Motorola's experience has shown. Partly as a reward for staying the course after Tiananmen, Motorola was allowed to own 100% of its key operations, while its telecom rivals had to form ventures with state partners.

But succeeding in today's China is about a whole lot more than *guanxi* and getting your products past customs. The big winners are investors who have nurtured Chinese managerial talent and given them the reins to run vital operations. They localize manufacturing, parts sourcing, and R&D to the greatest extent possible to lower costs and leverage China's immense talent pool. The winners treat partners as equals when joint ventures are a plus, and part ways when they aren't. They also keep a grip over distribution and after-sales service networks to ensure customers are satisfied. And they invest heavily in training to integrate Chinese engineers and sales staff into their global organizations—and keep them motivated so they won't jump ship. "Retention of skilled workers is on every company's mind now in China," says Dayton Ogden, chairman of recruitment firm Spencer Stuart Management consultants. "You have to make your company a place where people want to stay."

Success also requires an ever more sophisticated understanding of the Chinese market. China's emerging consumer class, for example, cannot be treated as an undifferentiated mass. Tastes vary by region, and many upwardly mobile professionals see cell phones with all the latest features as fashion statements. Others demand top performance at a low price. It's also a mistake to focus exclusively on rich cities like Guangzhou and Shanghai. "To continuously grow your business, you must go to level-two, -three, and -four cities," says Sun Cheng Yau, head of Greater China for HP. In smaller cities, some members of HP's growing network of 200 service reps even have to work out of their own homes.

Few companies pay better attention to all these details than P&G. It has invested more than $1 billion in China since 1988 in four factories and a Beijing R&D center. P&G sells 17 brands, from Head & Shoulders shampoo and Cover Girl makeup to Pringles potato chips and Pampers diapers. It leads each category in which it competes, except detergent. Even here, Tide is No. 2.

Hundreds of P&G research managers live with Chinese families in cities and on farms to learn how they use everything from detergent to toothpaste. The insights have helped P&G adopt a multi-tier pricing system for some brands. The company sells cheaper, basic versions of Tide and Crest in small cities and villages, for example. In beauty care, it has created different versions of Olay moisturizing cream—one for supermarkets and a pricier version with skin-whitening and antiaging properties sold only in upscale department stores. "We have extended the brand to meet different needs," says Christopher Hassall, a P&G vice-president for Greater China. P&G is using the strategy for Olay and Crest in other developing nations and may try it in the U.S.

## Sitting Pretty

Smart marketing also is enabling some U.S. companies to succeed even in industries where Chinese manufacturers are ferociously competitive. Haworth Inc. is an example. At a time when hundreds of U.S. furniture makers are shutting down due to cheap Chinese imports, Holland (Mich.)-based Haworth is selling locally all the office furniture it can produce in its Shanghai factory—even though Haworth products usually cost 30% to 50% more than models by local producers. One of its secrets: a team of Haworth designers and psychologists who, free of charge, develop an entire workplace "environment" for potential clients after interviewing executives and staff. That appeals to multinationals, and a growing number of Chinese companies, concerned about retaining and motivating talent. Haworth also welcomes passersby to try out its ergonomically designed furniture, and enjoy free cappuccino and wireless Internet connections, at its Shanghai Creativity Center in the trendy Xintiandi district. "You have to give people a chance to experience your product before they buy," says Haworth Asia Vice-President Frank F. Rexach. Since adopting the strategy three years ago, "business has started to explode," says Rexach. Each month, Haworth sells more than 100,000 chairs priced at up to $1,200 apiece and 75,000 workstations.

Carmakers also are learning to look beyond the wealthiest Chinese consumers. GM had enjoyed enormous success with its Buick Regal, which starts at $25,138, since production began in 1998 with partner Shanghai Automotive Industry Corp. Now, GM is trying to reach the gamut of consumers by expanding its line to include imported Cadillacs like the XLR, which retails for $158,000, locally made Chevrolet Spark sedans starting at $5,654, and even minivans. GM launched three Chevrolet models in the first six months of 2005. And it built a network of 1,000 distributors. "One thing you learn in China is that you have to move fast," says GM China Group President Kevin E. Wale.

Such diversification is becoming essential to remain a serious player. As China emerges as the world's biggest market for everything from cars to digital TVs, it increasingly will influence global trends. Already, many cell phones sold in China have features not available in the U.S. At Motorola's labs in Shanghai, Chengdu, and Beijing, engineers are working on phones that surf the Web and double as MP3 players.

All the lessons from the corporate pioneers will come in handy to first-time investors. But they needn't follow the same trail. Changing rules mean new entrants can leap in with different strategies. Chicago-based IGA aims to do just that in the grocery business. The nonprofit alliance of grocers would seem to have little chance against retail giants such as Carrefour and Wal-Mart Stores Inc., which have arrived in force. But IGA has signed up five Chinese retailers with a combined $1.6 billion in annual revenue. The group is trying to convince Beijing officials that it can help homegrown retailers compete with the giants by lowering costs via group buying. IGA also can help retailers export their own packaged foods, clothing, and even DVD players under its brand through its 4,500 worldwide affiliates. "We are giving local players the chance to make contact with the international market," says CEO Thomas S. Haggai.

As Beijing opens areas like tourism to outsiders, companies need more flexible business models. Parsippany (N.J.)-based Cendant Hotel Group Inc., which opened its first Ramada hotel in China in 1993, now is launching its Super 8 chain of motels, a sector Beijing is encouraging to offer more affordable rooms to tourists and business travelers and to create more jobs in services. Cendant opened 10 motels in early 2005, mainly in city centers, owned by Chinese franchisees. It wants around 60 within three years. "Overlay the personal income of China's growing middle class with a country with 21,000 miles of highway and big events coming up like the Beijing Olympics," says Cendant CEO Steven A. Rudnitsky, "and we are very bullish on business opportunities."

To many smaller U.S. companies, China still seems far too intimidating. But with hundreds of manufacturers succumbing each year to brutal mainland import competition, more are concluding they must take the China plunge. More than half of new American Chamber of Commerce members in China are managers from small and midsized companies. Chicago-based Phoenix Electric Manufacturing Co., a 100-employee, $20 million maker of electric motors for power tools, kitchen appliances, and other products, recently opened a second Chinese factory, in Suzhou. For Phoenix, the move was "a matter of survival because our customer base is moving here," says Chairman John S. Bank. It enabled Phoenix to keep its biggest clients, such as General Electric Co. and Emerson Electric Co., which have shifted most of their consumer-electronics production to the area.

No doubt China will keep trying the patience and pocketbooks of U.S. companies. It will be many years before China develops the intellectual-property rights protection, transparent policymaking, and level playing field that will make it anywhere as predictable as the West or Japan. But one by one, most of the obstacles that for so long made China a money pit are diminishing. So, too, is the rationale for companies who thought they could be global players without getting into China.

---

# A Thousand Chinese Desires Bloom

*A large study gives insight into the mindset of China's increasingly varied consumers, a complexity foreign outfits need to come to grips with*

Many foreign companies still tend to treat Chinese consumers as an undifferentiated mass. Their priority is getting products into the country, figuring they can then formulate an advertising campaign based on clichés of what people in developing nations want.

In fact, China's consumer market is quickly becoming increasingly sophisticated—and segmented. Savvy corporations are learning to tailor their products and pitches to the tastes, aspirations, and demands of distinct elements of the population.

"People from the outside think this is just a gold mine," says Grey Global Group's Josh Li, managing director of the marketing outfit's Beijing office. "Actually, this is a very complex market, with many diverse lifestyles."

## The Chinese Dream

To get a good picture of China's emerging consumer class, Grey collaborated with the British Council, a government-funded organization that promotes education and culture, to conduct a detailed study of Chinese aged 16 to 39 living in 30 big cities.

They collected data from home visits with 70,000 people—an enormous sample size—that Grey figures is representative of 50 million to 60 million people. The study was supplemented with data from a Chinese research institute survey of 10,000 university undergraduates.

The main trend that emerges is that the younger generations in China are very confident about their future, says Viveca Chan, an early pioneer in studying Chinese consumers, who was until recently head of Grey's Asia operations. "When I went to school, everyone talked about the American Dream, and everyone in China aspired to go there," Chan says. "Now, the Chinese Dream is starting to happen."

## Pragmatic Youth

Another clear finding is that young Chinese adults are extremely driven and are obsessed with getting ahead. "If you talk to them, they are very eager to get connected to the business world, the reality world," says Li. "This is entirely a new generation for China."

Li, who is 36, says when he was in college he was very much involved in politics and took part in the 1989 pro-democracy movement. "Now, students don't care about those issues. They care about getting a good job and are quite willing to join the Communist Party to get it, even though they don't believe in communism."

But this doesn't mean all young Chinese think only about making money. "At the same time, they are looking for fun," he says. "They are looking for safe rebellion and calculated risks. There's a lot of unemployment, so the competition for jobs is huge."

## Precious Info

This kind of information is valuable for marketing companies as they try to figure out which buttons to push. The study, called the Chinese Media and Marketing Survey, found that the younger Chinese generation can be segmented into consumer groups with distinct psychological perspectives and values.

The biggest consumer category, 34% of the sample, is what Grey labels "advancers." They are obsessed with their self-image, and money is important to them. Most are male, and 69% are married.

"This is the big market, the backbone of China's consumer market," says Li. "And they have a lot of influence over those below them." These are the buyers Volkswagen, General Motors, and the major cellphone suppliers are after.

## Key Target

Another 17% of the young adult market are regarded as "experimenters," meaning they are most likely to be the first, say, to buy a PDA with the latest features. About 11% of those sampled can be classified as "young and hip"—they are the type who want iPod music players and trendy clothes. They tend to admire the same celebrities as Taiwanese or Hong Kong youth. And 11.6% are classified as "motivated"—mainly concerned with getting ahead in their careers.

The richest segment, labeled the "achievers," account for about 5%. These are the people who often end up in top executive positions and are a key target market for companies like Oracle.

## Influential Segment

This privileged group is always influential in Chinese society, Li says, because of the prestige associated with success. Especially popular are wealthy tycoons who are socially responsible, such as Hong Kong's Li Ka-shing, who donates heavily to educational causes.

A final, and surprisingly big, segment of the Chinese young adults are simply the "independents," those who pride themselves on charting their own course and not following the pack. They account for 8.6% of young adults.

Perhaps the most interesting aspect of the Grey study, however, is the way it breaks down the psychological makeup of today's young Chinese adults. Researchers asked a number of questions about basic values. In many ways, attitudes seem like those of young Americans in the post–World War II era. Among the major characteristics:

- **Individualism.** Roughly two-thirds of young Chinese prefer to do things themselves, rather than rely on others. The same percentage also say they don't judge others on how they live their lives.

- **Craving a better life.** Only 39% of Chinese are happy with their life as is. And a mere 18% say they have enough money to enjoy life. Fifty-nine percent say they need to take risks to be successful. For consumer products companies, this means there is a huge desire for new trends.

- **Career ambition.** Eighty percent of younger Chinese say they are working very hard for their career. Two-thirds agree with the statement, "It is important that my family thinks I am successful."

- **Liberated women.** Men should do housework, according to 64% of men and women surveyed. The divorce rate now is about 22% in China overall but higher and rising in urban areas.

- **Internationalism.** Two-thirds of young Chinese adults say they are interested in other cultures and in international events, while 52% say they are attracted to lifestyles of developed nations. But marketers shouldn't take these opinions too literally. Says Chan: "They don't walk the talk. They still eat noodles, not pasta. Lifestyles are very difficult to change."

- **Value of knowledge.** Some 75% say it's important to be well-informed. "This is an important trend," Li says. "The market is characterized by mobility. People believe they will have a better life with more knowledge." It helps explain why the education market, especially for business and professional improvement programs, is booming across China, as are sales of business books.

- **Longing for enjoyment.** There is growing demand for spiritual experiences. Sixty-two percent say they spend time outdoors to understand nature, one-third say they exercise regularly. "However, this is an aspiration," cautions Chan. "The survey also shows 51% are willing to sacrifice leisure for making more money."

- **Social consciousness.** Young Chinese adults care more about the environment, charity, and public interests in general than older Chinese. Sixty percent say they have often taken measures to protect the environment, and 59% say they appreciate enterprises or brands that support charity.

Add all of these findings together, and you get a profile of a population that's making a dramatic departure from thousands of years of tradition. What's more, attitudes are changing with remarkable speed. They are putting a greater value on creativity, self-expression, and control over their own lives.

For Western companies, understanding this evolving mindset—and dispensing with old stereotypes—will be vital for success in the China market.

# China: Go West, Westerners

*With growth slowing in the crowded and costly coastal centers, Beijing is ushering investors into the hinterlands*

It was a Chinese-style road show. In a sumptuous compound of sculpted gardens and plush banquet halls in south Beijing, executives from a long list of multinationals, including Boeing, Caterpillar, Goodyear, Alcoa, Unisys, and Microsoft, sipped cocktails and dined on such Sichuan delicacies as twice-cooked pork, diced duck with pepper on pastry shells, and dan-dan noodles. Their hosts for the Oct. 26, 2005, event were a delegation of top officials from Sichuan, a western province 2,000 km from Beijing that is eager to lure new investment away from the coastal cities that have been the center of China's business boom.

The Sichuan officials had much to offer. A manufacturing worker there earns an average of $126 a month, a little more than half what he might make in Guangzhou or Shanghai. There's also abundant energy, brand new highways and power grids, and a vast interior market. "We sincerely hope that multinational corporations can take an active part in the development of Sichuan," local Communist Party Secretary Zhang Xuezhong intoned over repeated toasts of rice liquor and Chinese red wine.

## Worried about Protests

In 2003, President Hu Jintao and Premier Wen Jiabao placed urgent priority on developing China's hinterlands. Three years before that, the Develop the West policy was launched by their predecessors. Since then, China's bureaucrats have unleashed a charm offensive to persuade more companies to move inland.

Anxious about a rising tide of industrial and farmer protests in central and western China, Beijing is giving top billing to narrowing the yawning income gap between rich coastal cities and the rest of the country. Billions of dollars have been spent on bridges, expressways, and power plants to boost the economies of inland China. Now provincial delegations increasingly are trekking to Beijing, Shanghai, and Guangzhou to trumpet their edge over the coast.

"In Sichuan, we provide year-round reliable energy for investors— we don't have the problems of the Yangtze River Delta," bragged Xu Mengjia, the mayor of Yaan, a Sichuan city of 1.5 million. He was one of five Sichuan mayors who attended the Beijing coming-out party.

## Easy Sell

These days those mayors have an increasingly easy sell with multinationals and local companies alike. After years of easy expansion, coastal China, and particularly the Pearl River and Yangtze River deltas, is facing growing pains. Labor and land costs are rising fast in Shanghai, with commercial rents up nearly 40% over the past several years, while industrial space is simply not available. Labor costs are inching up in Guangdong too, but the bigger problem is finding any workers at all for its huge manufacturing sector.

"The operating environment in coastal areas is getting worse and worse," says Zhai Suoling, general manager of a toy factory in Dongguan. "Lots of manufacturers are moving to inland cities." Indeed, while foreign investment in central and western China was up 7% in 2003, it actually fell by 0.2% in eastern China.

Companies, including General Motors, Honda, Intel, and Motorola, now run operations in interior provinces. They report no shortage of skilled labor—and increasingly vibrant consumer markets. "Companies that don't look at inland China will find themselves disadvantaged," says Emory Williams, chairman of the American Chamber of Commerce in Beijing, which reports that 50% of U.S. member companies have already invested in second-tier cities.

Amcham-organized delegations, including executives from Chevron, Rockwell Automation, and Ohio-based manufacturer Eaton, recently scouted new investment opportunities in Xinjiang, whose capital

Urumqi is 2,500 km (640 miles) from Beijing, as well as Inner Mongolia and Yunnan, which borders Vietnam. "When I talk to manufacturers, they say they will never build another plant in Shanghai—it's too expensive," says Michael Hart, Shanghai-based head of Greater China research for real estate consultancy Jones Lang Lasalle. "They need to go further inland to find land and people."

## Lower Turnover

Moving west is now easier than ever due to the massive buildout of interior infrastructure. Almost $9 billion has been spent on new airports alone in a five-year period, with twice as much allocated for the next five. In the coming years, a recently approved national highway plan will double the 34,000-km highway network—already the world's second most extensive after the U.S. interstate system. "When the Chinese government talks about building infrastructure, they will do it on time and on a scale that defies belief," says one Shanghai-based Western logistics expert.

Not surprisingly, managers of businesses with cutthroat margins, like toys and shoes, have been the first to migrate. Take Taiwan native Zhai Suoling, whose factories in the city of Dongguan in Guangdong Province build wooden dollhouses and toy wagons that sell in big-box stores like Wal-Mart and Kmart. In 2004 he built a $2 million factory in Tonggu, Jiangxi, where 200 workers make wooden toy pieces that are then trucked 12 hours to his Guangdong factory for assembly.

A new road between the two provinces will soon cut transit time to nine hours. With land 50% cheaper in Jiangxi than in Guangdong, and energy and water 25% less, the move was a no-brainer, Zhai says. Workers in his new factory are also paid a little less, but more important, he says, is the low worker turnover—close to zero in Jiangxi, versus 40% in Guangdong. "Having a stable labor force and smooth operation is key to my business," Zhai says. "I plan to move more and more production out of Dongguan."

## R&D's Edge

Even deep in China's hinterlands, thousands of kilometers from the bustling coast and its ports, some cities are succeeding in wooing foreign investment, including high-tech industries that can utilize air freight to transport products and the Internet for logistics. Well before the recent road show to Beijing, the gross domestic product of Sichuan Province was growing 12.7% a year. It has pulled in more than $6 billion in investment from the likes of Toyota Motor, hypermarket chain Carrefour, and French cement maker Lafarge. In the provincial capital of Chengdu (population: 10 million), western China's most affluent city, streets are lined with Audi and Buick dealerships and boutiques for luxury goods by Louis Vuitton, Gucci, and Cartier.

Chengdu was an early beneficiary of the Go West movement: It nabbed a Motorola research and development lab in 2001 by promoting lower costs as well as access to engineers from its strong universities. When Motorola decided to expand outside its original downtown location in 2003, the municipal government agreed to pay for the new research center. (Neither the company nor Chengdu officials will say how much.) Inside, some 330 Chinese engineers and technicians are developing software for Motorola phones.

"R&D has the advantage that we don't have to ship freight," says Motorola Software Center manager Stone Shi. Since Motorola arrived in Chengdu, Alcatel, Ericsson, Nokia, and Microsoft have all set up R&D or tech centers in the sleek industrial parks that skirt the city.

## Sometimes Unreliable

For many manufacturers, the market is right outside their door. Intel justifies the $450 million it is spending on two assembly plants for chipsets in Chengdu by pointing out that computer sales in the region are growing by as much as 45% a year. Boise (Idaho)-based semiconductor maker Micron Electronics has just announced it will sink $250 million into a new plant in the ancient city of Xian in the neighboring province of Shaanxi. "Both cities have very young and energetic, ambitious, results-oriented politicians," says Ian Yang, Asia Pacific general manager for Intel.

What about coastal China? Foreign investment there still dwarfs what is going on in western China. Infrastructure in many parts of the interior is still primitive and unreliable. And regardless of any cost savings, multinationals want their regional headquarters near the political, regulatory, and financial centers of Beijing and Shanghai.

Nevertheless, it is clear that vast new regions of China are now open for business, or soon will be. The next round of banquets sponsored by officials from areas like Sichuan is sure to be well attended.

## GM and VW: How Not to Succeed in China

*The two giants are losing sales to rivals offering cheaper cars with features Chinese buyers love*

During the Shanghai Auto Show in April 2005, Volkswagen and General Motors Corp. put on a brave face. At Volkswagen's 5,000-sq.-meter stand, car buffs could sample tropical fruit, salmon, and chocolate while ogling the new 200-horsepower Golf GTI and the Audi A6L—a China-only version that's 10 cm longer than the standard A6 to make the back seat roomier for execs with drivers. At GM's display, models in slinky outfits posed beside the chiseled 3.6-liter Cadillac CTS, the new Chevrolet Aveo compact sedan, and—to give Chinese buyers a taste of GM's former grandeur—a 1959 Cadillac Eldorado.

But all the flash in the world can't hide the challenges the two companies face in China. Both came early to the mainland—GM formed its Shanghai joint venture in 1997, while VW arrived in 1984—and quickly dominated the market. But now they're getting trounced by new entrants offering smaller, cheaper cars. Led by the success of its Elantra compact, starting at $13,600, Hyundai Motor Co.'s unit sales in China soared by 156% in the first quarter of 2005 over the same period the previous year according to market researcher CSM Worldwide.

Guangzhou Honda Motor Co. sold 76% more cars as buyers snapped up its $10,360 Fit. And domestic champ Chery's sales climbed 42%, driven by the explosive response to its $3,600 QQ. VW, meanwhile, has seen its 2001 market share of 40% tumble to less than 20% in 2004. In the first quarter of that year alone, sales plunged by nearly two-thirds. GM's sales from its Shanghai operation—its biggest China venture—dropped 35% in the same quarter, and its overall profits in China plummeted 80%, to $33 million.

The reason for the shift is simple. Just a few years ago most auto sales were to state-owned companies that didn't worry much about price. Today most buyers are individuals who want the best deal for their money. And rumors that Beijing is mulling a tax on vehicles with big engines are only accelerating the trend. "Now the common people are buying cars," says Yale Zhang, head of the Shanghai office of CSM. "They want affordable, small [vehicles], of good quality and with a good brand."

The problems at GM and VW, though, go deeper than just the change to more modest cars. Their woes also stem from the fact that they got to China so early. As first movers, the two benefited from high tariffs that kept out imports and allowed them to milk the market for immense profits. But the tariffs also allowed them to avoid necessary cost-cutting. And they faced cumbersome restrictions from Beijing. Volkswagen, for example, has had to develop a separate distribution network for each of its two China manufacturing operations. It was "a mistake of the past," says Bernd Leissner, president of Volkswagen Group China. And Beijing demanded that GM focus largely on the expensive Buick Regal. Honda and Hyundai, by contrast, have been able to get into China with far less meddling from Beijing. Locals such as Chery have seen little interference from bureaucrats.

## A Smooth Ride

The newcomers have also done a better job of making cars Chinese consumers want to buy. Before Hyundai launched the Elantra in 2004, the company sent 20 engineers and marketing experts to China for three months to suss out what buyers were looking for. As a result, the Elantra sold in China has a strengthened chassis and wider tires to ensure a smooth ride on the mainland's rough roads. There's also a computer that boosts fuel efficiency, and a hands-free kit for China's mobile-phone-mad consumers. While GM and VW did their share of market research, their hands were tied by restrictions on what kind of cars they could make.

There's more competition coming, too. Capacity in China grew an estimated 30% in 2005. Chery showed off a range of new models at that year's Shanghai show, including a sporty concept car called the S16, while Hyundai plans to introduce three models to China in 2006. Indeed, Hyundai sees China as a step on the way to the big leagues. It plans to invest $1.1 billion by 2008 to triple its annual production capacity, to 600,000, from 2005's 200,000. Ford Motor Co. is planning a $1 billion investment in China on top of the hundreds of millions it has spent already. The money will go toward a new engine plant in Nanjing and a new production line for its four-door Focus sedan at an existing factory in Chongqing. Nissan Motor Co. plans to add 250 new dealerships, to bring its total to 400, and hopes to boost sales to 350,000 cars by 2007, up from an expected 140,000. "Being late or in advance doesn't matter," says Nissan Chief Executive Carlos Ghosn. "Make a good product and have good service, and you'll be successful."

In response, both GM and VW are moving to revamp their operations, most notably by replacing top management in China. VW announced in 2005 that Winfried Vahland, currently deputy chairman of the Board of Management at subsidiary Skoda Auto, will take over for Folker Weissgerber, its board member responsible for China. At GM, longtime China boss Philip Murtaugh, who oversaw the flagship Shanghai venture from the start, stepped down in 2005 amid rumors of disagreement with headquarters over the pace of China growth. The company denies any conflict.

The two early leaders are also looking to beef up their offerings of smaller cars. VW already sells its $9,000 Golf and $12,000 Polo in China and is planning at least two new models annually, but declined to provide details. And GM is pushing its sub-$8,000 Chevy Spark—a car that, GM says, Chery copied with its QQ. (Chery declines to comment on the case; a lawsuit on the issue is pending.) Unit sales of the Spark tripled in the first quarter of 2005, although remaining less than 25% of QQ volumes. Some doubt whether either has done enough to get back in the game. "Prices for GM and Volkswagen vehicles are still too high," cautions Jia Xinguang of the Beijing-based China National Automotive Industry Consulting & Development Corp. VW CEO Bernd Pischetsrieder counters that the company doesn't want to get into a price war that would destroy margins. "Market share [in China] is important for us, but not at any price," he told shareholders at VW's 2005 annual meeting in Hamburg.

Both GM and VW have outlined ambitious cost-cutting programs in China and are urging more suppliers to start producing in the mainland as well. Competition, though, is sure to increase as ambitious newcomers keep chipping away at the early leaders. China used to be an easy game. Not anymore.

---

# China: Let a Thousand Brands Bloom

*Multinationals are competing with local companies for a more discerning Chinese consumer*

In 2000, General Motors Corp. offered just a handful of car models in China—mostly large, high-end Buicks costing around $40,000. That limited selection worked in a market dominated by fleet sales to government offices and enterprises: What these customers wanted were large sedans for hauling big shots. "We were targeting institutional buyers, who were our big market back then," says Kevin Wale, president of GM China.

Fast-forward to the present, and it's hard to believe GM is the same company. The automaker now offers a fast-expanding range of models in China, each aimed at a specific customer segment. For China's newly rich, there are $75,000-plus Cadillac SRX sport-utility vehicles and $55,000 CTS sedans. A bit lower down, the $30,000 Buick Regal continues to be a top seller, but it's now positioned as the vehicle of choice for cost-conscious entrepreneurs who want a prestigious car. For their midlevel underlings, there's the $15,000-to-$20,000 Buick Excelle—offered in various models. And for younger urbanites buying their first cars, GM's Chevrolet marque now has the $19,000 Epica sedan, the $10,000-to-$12,000 Aveo hatchback, and the $5,700 Spark minicar. Meanwhile, in the countryside GM offers the Wuling, which goes for $4,000 to $6,500. This boxy minivan can carry seven passengers, a couple of hogs, or a dozen sacks of potatoes. "We had a very limited product line in China," says Wale, who took over GM's top China job in 2005. "Now we have an extremely well-developed range of brands and cars." And they're available at nearly 1,000 outlets across the country, up from just nine in 1998. Add it all up and it means lots of metal moving off the lot.

## $37 Washing Machine

GM isn't alone in discovering that China is not a monolithic market. The country, with 1.3 billion citizens speaking more than 100 dialects, is wildly diverse. What people eat, wear, and drive differs greatly from north to south, east to west, rich to poor, young to old, city to countryside. Urumqi in the northwest is further from Guangzhou in the southeast than Oslo is from Rome, and the desires and needs of people who have benefited from the economic changes of the past two decades barely resemble those of individuals who have been left behind. "It's clear that you can't treat China as just one country," says Glenn Murphy, managing director of ACNielsen China in Shanghai.

And while it was once enough for companies to focus on the 100 million or so Chinese living in Beijing, Shanghai, Guangzhou, and a handful of other big cities, today they're scrambling to offer products tailored to more segments of the population—rural, urban, middle class, wealthy, and poor. That means an explosion of choice for consumers.

Appliance- and gadget-maker Samsung has discovered that customers living in steamy Guangdong Province need larger refrigerators than those in the more temperate north, so it started shipping bigger fridges to the south. Household-goods company Procter & Gamble Co. has won over consumers in China's hinterlands with a budget detergent called Tide Clean White, while holding on to city customers with the more expensive Tide Triple Action. And Nokia Corp. now pumps out scores of phone models aimed at every conceivable type of user and has more than 100 sales offices in virtually every corner of China, up from just three in 2002. "We were trying to run China by just managing it centrally as one market," says Colin Giles, Nokia's senior vice-president for sales and marketing in China. "When we started to roll out local distributors, we realized how diverse the market really is." Since it revamped its strategy, Nokia has clawed its way back to the top spot among cell-phone brands sold in China after slipping several years ago.

It's not just the multinationals that are segmenting the market. Chinese companies are doing the same. Appliance maker Haier Group, for instance, sells dozens of washing-machine models in China, including a tiny one targeted at rural customers that costs just $37. Lenovo Group Ltd. manufactures not only PCs that cost $2,000 or more and double as home-entertainment centers, but also simple machines costing just a couple of hundred dollars that are aimed at poorer rural families who want their children to become computer-literate. And local automaker Geely Automotive Ltd. today offers five models, up from just two in 2003. The $17,000 Mybo is marketed as a family sedan for city drivers, while the $3,700 Haoqing is aimed at recent college grads just buying their first set of wheels.

Learning about these emerging groups of consumers is the No. 1 task for multinational and domestic companies alike. They're meeting it by conducting focus groups and surveys across the country to anticipate shoppers' needs and desires. To succeed in China, you have to "understand the psychographic profile of Chinese consumers, their emotions, and what they identify with in a brand," says Viveca Chan, brand expert and former China head for the advertising agency Grey Global Group.

Grey has divided young Chinese into 11 categories based on their lifestyles and aspirations—everything from independent types who don't follow consumer trends to shoppers on the cutting edge.

Other companies are spending lots of time with customers. In the spring of 2005, GM designers and engineers flew to Guangxi Province to visit microvan buyers at their homes and farms. James Shyr, director of design, recalls sitting on the sidewalk, smoking with drivers and talking about the features they like and dislike. "They use their microvans to run around from Monday to Friday hauling a lot of goods, but on the weekend they clean it up and take it for an outing," Shyr says. So instead of the greater luxury Shyr's designers might have wanted, they stuck with a more utilitarian design that is better suited to rural lifestyles.

Similarly, Motorola Inc. dispatched teams of researchers to far-flung locales. The company, which stumbled in China in 2003 when local rivals started to eat into its market share, discovered that even consumers far from the bright lights of Shanghai and Beijing are becoming more discerning. "In the lower-tier cities, the young people look at value, but they're also very individualistic," says Motorola China boss Michael Tatelman. The result: Motorola designers are devoting more time and energy to the lower end of the market, and even the company's least expensive phones allow users to download MP3 songs and customize their ringtones. And while Motorola doesn't design phones specifically for rural China, it is now better at getting the right handsets to each location—a bigger supply of cheaper phones in rural areas, and snazzier ones in cities. "The demographic differences have always been there, but we've become more sophisticated in our ability to identify them," Tatelman says.

As marketers figure out how to reach China's variegated consumers, rural China looms ever larger. It numbers some 750 million residents, and in the first half of 2005 per capita incomes in rural areas were up by 12.5%. Local competition is stiff. Wahaha, for instance, is China's largest beverage producer because it developed its distribution in rural areas. Wahaha's marketing sometimes consists of simply painting the company's logo on village walls. "Distribution is a huge challenge for the [multinationals] in rural China," says Fu Guoqun, a professor of marketing at the Guanghua School of Management at Beijing University.

Yet the multinationals keep getting more sophisticated in tailoring their message for both urban and rural consumers. P&G, for instance, reaches China's city strivers by sponsoring a popular reality TV show called *Absolute Challenge*, which has featured contestants vying to win a job as a product representative for Crest or Cover Girl. At the same time, P&G has blanketed village kiosks and mom-and-pop stores with advertising materials emphasizing the value offered by Tide Clean White and low-end versions of Crest and Oil of Olay skin cream. Breaking out of China's cities is a challenge, but one that more and more companies, local and foreign, know they must take on.

---

## Sitting Pretty in Shanghai

*Haworth Furniture made a ho-hum start of its China venture. When its approach to the market clicked, so did its fortunes.*

Frank Rexach, who runs the Asia operations for Haworth Furniture, likes to keep things light and mobile. Rexach doesn't have his own office at his home base in Shanghai. He simply uses whatever cubicle is available and brings his computer and files in a piece of rolling luggage.

Fluent in Mandarin, Rexach likes to chat with everybody on the staff. "As a leader, you have to be seen as locally integrated in your local organization. They really look to see if you are on an expat assignment and just enjoying the perks," he explains. "Some staff call me an egg—white on the outside, yellow on the inside."

Unconventional approaches are working well for Rexach—and especially well for Haworth, a $1.4 billion Holland (Mich.)-based maker of office furniture. The family-owned company has seen its Middle Kingdom sales grow 50% annually from 2002 through 2005, From its

250,000-square-foot factory in Shanghai, Haworth is selling more than 100,000 chairs a month, priced at $250 to $2,000 apiece, and around 100,000 office workstations, which go for up to $2,500 apiece. Rexach also has nurtured a booming business in India, where many huge call-center operations are buying up to 5,000 Haworth chairs and workstations at a time.

## Investing in People

What's particularly impressive is that Haworth is beating many Chinese manufacturers at their own game—and doing it on the locals' turf. In recent years, U.S. furniture makers have been under siege from Chinese imports. Hundreds of U.S. furniture factories have shut since 2000, unable to compete with high-quality Chinese-made furniture costing 30% to 40% less. Few U.S. furniture makers have even contemplated taking the fight to China by manufacturing there and selling to the domestic market.

Haworth's secret? In short, recognizing that the China market is fast becoming just as sophisticated and demanding as the U.S. and Europe. As in the West, corporations in China are growing more concerned about keeping and motivating talent. As a result, they are willing to pay more for quality and extra service, rather than make decisions only on price.

True, most of Haworth's customers are multinationals like General Electric, 3M, SAP, and Siemens. But some of Haworth's corporate clients aren't customers in the U.S. or Europe, where it faces stiff competition from rivals like Steelcase and Herman Miller. Also, Haworth is making inroads with big Chinese corporations such as China Mobile, a major customer.

## Different Strokes

Haworth wasn't always so successful in China. In 2001, its Shanghai factory was operating at 20% capacity. Haworth had been importing key components from North America and Europe and assembling them in Shanghai for the China market. "It was just an extension of our U.S. business model," says Rexach. Haworth had a Shanghai showroom, but didn't do much to promote itself. "The attitude was, 'We are Haworth. You should buy us,'" he says.

The turnaround happened after Haworth brought its more modern business model to China. First, Rexach moved to locally designed and sourced furniture, rather than only pushing models designed in the U.S. It now strives to deliver custom-made furniture to Chinese clients within three weeks. Second, Haworth developed a marketing strategy that Rexach describes as an "outside/inside approach of knowing what people really want."

Rexach set up the Shanghai Creativity Center. The center, on the second floor of a modern office building near Shanghai's trendy Xintiandi district, has a commanding view of a park and manmade lake. The showroom is filled with a variety of attractive chairs and posters of top Haworth designers around the world. The center has been so successful that Haworth is setting up a similar one in India.

## Community Resource

Rather than actually sell furniture, the center's aim is "to provide value-added service for clients, whether they were buying furniture or not." Pretty much anyone off the street is allowed to come in, plunk themselves down in a comfy, ergonomically designed chair, and read or connect their laptop PC into the free wireless local area network. Staff even offer free cappuccino. Prospective customers also are encouraged to hang out and try various workstations.

"You have to give people a chance to experience your product before they buy," Rexach says. Also, since some showroom pieces remain designs in progress, Haworth wants the feedback.

What's more, all sorts of community organizations are allowed to use the center free of charge for events such as seminars by local chambers of commerce, fashion shows, and university alumni fundraisers. The idea is to make the center a community resource in Shanghai, which lacks much public space.

## Shrinking the Market

Haworth also introduced the "ideation" concept, which it uses in the U.S. and Europe. Essentially, Haworth provides a free consulting service. Its staff "work with the client at the highest levels of the organization, to learn their business goals and their challenges in attracting and retaining people, and to design the space around them," Rexach explains.

In Shanghai, Haworth employs two psychologists who study a potential clients' needs and the issues they are facing in the workplace, such as the lighting, the space between staff, and the way in which people work together. Haworth then suggests designs for a workplace environment with a complete suite of furnishings.

The goal of the "ideation process," and of providing valuable services, is to keep clients loyal. "We definitely have won business this way," he says. "A lot of it is relationships and word of mouth."

## Universal Truths

Rexach figures Haworth faces about 20 serious rivals in China, versus just three or four in the U.S. The toughest are big Taiwanese and Japanese office-furniture makers. But there is also a growing pack of domestic suppliers that offer cheaper knockoffs. Rexach says his goal is to narrow the price gap between his wares and those of local competitors to no more than 20%.

Whether or not Haworth's success can be directly tied to touchy-feely consulting or free use of its facilities is hard to measure. But whatever it is doing right, Haworth's success demonstrates that it is increasingly possible to succeed in today's rapidly modernizing China, even in the toughest manufacturing businesses. What works best, it seems, are the same kind of highly sophisticated marketing strategies that the U.S. market expects and demands.

---

# India's New Worldly Women

*The country's younger generation is shedding submissive attitudes, wants careers, and longs for wealth. And marketers are paying attention.*

When the first American music videos and popular TV shows began appearing in Indian homes in the early 1990s thanks to satellite and cable, many pundits predicted Indian society would never be the same. For the first time, young Indian women saw a regular dose of sexy, scantily clad divas shimmying. Female viewers also saw independent, successful women—think Ally McBeal—and fun, sensitive guys a la *Friends*. Sex and divorce were openly discussed in these TV imports and couples kissed passionately—then still a taboo in Indian TV shows and movies.

Indeed, the impact on younger generations of Indian women has been profound. Whereas Indian women traditionally have been submissive to parents and husbands and valued frugality and modesty, a number of sociological studies show that young Indian females now prize financial independence, freedom to decide when to marry and have children, and glamorous careers.

## Tomorrow's Buyers

"A generation back, women would sacrifice themselves and believed in saving," says Nisha Singhania, senior strategic planning director of Grey Worldwide India. "Today, it is spend, spend, spend. It is OK for a woman to want something for herself, and people will accept it if she goes out into a man's world making a statement."

Because today's young women are the key consumer group of tomorrow, these shifts have big implications for marketing companies. And the trends come out clearly in two recent studies by Grey Global

Group. One study examined 3,400 unmarried women aged 19 to 22 of different income and social levels. Altogether, the project involved 40 focus groups in five large metro areas and five smaller cities.

In some cases, the researchers lived with the women for a while to study them more closely. The researchers supplemented this data with interviews of journalists, teachers, and psychologists.

Among the findings:

- **Guilt-free materialism.** Fifty-one percent of young single women in major metro areas say it's necessary to have a big house and big car to be happy. In smaller cities, 86% agreed with this statement. "This shows that the less women have, the greater are their aspirations," says Singhania.

   One woman interviewed was making just $200 a year but said she wants to own a jet plane. "A typical comment in recent interviews was, 'I want money, fame, and success,'" says Singhania.

- **Parental ties.** Traditionally, parents regarded girls as somebody else's future property. They arranged marriages for their daughters, and then the daughters would go away and take care of their in-laws, so parents needed and doted on sons. "As a girl, you never spoke to your parents. They spoke to you," Singhania says.

   But today's young women are rebelling against that. Sixty-seven percent say they plan to take care of their parents into their old age—and that means they need money.

   Unilever played on that sentiment with a recent controversial—but successful—ad for its Fair and Lovely line of beauty products. A daughter came home and found that her parents had no sugar for coffee because they couldn't afford it. She became an airline hostess after using the Fair and Lovely products to make her beautiful. She then visited her parents and took them to a first-class restaurant.

- **Marital freedom.** Now many women say they'll marry when ready—not when their parents decide to marry them off.

Sixty-five percent say dating is essential, and they also want to become financially independent before they marry. More than three-quarters—76%—say they want to maintain that independence afterward. Sixty percent say they'll decide how to spend their own salaries.

What's more, 76% say they'll decide when to have children. "They now regard this as the woman's decision completely," observes Singhania. In big metro areas, 24% say they never want children, and that number reaches 40% in smaller cities.

- **Individualism.** Female role models in Indian culture used to personify perfection, Singhania says. Now, 62% of girls say it's OK if they have faults and that people see them. "They don't want to be seen as Mrs. Perfect," she says. "Popular characters are Phoebe of *Friends* and Ally McBeal. They like women who commit blunders."

- **Careerism.** A decade ago, most young women saw themselves as housewives. After that, most said they wanted to be teachers or doctors. "If they had a profession at all, it had to be a noble cause," Singhania says. "Now, it is about glamour, money, and fame."

  A surprising 45% of young single females say they would like to be journalists. Singhania says that's largely because prominent female journalists, especially TV reporters, are seen as very glamorous.

  Another 39% say they would like to be managers, 38% are interested in design, and 20% think they want to be teachers. Interestingly, 13% say they would like to be in the military. The percentage of those saying they want to be a full-time housewife was minuscule.

- **Modern husbands.** "The relationship with the husband used to be one of awe," Singhania says. "Now, women want a partner and a relationship of equals. They want to marry a man like Greg of *Dharma and Greg* or Chandler of *Friends*." A recent Whirlpool ad shows a man washing the family clothes before his wife comes home from work, while a Samsung home-appliance ad shows a husband and wife cooking together.

For Indian society, the changes in young women's outlook on life is revolutionary. For marketers, they offer interesting new opportunities to exploit.

---

## Getting the Best to the Masses

*A wave of innovation is yielding high-quality goods that India's poor can afford*

In the fall of 2004, at the Tata Motors factory just outside Pune, south of Bombay, a group of young designers, technicians, and marketers pored over drawings and examined samples of steel and composite plastics. By early 2005, they had designed a prototype for Tata Group's most ambitious project yet: a compact car that will sell for $2,200. The company hopes the car will beat out Suzuki's $5,000 Maruti compact to become India's cheapest car—and an export model for the rest of the developing world. "This is the need of the day in India—a people's car," says Ratan Tata, chairman of the $12.5 billion Tata Group. The car is expected to hit the market by 2008. Investors, executives, and workers in the developed world have all felt the impact of India's booming software sector and call centers. But those are examples of Indians providing solutions for rich nations. Now, Indian entrepreneurs and companies such as Tata Group want to provide products and services to the nation's masses. With 1 billion people, 70% of whom are poor, India needs low-cost, high-quality goods and services. Most Western output is too expensive or complex for the Indian market.

India's engineers and professionals are focusing on finding fresh solutions in fields from manufacturing and health care to finance and education. They're not only making use of the country's cheap labor and materials but also finding practical ways to get the job done on a mass scale. Says Vivek Paul, chief executive of software services giant Wipro Technologies, the world's largest supplier of outsourced research: "Thanks to the lowered cost of R&D now possible out of India, there are new avenues opening up that weren't possible before."

## Massive Clout

This quest for the best for the least could amplify India's impact on the global economy. "Future innovations will flow from the rise of capital-scarce but labor-abundant nations like India and China," says Diana Farrell, director of McKinsey Global Institute. Already, Indian companies are eyeing markets in Asia, the Middle East, Africa, and Latin America.

It remains to be seen, of course, how many of these goods and services find their place in Europe and the U.S. But thanks to increasingly demanding and sophisticated consumers, low-cost innovations have begun to spread across India, capturing the attention of analysts such as McKinsey's Farrell and University of Michigan business guru C. K. Prahalad. He is author of *The Fortune at the Bottom of the Pyramid: Eradicating Poverty through Profits*, which focuses on inexpensive goods and services created in India, Brazil, and elsewhere.

Tata is the best example of Corporate India getting involved in these innovations. Tata has already developed the Indica, a compact hatchback that retails for $6,600 and is exported to Europe. In the process, Tata engineers figured out how to use the skilled but cheap local labor instead of the industrial robots that would have been used in Japan or the U.S. on a car like the Indica. That decision shaved roughly $1 billion off the design and production cost. As a result, the Indica can break even on an output of 80,000 vehicles—about 30% less than the volume that global auto companies need to profit from such a car.

The $2,200 Tata compact—which will appeal to the 5 million Indians who own motorbikes but can't afford the standard economy car—pushes the envelope on cost even further than the Indica. Tata's specialists are also designing a new business model. If all goes according to plan, the new Tata car will be made and distributed not only from the Pune factory but also in knocked-down kits to franchisees across the country. The franchisees will assemble the new auto in mini-factories, as well as sell it, creating thousands of local jobs. That will save Tata millions—it's easier to ship kits than fully loaded cars—and the savings will show up in the car's low price. "Tata has the expertise to deliver such a mass market product," says Kumar Bhattacharyya a, director of Warwick Manufacturing Group, the British auto think tank, who has seen early versions of the new Tata car.

The company is also experimenting with cost-saving manufacturing techniques. Instead of welded bodies, for instance, Tata may choose bolted or glued panels. The challenge will be to meet stringent safety norms at the same time. The company is also planning to outsource about 80% of component manufacturing to inexpensive Indian suppliers.

## Fresh Eyes

The new Tata car is innovation on an industrial scale. But mass-market techniques, Indian-style, can be applied to health care too. Witness the Aravind Eye Care Centre in the southern Indian city of Madurai. Designed by an ophthalmologist named G. Venkataswamy, the centre has developed inexpensive cataract surgeries for $50 to $300, compared with just over $2,000 in the U.S. The procedure's price even includes the cost of a locally made intraocular lens, inserted during surgery to restore sight.

Well-to-do Indians are charged the higher fee, which partially subsidizes operations for the poorest. But the key to keeping costs down is the huge volume of surgeries and the efficient system the doctors have developed. At Aravind's three hospitals, 80 doctors perform 50 surgeries a day. At any one time in the operating room, four doctors are working on patients side-by-side. Patients are returned to their village the next day, where paramedics complete the postoperative care. In technical jargon, this is "process innovation." India seems to excel at it. "Process innovation is a critical step in making products and services affordable for the poor," says the University of Michigan's Prahalad.

Moreover, doctors say, the assembly-line procedure doesn't hurt the result. "The quality is stellar," says Burjor P. Banaji, a well-known ophthalmologist in Bombay. Aravind says it manufactures the intraocular lenses used in the operation for $5 each—a big savings from the $50 the hospital once paid the American company Allergan for lenses approved by the U.S. Food & Drug Administration.

If Aravind's cataract surgery is a triumph of process, the prosthetic Jaipur Foot is a triumph of product. The $30 artificial limb was developed in the late 1960s by Ram Chandra, a temple sculptor from the north Indian city of Jaipur. He observed that patients in his city had trouble using imported artificial limbs, which can't accommodate Indian postures like squatting. So he set out to improve things.

## Secure Voting

The Jaipur Foot is made from a rubberized material and is more flexible than many standard prosthetic feet available in the U.S., which cost from about $250 to $1,500, depending on their range of motion. And the Jaipur Foot is suitable for long periods of immersion in water—essential for farmers who stand barefoot for hours in rice paddies. Its movement at the knee and ankle allows Indians to comfortably squat, sit cross-legged, and walk barefoot, as is often their custom. The prosthetic limb costs so little because it's made from cheap yet sturdy materials, and its labor-intensive assembly does not require the use of high-cost machinery.

Distributed by a charitable organization known by the acronym BMVSS, the Jaipur Foot is exported across the developing world, from Afghanistan to Rwanda. In 2002, the BMVSS created a partnership with India's satellite space-research program, the Indian Space Research Organization, to improve the limb and further reduce its cost. The Jaipur Foot will soon be manufactured using polyurethane, a lightweight material normally used for making rocket propellant. The new outer material will reduce the weight of the foot by half and cut production costs by about 10%, to $27.

There are many more low-cost Indian innovations—from Bharat Electronics Ltd.'s tamper-free electronic voting machine to Tata Consultancy Services' computer-aided literacy program. Bharat Electronics sees huge export potential in its $200 suitcase-size voting machine, which illiterates can use to cast their electoral ballots. Unlike the electronic voting machines used in the U.S., which are networked through personal computers, the Indian machines run on software embedded in a microprocessor that cannot be reprogrammed. That means they can't be hacked.

Computers are also helping literacy grow in India. For just $100,000, TCS software engineers developed a program to teach India's 200 million illiterates to read in their own language. Words float across the screen while a narrator repeats the sound that most closely represents the word, such as "m" for "mother." In one test, TCS engineers found that in 10 weeks, adults learned enough to sign their names and slowly read a newspaper.

India's largest private bank, called ICICI, has also created innovations through small loans given to self-employed farmers and craftspeople. Following the example of mortgage-backed securities, ICICI decided to bundle $5.3 million of loans from India's two best microfinance institutions, and sell them as securities yielding double-digit returns. By connecting capital markets to India's small entrepreneurs, the bank demonstrated that securitization could eventually create a new instrument for microborrowers across the world.

Banking. Education. Health care. Autos. In these areas and beyond, Indians are increasingly demanding better products and services at an affordable cost. Strong economic growth will only enlarge that demand. The phrase "Made in India" may come to represent low-cost innovation in the new global economy.

---

# GE's Indian Adventure

*The multinational's top exec in the country explains where it fits in the "One GE" strategy*

Until recently, few multinational players believed in India's potential and future. Most stayed away and have only just begun to make an impact in the country. But not General Electric. It has had a significant presence there for years, with joint ventures in consumer finance, lighting, and medical equipment. But GE really began to take off with the establishment of GE Capital International Services (GECIS), the back-office operation that serviced all of General Electric worldwide.

GECIS—now an independent company, of which GE owns less than half—was the brainchild of former GE CEO Jack Welch, who saw the raw talent of India and invested it in GECIS. Welch's "low-cost and high-quality" mantra is the reason other multinationals are flocking to India for services in everything from pharmaceuticals to technology and design engineering.

Under Jeff Immelt, Welch's successor, GE has even greater ambitions in India. It sees a country in transition, a perfect market for its products. Immelt wants GE's revenues there to go from $800 million currently to $5 billion by 2010. Scott Bayman, GE's country head in India since 1993, has overseen GE's India strategy. At his spacious office in New Delhi, he recently talked to *Business Week* India Bureau Chief Manjeet Kripalani about how GE plans to achieve its goals for India. Edited excerpts of their conversation follow:

**Q: How much has changed for Indian companies since you first came here?**
A: Ten years ago, Indian companies didn't need much capital. There was no market, no exports. Today, there's more capital available in India, and Indian companies have plenty of access to it. Their ability to finance projects themselves today is huge. China needs foreign direct investment, and India does not. What India needs is the knowledge that FDI brings.

**Q: Does GE have local competitors here?**
A: The majority of our competitors are still global competitors, not local ones. However, the scale isn't so large. Philips is in health care, for instance, but here it does mostly lighting and electronics. The big difference with GE is that we have localized the services we provide, with local software development. No one is doing this much here, among the multinationals.

**Q: At what stage of growth is GE in India now?**

**A:** We're at the third stage now. We came in early, in 1993, looking for the local market. We got into consumer finance and power-equipment supply. We had bumps along the way, we rationalized and shut down some businesses, but we learned. We developed people and now are 99.99% local.

When we realized the market wasn't maturing fast enough, we looked at what else to do. We couldn't find software engineers in the U.S. and found them in India. And that's what led us to back-office operations in 1998. So we started GECIS in India. That was phase two. Phase three began in 2004—which is actually phase one again, i.e., we're looking at the local market. Our new plan is to grow from $700 million in 2004 to $3 billion in 2008.

**Q: Where will this come from?**

**A:** This is part of our "One GE" strategy. It will be spread across our individual businesses. For instance, in power generation, we're involved in gas, hydro, and wind generation. We offer aircraft engines and leasing services—India has all these new airline start-ups. We will pursue real estate development and ownership. We'll develop financial services for both consumer and commercial markets.

Our engineered plastics business will be driven by the growth in the auto industry here. In health care, we're looking at growth in government hospitals and in medical tourism. We'll provide medical equipment and lighting.

**Q: Are you developing local products?**

**A:** Yes, we will. They'll have fewer bells and whistles and may have more portability to go from village to village, like ultrasound equipment or X-ray machines.

**Q: How integrated is the Jack Welch Research Centre in Bangalore with GE?**

**A:** The centre now has 2,500 scientists in Bangalore and 1,000 more in Hyderabad. About 40% of the GE engine for the [Boeing] 747 Dreamliner was developed in Bangalore. It's all integrated with what GE does with software. India is integrated into our company.

**Q: Jeff Immelt announced a $250 million investment in a medical facility in New Delhi in May 2006. Can you give us some details about that?**

A: That's Medicity, an integrated health-care and research facility in Gurgaon, just outside of Delhi. It's not an investment; rather we'll be supplying equipment [for high-end medical diagnostics, clinical research and development, power generation, lighting, water treatment] and operating it.

**Q: What's in it from you, apart from the $250 million in equipment that's your investment?**

A: It's GE's first such collaborative venture worldwide. India gives us a lot of throughput in equipment that will help us do engineering design here. We see this as an opportunity to get into some cutting-edge facilities in India. We want to do further product development here. It will also give us a platform for doing clinical trials.

For us, it's an opportunity to create the best of all the institutions, like Johns Hopkins, but in newer facilities, using leading-edge doctors and thought leaders.

**Q: So India is a business-to-business proposition for you, not a business-to-consumer?**

A: Our products have to be global. Here we're all about how to support our customers' business models. We're more B2B, than B2C. This model fits better.

**Q: What will your role be?**

A: I'll be spending my time adding people, increasing service capabilities in local markets. We'll be growing further and will localize our new employee base as soon as possible. We bring expats to infuse the culture and develop a local management team that can take the company further. Worldwide, our employees have the same annual performance review, salary style, stock options, and processes on everything like Six Sigma.

**Q: Where does India stand in the world of GE?**

A: In 2008, India will be the fastest-growing region for us. No, it won't be large dollar-wise, just $3 billion by 2008, and GE will be a $190 billion company by then. But India will be much more significant. By 2015, India will be the third- or fourth-largest economy on earth.

**Q: It won't be easy making your goals. India is still a fairly restricted economy.**
**A:** We're banking on India getting its act together, especially in infrastructure and health care. That's where One GE comes in—we can provide all the services India needs.

Almost every global company has woken up to India. I've met most of the companies coming here or making plans to be here. The question is: How big an export market this country can be, how soon can infrastructure be fixed and made world-class?

**Q: India seems so behind China. Can India ever compete?**
**A:** If India gets its infrastructure together, absolutely it can compete.

---

# How Cummins Does It

*The engine maker runs different game plans in India and China*

In an age of just-in-time delivery, it's probably not the best place to put an engine plant. Until recently, reaching the Dongfeng Cummins Engine Co. Ltd. complex from Wuhan, the nearest city with daily flights from Beijing, required a 5½-hour drive on a two-lane highway winding through the hills of rural Hubei Province to the dusty industrial city of Xiangfan. Even today, heaps of freshly picked watermelons lie along the road into town in the summer. For plant manager Jerry Gantt, 58, Xiangfan's only African American and a former offensive lineman for the Buffalo Bills football team, the five-year assignment has meant many tough adjustments to culture, business practices, and diet. "It's been a challenge," says Gantt, a 15-year Cummins Inc. veteran. His happiest day, he jokes, was when the first McDonald's restaurant opened in Xiangfan a few years ago.

Cummins didn't have a choice where to locate the diesel-engine plant when it opened in 1995—two decades after then-Chairman J. Irwin Miller was one of the first U.S. executives to visit Beijing. That was the decision of the Chinese government and Cummins' 50-50 partner Dongfeng Motor Co., a state-owned maker of cars and trucks. But like many multinationals that decided to get into China early, Cummins has learned to play the cards it was dealt. That's been true in India too. The Columbus (Ind.) company opened its first diesel engine venture in India in 1962. But for three decades sales were limited by bureaucratic controls on everything from pricing to product lines.

Yet their persistence has paid off. China and India now account for nearly 10% of Cummins' $10 billion plus in annual sales—and are expected to reach $5 billion by 2010. Dongfeng is now Cummins' No. 2 customer, after DaimlerChrysler, and has proved to be a valuable partner. The Xiangfan factory, profitable from the outset, churns out 120,000 truck engines a year. It has boosted output fourfold since 2001 while trimming the workforce by 10%, to 1,900. Meanwhile, Indian partner Tata Motors Ltd. is Cummins' No. 3 global customer, and a Cummins engineering center in Pune is becoming vital in designing engines, power generators, and components. Cummins is also winning orders in promising niches. For example, it is fitting thousands of buses in Beijing and New Delhi with hybrid engines that burn liquefied natural gas. In both nations, Cummins is expanding aggressively in every line of business. "Both China and India are probably the largest growth opportunities for Cummins," says Chief Executive Officer Theodore M. Solso.

Cummins needs the lift. In North America its potential market for big truck engines is shrinking as customers such as DaimlerChrysler, Volvo, and Navistar shift orders to their own affiliates. In 2007, Cummins will confront a new challenge when new U.S. emission standards kick in, which could raise costs. This makes expansion in China and India "particularly important," says Citigroup analyst David M. Raso.

Cummins has succeeded in nations renowned for being tough for foreign investors. It has pushed to localize manufacturing. By nurturing solid partnerships, it has minimized capital costs and gained a marketing edge. It has put a high priority on training and empowering local managers. Seven of Cummins' top 10 China managers are mainlanders. Top expatriates stay for long stints rather than use posts as two-year stepping stones. Cummins also has moved 100 Asian managers and their families to Columbus, where they are climbing the corporate ladder.

Beyond that, Cummins plays India and China differently, highlighting the two economies' diverging structures and strengths. Some major contrasts:

## Partnerships

When Cummins entered India in 1962, it formed a venture to make heavy engines and power generators in Pune in which it owned 50%. India's Kirloskar family owned 25%, and the rest floated on the Bombay Stock Exchange. When the Kirloskars sold much of their stake in the mid-1990s, more liberal investment rules allowed Cummins to boost its share to 51% in what now is called Cummins India Ltd. That gave Cummins clear management control and more flexibility to invest in new opportunities. It operates a fleet of rental trucks and a truck-stop chain, and sets up and helps run power plants. It also does back-office accounting, human-resource, and info-tech support work for Cummins worldwide. It even owns a $50 million company providing IT services to clients like Unilever and BNP Paribas.

Otherwise, Cummins is sticking with its original partners. It still shares ownership of another Indian venture formed in 1996 to make lighter truck engines with Tata Motors, India's premier maker of cars and trucks. And in China, it says it is committed to keeping its 50% stake with Dongfeng. Cummins' Fleetgard Division also has a 50-50 venture with Dongfeng in Shanghai making fuel and air filters. Plus, Cummins has a new joint venture with Shaanxi Automobile Group to make engines for heavy-duty trucks. The eagerness to share ownership is unusual. Many multinationals that Beijing pushed into marriages with state companies in the 1980s and 1990s have since maneuvered for full control. "Most foreign companies think it's a mistake" not to have clear control of their Chinese operations, says Steven M. Chapman, who ran Cummins' China operations for six years before recently assuming his new U.S. post as group vice-president for emerging markets. "But I really insist we be able to trust each other as absolute peers." Chapman, a Mandarin speaker, negotiated Cummins' first deal to assemble engines under license in 1985 and has worked with five Dongfeng chairmen.

There is an obvious reason to stay with Dongfeng. As China's top truck maker, it buys 70% of the plant's engines. Dongfeng also has the funds for rapid expansion. In three years, sales at the Xiangfen venture have zoomed from $63 million to $554 million, yielding $89 million in operating earnings for Cummins. Another big expansion is in the works.

In a nation where relationships are paramount, an ally like Dongfeng can be invaluable. Over the years, Cummins executives say they've developed deep connections at many levels in the company. "Our partner is very good at working through the red tape and speeding up approvals, which helps us ramp up quickly," says Cummins East Asia Managing Director John Watkins.

Dongfeng's business acumen also helps. Cummins sells an array of engines and parts to local vehicle and equipment makers. Its toughest competitors are mainland manufacturers that are improving quality and service—and undercut Cummins by up to 40%. Fleetgard competes against 1,600 other makers of filters in China. "We have the products and the technology, but we need a partner to get access to the market," says Ivan Lok, manager of the fast-expanding Fleetgard plant in Shanghai. Cummins has 100% control of its network of 200 distributors and service centers, however.

## Local R&D

In China, Cummins is about to open its first development center, also a 50-50 tie-up with Dongfeng. It will focus mainly on custom-designing engines for China. There also is talk of developing emerging markets.

In India, the two-year-old Cummins Research & Technology India center in Pune is playing an important role in helping the company slash development costs and time in its bid to best such archrivals as Caterpillar Inc. in building a new generation of diesel engines. Cummins is tapping India's immense pool of skilled, low-cost engineers. Pune is a software and auto hotbed, where pristine industrial parks abut narrow streets jammed with cars, cattle, and rickety three-wheel taxis.

The center's 100 engineers specialize in 3-D computer modeling and simulated testing of engines and components. They collaborate with R&D teams in each of Cummins' 20 other development centers worldwide. "We're involved in just about everything Cummins is doing," says John O'Halloran, a 12-year Cummins veteran dispatched in June 2003, to build and staff the center. In one area, a computational fluid dynamics team led by Ritesh Dungarwal, 26, an aerospace engineering graduate from the Indian Institute of Technology Bombay, simulates the combustion process inside a virtual prototype of a future engine. By mapping the movement of each fuel particle after it is ignited, they learn the size of droplets, how many are burned up, and how many are kicked out in the exhaust. Such data help determine fuel efficiency and emissions. At other pods, staff test engine components to see how they hold up to stress and whether fuel and air flow past at optimal levels. They tweak designs, and U.S. engineers review the work overnight.

Cummins engineers in the West do similar work, of course. But because such labor is so expensive, "we had to be very selective in the past," says O'Halloran. "You can come up with hundreds of things to simulate in a computer. But we were constrained by the number of engineers, so you had to decide which tasks were most critical." Now, hundreds of parts can be modeled, tested, and perfected. That should translate into higher performance, lighter engines, and lower costs. Another benefit is that Cummins now builds half as many physical prototypes as it used to, thus cutting development time by up to two-thirds. Pune "eventually will play a significant role in developing major engine platforms," he says.

## Exports

Given America's lopsided trade deficit with China, you would assume Cummins uses it as a major export base. Just the opposite. Cummins ships up to $400 million worth of engines from the U.S. to China a year—four times more than it imports. China's booming market absorbs all of the engines it makes there.

India, however, is a great base for exports. The Pune factory ships one-third of its generators to the U.S., Britain, China, South Africa, and other nations. It also exports engines for everything from mining equipment to marine frigates. Why use India, with its clogged roads and seaports, rather than China's superefficient industrial zones? For one, Cummins and its partners have been designing products for the price-conscious Indian market for years, providing an edge in developing nations. And while China is unbeatable in mass-volume manufacturing, India is well-suited for low-volume production of complex industrial goods. "In any component, subsystem, or piece of machinery that requires a high engineering content, India has the advantage," says Cummins India Chairman Anant Talaulicar.

Investing in local manufacturing. Grooming managers for the long term. Exporting when it makes sense, and tapping local engineering brainpower. Many multinationals are now emulating these strategies in China and India. Cummins figured it out well before the competition.

6

# The Leap Ahead

NEITHER CHINA NOR INDIA HAS YET produced many important breakthroughs in science or technology. But it is only a matter of time before India and China are at the forefront in technological innovation. They boast the world's greatest numbers of new scientists and engineering graduates, mounting R&D expenditures, and deepening ties with top foreign tech companies and schools.

"A New Labor Partner for the U.S.?" argues that China need not be viewed mainly as a future technology rival to the U.S. Indeed, China's advantages, such as low costs, government support, and skilled researchers are still largely outweighed by such shortcomings as an immature financial system, intellectual-property right theft, and weak links between universities and top companies. Moreover, China's biggest role may be as an extremely valuable ally with multinationals in the search for everything from cancer treatments and alternative-energy technologies to new materials. Nevertheless, China has big ambitions to become a science and technology power in its own right. "High Tech in China," written in 2002, was one of the first articles to take stock of China's rapid advances in a variety of fields.

Another factor in China's favor is its breathtaking rise as a leading manufacturer in a raft of next-tier industries. Thanks to massive foreign and domestic capital investment, described in "China Ramps Up," China is rapidly acquiring huge state-of-the-art capacity in industries such as steel, petrochemicals, semiconductors, automobiles, and flat-panel displays. As China becomes a global manufacturing leader in these areas, it also will likely become a vital innovation center.

India, meanwhile, is leveraging its wizardry in software and abundant low-cost engineering talent to develop its own innovative products. "Scrambling up the Development Ladder" shows how Indian engineering houses are assuming greater roles in helping foreign clients develop everything from auto components and consumer electronics to industrial machinery and medical devices.

India has become such a crucial source of low-cost engineers that many U.S. technology start-ups establish R&D operations in cities like Bangalore, Hyderabad, and Pune from the beginning. Venture capitalists are pushing this trend, as explained in "India and Silicon Valley: Now the R&D Flows Both Ways." The venture capital industry in India itself remains nascent, but a handful of promising homegrown companies marketing their own branded software, drugs, chip designs, and other tech products is starting to emerge. Foreign tech companies also are beefing up their Indian R&D centers to boost innovation, rather than merely take advantage of lower wages. "IBM's Passage to India" and "A Brain Trust in Bangalore" offer examples.

---

# A New Lab Partner for the U.S.?

*China's rapid rise in science could make it a valuable ally in breakthrough research*

On a July afternoon, China's newly built Shanghai Institute for Antibodies is quiet. No researchers yet toil amid the recently installed rows of DNA analyzers, mass spectrometers, and other state-of-the-art scientific tools. But the hush is temporary, promises Guo Yajun, the center's chairman. Soon, 100 Ph.D. researchers and 200 technicians and other staffers will be developing cancer treatments at the new $60 million facility in Shanghai's Zhangjiang Hi-Tech Park.

"Everything is brand-new here," says Guo, 50, a professor of oncology and immunology at University of Nebraska's Eppley Institute who splits his time between the U.S. and China. "The equipment is much better than my lab in the U.S."

Researchers with U.S. experience like Guo are helping to power a remarkable surge in Chinese science. Zhangjiang Hi-Tech Park has become a hotbed of new biotechnology research facilities. Eight government-run labs, including the Shanghai Transgenic Research Center, are located in the park, which is also home to 34 local and multinational drugmakers. Roche Holding Ltd. opened a research and development center nearby in 2004. And Chinese government spending on R&D is on the rise. It has more than tripled since 1998, and the number of scientific papers from Chinese researchers has more than doubled in that time. If current trends continue, says Richard B. Freeman, economics professor at Harvard University and director of labor studies at the National Bureau of Economic Research, "By 2010, China will produce more science and engineering Ph.D.s than the U.S."

Such dramatic statistics are setting off alarms in the U.S., where Cassandras are quick to warn of a possible end to American preeminence in science. "There is a good chance that U.S. competitiveness in vitally important high-tech areas will fall behind that of China" and other countries, Johns Hopkins University President William R. Brody told a congressional panel in 2006. Experts worry that China is investing heavily in key areas like biotech and nanotech while U.S. funding for the National Institutes of Health has leveled off after a five-year doubling. Spending in some areas of the physical sciences has actually declined in real dollars.

But that doesn't mean China will soon beat—or even seriously challenge—the U.S. in research and high tech. For one thing, China's advantages—low costs, government support, and skilled researchers—are still outweighed by shortcomings. These include an immature financial system that makes it hard for science-based start-up companies to raise money, a copycat culture wherein intellectual-property pirates regularly rip off patents and copyrights, and weak links between China's universities and its top businesses. "There's still a lot that needs to be done before China can be an innovative economy," says Lu Xianping, a 43-year-old native of western China's Sichuan Province who did post-doctoral research at the University of California at San Diego and worked in the U.S. for a dozen years. He is now president and chief scientific officer of Shenzhen Chipscreen Biosciences Ltd., a drug-discovery start-up he founded with six other Western-educated Ph.D.s.

More important, China's rise doesn't have to be America's loss. Besides leading to benefits at home, Chinese R&D will add to the world's pool of knowledge. "Science really doesn't have boundaries," explains Shu Chien, the China-born director of the Institute for Biomedical Engineering at the University of California at San Diego and a frequent visitor to the main-land. "Whatever the Chinese publish, we will see here in the U.S., and we can step on each other's shoulders to move ahead faster. If we look at it as a friendly competition, everyone gets better."

Experts increasingly see the chance of a win-win result from the combination of Chinese and American research might. That was one of the motivations for Wise Young, director of the W.M. Keck Center for Collaborative Neuroscience at Rutgers University, when he decided to set up a network of 17 clinical centers in China and train researchers to test new therapies. Born in Hong Kong, Young is a leader in the search for spinal-cord injury cures. A few years ago he had a visit from Chinese gymnast Sang Lan, who broke her neck practicing for the Goodwill Games in 1998. "She asked, if I discover the cure, how will it get back to China?" Young recalls. "I said that the only way China would get the therapy was if it actually did the clinical trials."

Young's clinical centers could help China become a leader in impor-tant new areas such as stem cells and nerve regeneration. They could also offer a way for Western companies to get their own treatments to market more quickly, Young says. Costs for conducting clinical trials in China are about one-fourth of those in the U.S. And while China was previously known for poorly regulating clinical trials, the government is beefing up standards in a bid to attract more Western companies to test drugs there.

## Tech for Today

Beijing is also working hard to lure American-educated Chinese scientists back to the mainland. One way to do that is by hiring returnees such as Han Jie, a University of Utah Ph.D. in materials science and engineering, to run government institutes. Han worked for IBM and for NASA's Ames Center for Nanotechnology before becoming director of a premier Chinese nanotech lab, the National Engineering Research Center for Nanotechnology in Shanghai, in the spring of 2004. Han and his team are moving to a new $15 million complex equipped with top-of-the-line facilities. Among other projects, the center is working on energy-efficient streetlights made from nanomaterials. "In the U.S., we try to build up technology for the future, but in China, I try to build technology that can be used today," Han says.

It's too early to tell what results labs like Han's will achieve. But experts such as Horst L. Störmer, a Nobel Prize laureate and director of Columbia University's nanotech center, have returned from visiting China's top nanotech institutes impressed by the science. Störmer is convinced the Chinese will become major players. "We talked at the same level," he says, adding that the Chinese were doing "top-notch research."

No doubt, some Chinese scientists will wind up becoming world-beaters, challenging their counterparts in the U.S. What's important is that researchers from both countries also expand their efforts at collaboration. That will pay off for all.

# High Tech in China: Is It a Threat to Silicon Valley?

Tang Tingao was apologetic as he guided a visitor through his lab at Fudan University in Shanghai in 2002. This is one of China's top institutions, and as head of Fudan's microelectronics institute, the

63-year-old Tang oversees some of the most advanced semiconductor research in the country. But by global standards, the conditions were primitive. The embarrassed scientist pointed to a row of old made-in-China furnaces for silicon preparation. In any other country, they would be obsolete.

They are fast becoming obsolete in Shanghai too. Despite a global technology slump, this city is in the middle of a high-tech spending binge. Government-linked Chinese companies and foreign multinationals are lavishing billions of dollars on new facilities. Chinese chip plants are mushrooming in a new science park just across the Huangpu River from the Fudan campus. In return for a toehold in the Chinese market, foreign companies helped Tang upgrade the equipment in his institute and train his staff. Such assistance could one day help Fudan become a semiconductor research hub for Shanghai, Tang says—"just like Stanford or Berkeley in Silicon Valley."

A Chinese Silicon Valley. In the mid-1990s, the idea would have been laughable. China was a place to make sneakers, not semiconductors. But to many of Silicon Valley's movers and shakers, the specter of Chinese competition is no longer a joke. Developments inside China—and a few beyond its borders—have reshaped the lens through which foreign multinationals view the world's most populous country. Over the next several years, China will become "a ferociously formidable competitor for companies that run the entire length of the technology food chain," predicts Michael J. Moritz, a partner at Sequoia Capital in Menlo Park, Calif., one of the Valley's premier venture-capital firms.

Consider some of China's milestones in science and tech:

- Chinese universities granted 465,000 science and engineering degrees in 2001—approaching the total for the U.S.

- Seven new semiconductor plants are cranking out chips, putting China on track to be the world's second-largest chip producer.

- A team at the Beijing Genomics Institute was among the first of several scientific teams to decode the rice genome, landing on the cover of the journal *Science.*

- Two homegrown vendors of network switches, Huawei Technologies Co. and ZTE Corp., opened offices in the U.S. and Europe and snatched contracts from the likes of Cisco Systems and Nortel Networks.

- China has been launching satellites for years and has begun manned space missions.

China's growing high-tech prowess and its ability to apply its expertise to defense matters were topics of discussion when Chinese President Jiang Zemin and President Bush met at the president's ranch in Crawford, Texas, in November 2002. Beijing's tech stature adds a new element to its often-troubled relationship with Washington. Bush wants China's support in the war on terrorism. At the same time, GOP hawks see China as one of the biggest long-term threats to U.S. security and economic preeminence. The hawks are opposed, however, by many executives from Corporate America who regard China as a lucrative market and are eager to offer the equipment and expertise it needs to meet its technological goals.

Mind you, China's achievements don't make it a high-tech superpower today. Despite scientific coups like the rice genome, China's companies can boast of little useful intellectual property and no paradigm-bending industrial innovations. China's equity markets are still largely closed to private start-ups, starving entrepreneurs of capital. Its software industry pales beside India's, not to mention Silicon Valley, and its stunted pharmaceutical sector hasn't come up with a single blockbuster drug. The country has yet to curb widespread piracy, a step that is essential for innovation to flourish. It also continues to suppress free speech and censor the Internet. And even now, says Andy Xie, managing director of Morgan Stanley in

Hong Kong, "America is sucking away all the best and the brightest in China."

Furthermore, by most standards of comparison, China's high-tech output doesn't measure up. Total research spending hovers at about $11 billion, versus more than $233 billion for the U.S. China's semiconductor production came to $2.9 billion in 2001, compared with $71.2 billion in the U.S. PC ownership and Internet penetration both hover at 2% of the population—far below Japan, South Korea, and most Western countries.

Nevertheless, China's early tech successes have convinced many Western executives that there are greater—and more worrisome— things to come. Even without strokes of innovative genius, China's energetic engineers can continue to clone the world's most advanced telecom and computer gear, as Huawei has done so successfully with network devices, and market them globally at rock-bottom prices. The total cost of an engineer in China, including benefits, is about $15,000 per year, notes Michael E. Marks, CEO of contract manufacturer Flextronics International Ltd. In Silicon Valley, the cost is 10 times that. For now, management at most Chinese companies is too weak for them to compete globally with Cisco, Intel, or Microsoft, Marks believes. Still, he says, "China has enormously talented engineers, and they all want to work. They are adding experience very rapidly. I would understand why U.S. electronics companies would be worried."

Most business folks already appreciate China's amazing achievement in manufacturing, raising itself from a Maoist backwater in the late 1970s to the world's most prodigious exporter today. And China isn't content to be a subcontractor. After more than a century of backwardness, the Chinese, who invented gunpowder, paper, and the compass, intend to regain their tech primacy. "You can't be economically very powerful but technologically very backward," says Wang Mingwei, head of the Chinese National Center for Drug Screening in Shanghai. "China is a proud nation and wants to have a say in the science arena, rather than be dominated by the Westerners and the Japanese."

Foreign companies privately might like to put the brakes on the Asian giant. But economics dictate that they do the opposite. To secure access to China's huge, growing market, dozens of foreign multinationals are entering research partnerships that are certain to upgrade the country's capabilities. Such pressure is frowned upon by the World Trade Organization, but try telling that to General Electric, Intel, Matsushita Electric, and Siemens, all of whom have shared valuable tech know-how. Microsoft Corp. has spent $750 million on a far-ranging research and training program. "China has discovered its leverage," says Erhfei Liu, Hong Kong–based chairman of Merrill Lynch China. "The Chinese say, 'If you want market access, give us technology.'"

In public, executives at Western companies make no apologies for technology transfer. "China is the most vigorous market for the U.S. [and] its most vigorous competitor," declares Intel Corp. Chairman Andrew S. Grove. But behind closed doors in Silicon Valley, Brussels, and Tokyo, China's science-and-technology agenda has become a sort of Rorschach test. For every executive like Grove who looks at the inkblots and sees opportunities outweighing risks, another senses palpable danger to Western interests. This camp is influenced by a variety of disturbing defense issues. A 2002 report by the U.S.–China Security Review Commission, a committee composed of a dozen congressional appointees, noted ominously that Beijing is hard at work acquiring "dual-use" technology that can not only boost the economy but also enhance the military and challenge American dominance in Asia.

Both responses to the Chinese Rorschach test—allure and alarm—are justified. And if there were only two viewpoints, the China-technology debate would be relatively clear-cut. But there are mitigating arguments that challenge the simple friend-or-foe construct. First, China's low-cost manufacturing base has driven down the price of consumer gadgets and all manner of industrial components. So shoppers in U.S. malls can take home $70 made-in-China DVD players, and industrial manufacturers such as GE can slash prices on everything from lightbulbs to aircraft engines. Second, as the world's scientific community grapples with overwhelming problems such as cancer, AIDS, and global warming, China's armies of newly trained scientists will be an important asset.

Individuals may attach different priorities to each of these points. But however you rank them, they lead to the same conclusion: China is destined to become a science-and-tech superpower. In the words of Gordon Astles, president of Asian operations for Cisco Systems Inc., China has "the sheer size, the will, the economic growth, and the openness to being part of the world. That says that they have a greater opportunity than ever before."

Beyond consumer gadgets and electronic components, China's impact on global technology is most evident in the ultracompetitive world of network equipment. Manufacturers such as Huawei and ZTE, which have long competed capably inside China, have targeted the breadbaskets of Western networking giants.

Huawei, which notched $2.4 billion in 2001 sales, won deals in Britain and Germany and launched a U.S. subsidiary dubbed FutureWei Technologies in June 2002. Huawei's international revenues rocketed 210% in the first half of 2002—an otherwise dismal period for equipment vendors. The company is counting on overseas sales to offset disappointing results in China, where the reorganization of state-owned China Telecom has stalled demand. ZTE, meanwhile, has opened research and development centers in New Jersey, California, and Texas and is targeting sales in Russia, India, and other emerging markets that are still growing despite the telecom depression in the West. "We are not as sophisticated as Lucent, Ericsson, or Cisco, but the gap has shrunk a lot," says Sun Zhenge, director of ZTE's technology center in China. "We will have the ability to exceed them in three to five years."

Networking executives in the West should not dismiss such talk as empty bravado. Because of China's inexpensive, highly skilled workforce, its equipment vendors can beat Cisco and Nortel on price by 25 to 50 percentage points. And while their high-end networking gear still trails that of North American rivals, Huawei and ZTE can compete when it comes to small or midsized networking products. "They're very serious about North America and Europe," says Michael Howard, principal analyst at market watcher Infonetics Research. "At every turn, Huawei will compete with Cisco at a much lower price."

In most respects, China's tech trajectory differs from the one Japan mapped out many decades earlier. Instead of trying to shut foreigners out of the market, Beijing encouraged domestic stars such as Huawei and ZTE to embrace alliances and research collaborations with foreign companies. "There's no 'not-invented-here' syndrome in China," says Zhou Zhen-hong, China managing director of Agere Systems, the Lucent Technologies spin-off, which has an R&D partnership with ZTE. Thanks to such efforts, Zhou believes that Chinese companies will be able to catch up to foreign rivals faster than Japan's lumbering giants could. Cooperation "closes the gap between the local companies and the multinationals," he says.

Like the network-equipment makers, China's cellular-handset manufacturers hope to build on their strength in their immense home market to become global players. China has the world's largest population of mobile-phone users. That means companies that serve the market gain vast manufacturing economies of scale. Plus, they are in a position to pioneer novel phone-based applications—such as wireless instant messaging—that could have international appeal. For now, Motorola Inc. and Nokia dominate the Chinese market. Nonetheless, handset makers are challenged hard in China by local rivals with names like Bird, TCL, and Konka.

Multinational manufacturers are responding by increasing their Chinese presence. Motorola has invested $3.4 billion in China, with a large part going to finance a giant chip plant in the northern city of Tianjin. Nokia has opened a sprawling industrial park for itself and its suppliers outside Beijing. German giant Siemens makes some 35% of its cellular phones in Shanghai and shifted a big chunk of its R&D team from Germany to Beijing. Siemens also is working with Chinese partners to develop a new standard for third-generation cellular service, aimed at the mobile Internet. "If China makes it, it will be a world standard," says Peter A. Borger, president of Siemens Shanghai Mobile Communication Ltd. Certainly, Siemens benefits. But a win in global-cellular standards would also vault China's players onto the international playing field.

Taiwan figures prominently in Beijing's tech strategy. Although the island's government remains at odds with Beijing's leaders, Taiwanese businesses have invested about $70 billion in China, and more of those investments are going toward big-ticket items such as semiconductor plants. The Chinese market "may take off pretty rapidly," says Morris Chang, chairman of Taiwan Semiconductor Manufacturing Co., the world's biggest contract manufacturer of chips. In addition, Taiwan's chip execs are now managing several contract-manufacturing plants in the Shanghai area. From this base, Taiwan-educated Richard Chang, a Texas Instruments Inc. veteran, wants to take on the world's silicon giants. He heads Shanghai's Semiconductor Manufacturing International Corp., a well-connected newcomer that includes among its investors Goldman Sachs and Toshiba Corp.

With support from Beijing, ethnic Chinese from around the world are following in the footsteps of the Taiwanese and forging new links to China. Shoucheng Zhang holds joint professorships in the physics departments at Stanford and at Beijing's Tsinghua University. The latter post was funded by Hong Kong billionaire Li Ka-shing, who aims to entice more overseas Chinese scientists to spend time on the mainland. Zhang has been bitten by the same bug: He's vice-president of Hua Yuan Science & Technology Association, a San Francisco nonprofit that promotes academic and commercial exchanges between the U.S. and China. The association boasts about 2,500 members in the U.S., including academic scientists as well as partners in prominent venture-capital firms such as IDG, Walden International, and WI Harper.

In short, Beijing is learning to harness Chinese intellect outside its borders and turn it into a competitive advantage. This has already contributed to strides in technical fields such as superconductivity, nanotechnology, and optics. Says Zhang: "China has been investing very wisely in the sciences. They are doing the right thing." And while no one has attempted to measure the overseas brain trust China could tap, it is clearly sizable, says Juan Enriquez-Cabot, director of the Life Science Project at Harvard Business School: "When you go into laboratories throughout the world, some of the brightest people are Chinese."

Among the foreign-born scientists and engineers working in the U.S., nearly 40,000 hail from China, more than from any other country.

The talent pool demonstrated its ability when China took on the arduous task of sequencing the rice genome, a feat that could one day lead to a cornucopia of hardy bioengineered crops and lay the groundwork for advances in genomic medicine. More than 500 researchers affiliated with the Chinese Academy of Sciences (CAS) worked on the project. But it might not have come to fruition without Seattle-based Gane Ka-Shu Wong, a Canadian physicist and post-doc at the University of Washington School of Medicine who was one of the project's instigators and lead scientists. The Cornell University–educated Wong and his colleague, Jun Yu, realized their task would require a team of skilled but inexpensive technicians. So in 1998 they persuaded CAS to set up the Beijing Genomics Institute, which housed the rice project. "We needed people to turn the cranks," explains Wong. "It's factory work."

One area where China clearly lags the West is the field of computer software. But Beijing has adroitly applied pressure on U.S. companies to help it catch up. For example, Microsoft's mammoth financial commitment to upgrading China's skills was prompted partly by the need to play in the world's largest potential consumer-software market. There was also, however, a concern that the Chinese government would throw its might behind "open-source" programs such as Linux, which could be a disastrous blow to Microsoft's Windows franchise.

Microsoft isn't the only one feeling the heat. China's population gives it extraordinary leverage in the design of next-generation programs. Take the area of network standards and operating systems. The Internet wasn't designed to support today's teeming cyberpopulation. Now, the global network is running out of "Internet protocol" addresses—a problem that is especially acute in the Chinese-speaking world. So Beijing is pushing for a rapid transition to a new generation of Internet hardware and software known collectively as Internet Protocol Version 6, or IPV6.

The U.S. has dragged its feet in this area because, among other things, the transition requires ripping out a lot of existing infrastructure and could render some of today's widely used computer and network software obsolete. But when it comes to the current generation of software, "China doesn't have a sig-nificant installed base," says AT&T software maven Steven M. Bellovin. "If China goes ahead and deploys Version 6 first, they could be the first to write new software while the rest of the world plays catch-up." This scenario meshes nicely with China's larger strategy. Developing a world-class software industry "is absolutely at the top of the agenda," says Derek Williams, Oracle Corp.'s Hong Kong–based executive vice-president. And in the case of IPV6, even if U.S. companies don't choose to help China, others will. Nokia has already con-nected 10 Chinese universities using a router platform and software developed partly at its R&D center in Beijing.

Certainly, the country has a lot of ground to make up. China's software industry generated revenues of just $850 million in 2001, compared with over $6 billion for India's. But it is growing rapidly. If Beijing gets results from its efforts to build software parks, provide incentive packages for programmers, boost English training programs, and enforce protections on intellectual prop-erty, the country could soon achieve parity with India in commercial software. In a few years, Gartner predicts India and China combined could reap nearly $60 billion in annual sales of software and application-service revenue. Those are revenues not booked in Silicon Valley.

This thought shouldn't elicit dread or dismay from Western executives. China is not demonic, and it is not monolithic. But it is poised to move up the technology ladder at a pace unprecedented among nations. The global industrial landscape will be permanently recast, as will the competitive balance among countries and companies. And no leap of technological imagination, threatening or benign, will be beyond China's reach.

---

# China Ramps Up

*It's adding massive factory capacity in tech-intensive industries such as autos and electronics*

The automotive world barely noticed, but a little bit of Chinese economic history transpired in June 2005 at the Xinsha Port in

Guangzhou. In a dockside ceremony replete with costumed dragon dancers, Honda Motor Corp. executives and Chinese officials celebrated the country's first full-scale export of cars made in China: 150 Jazz compacts bound for Europe. Guangzhou officials, who believe their booming city of 6.7 million is destined to become the nation's top auto hub, were thrilled. "From now on, high-quality autos made in Guangzhou will be shipped to more and more markets around the world," says Lin Yuanhe, the city's executive vice-mayor.

Officials in Changchun, Tianjin, Wuhan, and Shanghai are just as car-crazy. The mainland is in the grip of a massive capacity ramp-up by both global automakers and rising domestic outfits, from Chery Automobile to Shanghai Automotive Industry Corp. Plenty have plans to export China-made vehicles some day. "Where will these cars go but to international markets?" asks Hai Wen, deputy director of the China Center for Economic Research in Beijing.

Get ready for the next industrial leap. For years, China has been the cheap assembly shop for the world's shoes, clothing, and microwave ovens. Now, it is laying the groundwork to become a global power in much more sophisticated, technology-intensive industries that also demand tons of capital. Billions of dollars are flowing into auto, steel, chemical, and high-tech electronics plants. Driving this massive spending push is voracious domestic demand for all manner of goods as well as a big shift by multinationals to manufacture in China. As a result, China is rapidly becoming more self-sufficient in key materials and components, and setting the stage to be a major exporter of high-end products such as those listed here.

## Autos

By 2008, Chinese passenger car capacity could reach 8.7 million vehicles annually—double the number of expected buyers. Quality is increasing. At Honda's new $82 million export plant in Guangzhou, you'll see the same efficiency as at plants in Nagoya, Japan, or East Liberty, Ohio. Honda can crank out 50,000 1.2- and 1.4-liter versions of the Jazz compact, and there's plenty of unused land for expansion. At another jointly managed plant, where the Accord is produced, Honda officials were surprised to learn from in-house quality tests that the China-made version of the car is superior to the U.S.-manufactured model. The day is coming, declares Honda Senior Managing Director for China Atsuyoshi Hyogo, when the Japanese automaker "will use China as one of our export production bases" for global markets.

## Steel

For the first time ever, the Chinese steel industry became a net exporter in 2004, and shipments of rolled steel vaulted 54% during the first half of 2005. Asian steelmakers such as South Korea's INI Steel Co. and Tokyo Steel Manufacturing Co. announced price cuts in response.

It's too early to tell whether China will become a major exporter. With investment in construction and highways soaring, China's needs for steel remain high. But even if China simply manages to satisfy its own steel needs, that has big implications. In stainless steel, for example, China has quadrupled its capacity since 2000. That has allowed the country to shrink its imports from 65% five years ago to 40% in 2004—a worrying sign for big global steelmakers.

## Chemicals

The same thing is going on in petrochemicals. China has 50 projects under way involving at least $1 billion in investment—compared with just one in the U.S. today. Outside Shanghai, 5,600 workers are building a chemical complex a half-mile long for Germany's BASF and its Chinese partners in record time. Six other so-called crackers, built by Sinopec and other chemical companies, are expected to come on stream by 2010—an expansion that would push up China's annual ethylene capacity by 25% annually. China will still need to import the stuff, but it will be able to supply half of its needs in 2008, compared to one-third now.

## Semiconductors

China's chip industry is still in its infancy, but it is expanding rapidly. Consumer-electronics and telecom-equipment manufacturers are major buyers. Some 22 new silicon wafer fabrication plants are expected to be built by 2008. Fueled by this expansion, China's chip-design industry has grown nearly fivefold, to 450 companies, during the past five years. While China's silicon wafer fabs are still a generation or two behind those in the U.S., Taiwan, Japan, and Europe, they're good enough for chips in appliances and other consumer gear.

## Digital Electronics

By any measure, China is a consumer-electronics giant. It's the leading producer of color TVs, cell phones, desktop PCs, and DVD players. Now the industry also is poised to dominate in high-end products. That means China also may emerge as a global innovator. The country boasts more than 350 million mobile-phone users—the most in the world—and will likely overtake the U.S. in broadband households this year. Beijing also aims to convert to digital TV faster than in the U.S. and Europe. This makes China a crucial test market for new electronics technologies and products of the future, and it means China will help shape global standards as well.

The impact on world prices? "Chinese factories will drag down the profitability of global industries," predicts UBS Securities Asia Ltd. analyst Joe Zhang. If history is a guide, China's exports also will surge. China's global trade surplus now is on par with that of Japan, an economy almost three times as big. The Washington (D.C.)-based National Association of Manufacturers estimates China's sensitive surplus with the U.S. leapt 35%, to $220 billion, in 2005.

That means as China charges into these more sophisticated industries, a whole new strata of Western industries will likely face a crossroads. They will have to move even more forcefully into higher-tech, higher-value materials and products—or buy from China like everyone else.

## Scrambling up the Development Ladder

*By leveraging software wizardry and low-cost talent, India is eyeing the next level: Tech innovation*

Congenia, a two-year-old Italian drug company, can't match the cash of Big Pharma. So when it needed help in developing medicines to combat the diseases of aging, it turned to an unlikely source— India. Congenia in June 2005 tapped Tata Consultancy Services Ltd. for drug-discovery software and a team of programmers and life scientists in Hyderabad. The software, Bio-Suite, simulates the interactions of molecules with proteins, whittling down the universe of potential drug candidates from millions to thousands in about half the normal time. That also halves research costs.

With so much riding on its ability to discover new drugs, why would Congenia rely heavily on a company like TCS, which is mainly known as a low-cost supplier of computer services? Congenia Chief Executive Paolo Fundaro acknowledges he is taking a risk, but he's confident of TCS's skills. "There's no reason Indian companies shouldn't be on the front edge of tech in every field," he says.

This is a message Indian companies like TCS hope will spread far and wide. Over the past five years they've burst onto the world scene in software development, tech support, generic drugs, and back-office services. These businesses are nothing to sniff at. But in many cases they simply involve following orders from overseas clients or reverse-engineering.

Now, India is gearing up to reach the next level—technology innovation. By leveraging their software wizardry and cheap engineering and software talent, Indian companies are starting to develop their own products. Software companies such as i-flex Solutions Ltd., with its banking programs, are selling globally. "We have to build products that can be sold again and again, like Microsoft does. We have to continually go up the value chain," says Chairman Rajesh Hukku. In August 2005, in an affirmation of Indian software, U.S. software giant Oracle

Corp. agreed to pay $900 million for a controlling interest in i-flex—but leave the current executives in charge.

Hukku isn't alone. Pharmaceutical companies such as Nicholas Piramal India, Ranbaxy Laboratories, and Biocon are making strides in drug discovery and patenting their own compounds. This creative ferment could push Indian pharma output from $5 billion in 2004 to $25 billion by 2010, predicts consultant McKinsey & Co. And a NASS-COM/KPMG study predicts that Indian IT industry revenues—which swelled 32% in 2004, to $22 billion—could reach $148 billion by 2012. Industry leaders figure they have the chance to design and even make advanced products of all kinds. "The big opportunity for India is when it all comes together in manufacturing," says Ravi Gopinath, TCS's vice-president for engineering and industrial services. The Indians, in fact, hope to change the global game in industries from vehicles and machine tools to medical systems.

India, a manufacturing powerhouse? Still sounds off. In 2004, India exported $1.7 billion in electronics goods. That could reach $12.5 billion in 2010, projects Evalueserve Inc.

But India would still be a manufacturing minnow compared with China, which expects to export $175 billion worth of electronics in 2005. Besides, highways, ports, air terminals, and other infrastructure aren't yet adequate to support an export boom.

Yet India produces hundreds of thousands of industrial and software engineers yearly. And as more functions for cars, consumer electronics, and complex tools are packed onto semiconductors, the need for embedded software—an Indian expertise—is expanding fast. "That means India is well positioned to be a development hub in all kinds of industries," says A. T. Kearney high-tech consultant John Ciacchella.

## Still Growing Up

Internet connections and advances in interactive design software, meanwhile, make it increasingly possible to design, test, and reassemble industrial prototypes of highly complex products on computers. Using

3-D computer simulations of a virtual prototype, mechanical engineers and fluid dynamics specialists at Onward Technologies Ltd. in Pune are helping to design virtually every piece of a three-cylinder tractor engine due out in 2007 from a major farm-equipment company. Says Onward Chairman Harish S. Mehta: "This industry is in its infancy, but in two years you will see this really take off." Indian product engineering revenues rose 30%, to $2.7 billion, in 2004.

A handful of Indian outfits are rapidly moving along the path to hardware innovation. Wipro, Ittiam, HCL Technologies, and others are bringing together chips, circuit boards, embedded software, and industrial design—the whole stack of skills and technology needed to create a finished product. That can shave months and even years off product development, a godsend for Western companies under great pressure to cut costs.

India's industrial engineering firms are also moving beyond limited contract jobs for clients like Ford, General Electric, and Airbus and starting to cook up original prototypes for everything from machine tools to power generators. Bangalore's HCL designed a backup navigation system for the Airbus A340 and A320 jetliners in just 18 months. HCL clients often provide a mere two- or three-sentence description of the desired product and price target, and Indian engineers do the rest. "India will be very important for the world in hardware product development," predicts HCL Chief Executive Shiv Nadar.

The model for some Indian design houses is Taiwan. Big Taiwanese electronics companies like Quanta, Compal, and BenQ design and manufacture notebook PCs, cell phones, digital cameras, and other electronics for such brands as Dell, Hewlett-Packard, and Apple. Instead of mass-produced consumer items, though, India's niche could be industrial goods involving smaller production runs but high engineering content.

The breadth of research and development at TCS, which has 850 engineers just in its Bangalore center, and sister company Tata Technologies, a specialist in auto design, evinces the new vision for Indian tech prowess. Working from digital prototypes, Tata is helping a U.S.

automaker design the drive train, outer body, and interior layout of a future passenger car. For a leading U.S. developer of orthopedic implants, Tata engineers analyze CAT scans and custom-design replacement hips, knees, and wrist bones to fit patients awaiting surgery in American hospitals. For other U.S. clients, Tata has helped develop a forklift, a small earthmover, a golf cart, and high-security locks. For the Indian air force, it has even designed a test jet. Over the next half-decade, TCS plans to create a hybrid business model with 40% of revenues coming from licensing its technology and selling its own products, such as BioSuite.

## Smattering of Start-Ups

The Indians are starting to come up with original consumer electronics designs too. Ittiam Systems Ltd. of Bangalore specializes in integrating multimedia into low-cost devices. It licenses core designs to makers of in-flight entertainment systems, digital cameras, and video cell phones. Ittiam is preparing to release designs for portable iPod-like devices to play video downloaded from the Web.

A smattering of start-ups have taken the next step. They're both designing and selling their own cutting-edge hardware. Four-year-old Tejas Networks India Ltd., for instance, has become one of the leading sellers of optical networking gear in the rapidly growing Indian market. It has also begun selling its machines globally through Western networking suppliers. "The vision is to become one of the next Ciscos or Nortels of the world," says Chief Executive Sanjay Nayak.

What could delay India as it strives to innovate and build its own global brands? "It's a capital-starved country," says Sanjay Anandaram, a partner in JumpStartUp Fund Advisors Ltd., a Bangalore venture-capital firm. Start-ups with one foot in Silicon Valley have the edge. HelloSoft, a leading supplier of signal-processing technology for voice-over-Internet communications, raised $16 million from U.S. VCs in June, 2005. It was started by Indian entrepreneurs but its headquarters are in San Jose, Calif.

Indian start-ups don't have such ready access to cash. A recent scene inside the tiny conference room of JumpStartUp, located across from a crumbling Hindu temple, illustrates the problem. Weary from a red-eye flight from overseas, Sanjay Shah, CEO of three-year-old Skelta Software Ltd., a maker of corporate workflow programs, was making a presentation. JumpStartUp's partners, although sympathetic, peppered him with questions about how Skelta would gain credibility in the West and compete with Microsoft. Shah only wants to raise $1.5 million but sounded discouraged after the meeting. "I don't know how many VCs will be interested in funding me, and I don't see that changing fast," he says. "Without venture capital, India won't become powerful globally in software products."

But players like Shah don't need much money to make a difference. Engineering salaries are so low in India—even now, after rising 5% to 10% per year—that Skelta can afford to employ 30 engineers even though it only expects $2 million in revenues this year. This gives it an advantage over its main rival, SourceCode Technology Holdings Inc. of Redmond, Wash., which does much of its programming in the U.S.

Where there's hype, there's hope. Oracle's acquisition of i-flex shines a spotlight on India's nascent software products industry. And that could stimulate a flowering of new ideas and companies. "We're convinced that a good portion of the next generation of software companies will be emerging from India," says Oracle President Charles E. Phillips Jr.

I-flex Chairman Hukku urges his comrades to concentrate on developing software products tailored to particular industries.

That won't be the only path to software innovation, however. Trying something brand new is another option. Ramco Systems Ltd., for instance, which stumbled in its attempt to compete against Oracle and other leading corporate software makers, is being reborn with a new business model that could knock some of the established players off balance. Instead of selling packaged applications for accounting and manufacturing, which often don't fit a particular business, it builds software components that can be mixed and matched for a more custom fit. "They have been laboring away quietly," says University of Michigan management professor C. K. Prahalad. "This is going to surprise a lot of people throughout the world."

Indians know it's now or never. The advantages of low costs will last perhaps another 15 years, and competition from the likes of China, Brazil, and Ukraine is intensifying. "We are at a point in this country where if you don't innovate, you just won't exist," says S. Sadagopan, director of the Indian Institute of Information Technology in Bangalore. The Indians don't just want to exist: They want to flourish.

# India and Silicon Valley: Now the R&D Flows Both Ways

The ravages of the dot-com bust are still evident at Andale Inc.'s Mountain View (Calif.) headquarters. Half the office space sits abandoned, one corner of it heaped with discarded cubicle dividers and file cabinets. But looks are deceptive. The start-up, which offers software and research tools for online auction buyers and sellers, saw its workforce nearly quadruple back in 2003—with most of those jobs in Bangalore.

Andale's 155 workers in India, where employing a top software programmer runs a small fraction of the cost in the U.S., have been the key to the company's survival, says Chief Executive Munjal Shah, who grew up in Silicon Valley. In fact, Indian talent is adding vitality throughout Silicon Valley, where it's getting hard to find an info-tech start-up that doesn't have some research and development in such places as Bangalore, Bombay, or Hyderabad. Says Shah: "The next trillion dollars of wealth will come from companies that straddle the U.S. and India."

The chief architects of this rising business model are the 30,000-odd Indian IT professionals who live and work in the Valley. Indian engineers have become fixtures in the labs of America's top chip and software companies. Indian émigrés have also excelled as managers, entrepreneurs, and venture capitalists. As of 2000, Indians were among the founders or top execs of at least 972 companies, says AnnaLee

Saxenian, who studies immigrant business networks at the University of California at Berkeley.

Until recently, that brainpower mostly went in one direction, benefiting the Valley more than India. Now, this ambitious diaspora is generating a flurry of chip, software, and e-commerce start-ups in both nations, mobilizing billions in venture capital. The economics are so compelling that some venture capitalists demand Indian R&D be included in business plans from Day One. Says Robin Vasan, a partner at Mayfield in Menlo Park: "This is the way they need to do business."

The phenomenon is due in no small part to the professional and social networks Indians have set up in the Valley, such as The Indus Entrepreneurs (TiE), in Santa Clara: It now has 42 chapters in nine countries. Prominent Indians such as TiE founder and serial entrepreneur Kanwal Rekhi, venture capitalist Vinod Khosla, and former Intel Corp. executive Vin Dham serve as start-up mentors and angel investors. In early November 2003, Bombay-born Ash Lilani, senior vice-president at Silicon Valley Bank, led 20 Valley VCs on their first trip to India to scout opportunities. Of the bank's 5,000 Valley clients, 10% have some development work in India, but that was expected to rise to 25% by 2006.

Such opportunities for the Valley's Indians flow both ways. Hundreds have returned to India since 2000 to start businesses or help expand R&D labs for the likes of Oracle, Cisco Systems, and Intel. The downturn—and Washington's decision to issue fewer temporary work visas—accelerated the trend. At a 2003, tech job fair in Santa Clara, hundreds of engineers lined up, résumés in hand, for Indian openings offered by companies from Microsoft Corp. to Juniper Networks Inc. "The real development and design jobs are in India," says Indian-born job-seeker Jay Venkat, a young University of Alabama electrical engineering grad.

The deeper, more symbiotic relationship developing between the Valley and India goes far beyond the "body shopping" of the 1990s, when U.S. companies mainly wanted low-wage software-code writers. Now the brain drain from India is turning into what Saxenian calls "brain circulation," nourishing the tech scenes in both nations.

Some Valley companies even credit India with saving them from oblivion. Web-hosting software outfit Ensim Corp. in Sunnyvale relied on its 100-engineer team in Bangalore to keep designing lower-cost new products right through the downturn. "This company would not survive a day if not for the operation in India," says CEO Kanwal Rekhi. Before long, India may prove as crucial to the Valley's success as silicon itself.

---

# IBM's Passage to India

*Big Blue is making a big play in the subcontinent's tech sector, partly by hiring many more locals*

When IBM pulled out of India in 1978 in protest of new government regulations, it opened up the nascent Indian tech market to local players. Some of them grew up to be the tigers of the country's fast-growing software and tech services industries, including Infosys, Wipro, Tata Consultancy Services, and HCL Technologies. Now, those outfits are some of IBM's toughest competitors.

But IBM isn't off navel-gazing. It reentered India in 1992 and pumped up its game in the past two years—intent on turning its operations there into a huge competitive advantage.

## Too High?

You might say IBM has gone native. The company boosted its Indian staff from 9,000 at the end of 2003 to 23,000 at the end of 2005, and, according to an internal planning document made public by a union, the total was on its way to 38,000 by the end of 2005. The company says the 38,000 forecast is too high but acknowledges it is growing fast.

Already, IBM India just blew by Japan as the company's second largest country operation—after the U.S. "What you have seen in the past 5 years is nothing compared to what you'll see in the next 5 to 10," promises Mats Agervi, a tall, enthusiastic Swede who is vice-president for global delivery at IBM Global Services India.

IBM is under pressure to lower the costs of service delivery. Until the Indian software services companies emerged as serious rivals in 2003, its huge services workforce was distributed primarily within the regions where the work was done. One result was that its compensation costs—and therefore prices—were high. With the tech bust and the rise of the Indians, that strategy no longer worked.

## Brand-New

So IBM is in the middle of a massive retooling and migration of its work-force. It recently fired 14,000 services employees in Western Europe, the U.S., and Japan—even while it's hiring in India and Eastern Europe.

The India strategy isn't all about low-salary software coders, though. Not only does IBM have one of its eight basic research labs in Delhi but its 19 offices scattered across India include software labs in Bangalore and Pune, engineering R&D in Bangalore, and five data centers, including two brand-new ones. One of the new centers matches the capabilities of the company' so-called Level III facility in Boulder, Colo.—the best of the lot.

IBM isn't the only company expanding rapidly in India. Accenture has about 14,000 employees there, and Hewlett-Packard has 10,000, according to Technology Business Research Inc.

## Tapping into Talent

The Indian competitors are expanding their own workforces in India— and setting up programming and call centers elsewhere, as well. So far, though, "they're not in the same league. They don't have consulting, and they're not as global as IBM and Accenture," says analyst Bill Martorelli of Forrester Research.

Indeed, most of what IBM does in India is aimed at worldwide markets. It's developing a formula for distributing the workforce for its

$46 billion services business globally to tap into the right talent, local knowledge, and cost levels. So while it puts a smattering of sales and consulting people up close with customers, they're supported by thousands of programmers and business process operators in India, Brazil, and Eastern Europe. "You find ways to connect resources and capabilities all around the world—to get the very best from each location, whether it's skills or economics," says John Lutz, vice-president for on-demand business.

## Branching Out

One of the fastest-growing IBM operations in India is Daksh, the business process outsourcing (BPO) company it bought in 2004 for $150 million. IBM left Indian executives in charge. "We're still entrepreneurial and we're growing so rapidly," says Sanjeev Aggarwal, Daksh's CEO, who co-founded the company in 2000.

IBM doesn't break out Daksh revenues or say how fast it's growing, but India's NASSCOM software services trade organization lists it as the fifth-largest BPO operation in India.

Daksh started off as a customer service specialist, with e-mail and call centers. It landed high-profile customers such as Amazon.com and Yahoo!. But now it's branching into new areas, so-called transactional business process outsourcing. This includes finance, human resources, and procurement.

## Just as Powerful

The IBM connection has been good for Daksh. The parent company invested to help Aggarwal and his team build the business and has allowed them to tap scientists at IBM's research lab in Delhi to give them an edge over the competition. One piece of IBM Research technology automates the process of searching through documents for unstructured information—stuff that isn't packed into easy-to-follow templates and forms. That made it possible for Aggarwal to reassign 30 employees to more productive tasks.

Other benefits from the IBM connection are less tangible but just as powerful. In a fiercely competitive BPO market where rivals aggressively recruit each other's top employees, Aggarwal has been able to more than hold his own. His attrition rates are 50% per year in call centers and 20% in back-office operations, both substantially lower than the industry average. IBM's deep pockets allow him to pay among the best salaries in the industry.

## Keep Track

He also plays on IBM's reputation. One of his techniques is to reach out to the parents of employees, many of whom live at home. He sends letters to parents when their kids get awards or are promoted and invites them to open houses at the office so they know it's not a sweatshop. He shows them videos about IBM values. "The IBM brand is important to Indians," he says.

IBM's research operation in Delhi isn't just there to help with local technology and services projects. The lab, established in 1998, focuses on software and services for worldwide consumption. For example, scientists there created "eCoupon" technology for consumer products companies. It distributes electronic coupons to consumers and helps them keep track of them and use them before they expire.

Along with its research and global services operations, IBM is intent on expanding its footprint in the local Indian tech marketplace. IBM says sales rose 45% there in 2004. Although IBM declines to give the actual revenue numbers, a source close to the company says the total is on the north side of $500 million.

## Important Stop

Indian corporate clients have all of the sophistication of their Western counterparts. For instance, Bharti Tele-Ventures Ltd., India's leading telecom company, in 2004 outsourced much of its information technology operations to IBM in a 10-year deal potentially worth $750 million. IBM took over Bharti's operations and is transforming the way the company does IT. In an unusual twist, part of IBM's payments are linked to increases in Bharti's revenues.

The deeper IBM goes into India, the less it will seem like an outsider and the more it will become part of the local landscape. At the same time, India will be an important stop on the global talent supply chain.

"In the future you'll have two kinds of operations. You'll have innovation factories scattered around the world, and you'll have people within countries who can deliver to clients the value created in the factories," says Agervi, IBM's global delivery vice-president. Ultimately, if IBM gets this right, IBM India will produce a lot of both.

---

# A Brain Trust in Bangalore

*Sarnoff and other big tech names are setting up research operations in India—and not just because of the cheap labor*

They call it the monkey incident. A couple of months ago, a handful of engineers at Sarnoff Corp.'s lab in Bangalore, India, were conference-calling with colleagues at the research-for-hire outfit's headquarters in Princeton, N.J. They were sitting around a table in a meeting room when they heard loud banging from behind an air conditioner cover on the wall. One of them lifted the cover, and a baby monkey leaped into the room and raced around underfoot.

Two of the engineers were so surprised that they jumped up on the table. Then, "We all fled the room and closed the door," says Kiran Nayak, one of the participants, who recalls the incident with a huge smile.

It all turned out well in the end. In due time, the monkey returned to its mother, out on the building's ledge, and the engineers reclaimed their conference room and resumed talking about data-compression algorithms.

Such are the oddities of global research collaboration.

## "Highest Expectations"

Sarnoff is one of many Western tech research outfits that have turned to India for its combination of low labor costs, big brains, and English speakers the likes of which are available nowhere else in the world. Notables including Microsoft, Google, and IBM face plenty of challenges, but they're convinced that their investments in Indian research will pay off handsomely in the end.

"We have the highest expectations for Indian innovation. There's no question the raw talent exists," says Krishna Bharat, principal scientist at Google, who's starting up the company's new lab in Bangalore.

Sarnoff, a descendant of RCA's original TV-research lab, opened its doors in Bangalore in 2004 and already has 70 employees in two offices. Now it's in the process of consolidating in a larger space to make room for another 80 engineers.

## Third Wave

It's all part of Sarnoff CEO Satyam Cherukuri's master plan for creating a new model for tech research. "We're pioneering global networked R&D on behalf of our customers," says Cherukuri, who came to the U.S. 20 years ago from India for graduate school and has run Sarnoff since 1998.

Cherukuri calls this the "third wave" of tech research. The first wave was in-house R&D in large corporations. The second came with venture capitalists funding innovative start-ups that eventually grew to maturity or were bought by the big players. "This wave is about harvesting innovations anywhere in the world, with companies using their own employees or third-party researchers like us."

Sarnoff's India operations add to its small army of researchers, who are distributed worldwide. It has 400 engineers and scientists scattered in Princeton, Silicon Valley, Belgium, Japan, and, now, India. The company went through an extensive review of where it should expand next. While it considered 13 countries, it didn't take long to fix on India.

## Test Bed

Google, Microsoft, and IBM have similar strategies for distributing their research operations around the globe. IBM has long had a research outpost in Delhi, but added a software lab in Bangalore in 2001. Google and Microsoft have opened research labs in Bangalore in 2004 and 2005.

They can pick up an engineer just out of school for $5,000 to $10,000 a year in salary. But it's not just about the money. It's about the talent, says P. Anandan, managing director of Microsoft Research, India. Also, he says, "India's a test bed for developing technology for emerging economies and rural communities."

Doing research in India isn't without its challenges, however. Tim Mitchell, an Aussie who is Sarnoff's managing director in Bangalore, says it's tough to locate seasoned managers and engineers with the skills in analog-chip design that the company needs.

## Personal Projects

Google finds recruiting difficult as well. It announced early in 2004 that it hoped to hire 100 researchers before the end of the year, but by mid-2005 had landed just a couple of dozen. For the first year, the company concentrated on hiring and building a nucleus of senior researchers and managers. "The skill sets we're looking for are hard to come by in senior people," says Bharat, the chief scientist.

As a come-on to the top Indian technologists, the search giant promises them equal status to Google programmers and scientists in the U.S. and at other company outposts. Like all Google researchers and programmers, they're told they can spend 30% of their time on their own projects, in addition to working on assignments from supervisors.

So far, all of the projects the India team is working on are self-contained—meaning they don't have to do much coordinating with other Google researchers in the Silicon Valley, Tokyo, and Zurich. Eventually, Bharat says, there will be more collaboration and handoffs, taking advantage of the fact that the company has researchers positioned in three time zones to get projects done quickly.

## Cricket Gear

Sarnoff is further along in the collaboration sphere. Researchers keep in touch via phone, e-mail, and videoconference, and pass tasks off to one another as the day turns to night in one location and engineers arrive at work in another. This is no master-student relationship, however. "A guy in Princeton will ask us to follow up at the end of his day. Or if we're working on something, we ask them to do the same for us," says Prashant Laddha, a lead software engineer in Bangalore.

Sarnoff's Bangalore offices look much like technology offices elsewhere. A bunch of men in their twenties and early thirties labor away in small cubicles. One difference from their American kin: Rather than softball or bowling trophies, these guys keep cricket memorabilia on their desks. Several have motorcycle helmets stowed away, and the parking lot outside is jammed with cycles. The reason: Bangalore's narrow thoroughfares are so crowded with cars and buses that two-wheel transportation is the only way of getting to work in a reasonable amount of time.

The Bangalore researchers are working on a wide variety of projects, but one of them has already met with notable success. It's a good illustration of how networked global research is supposed to work.

## Video Feed

Since the lab was started, one of the goals was to help create a set of technologies for compressing and transmitting video wirelessly that could be sold, potentially, to a wide variety of customers. Rather than being an assignment from a client, Sarnoff conceived this as technology that it would develop and own itself.

The project is run by Sandip Parikh, Sarnoff's manager for multimedia technologies. He coordinates about 30 people, half in Princeton and half in India, who are working at least part-time on it. The aim was to produce high-quality video transmissions for low-power handheld devices, cell phones, and PDAs, at data speeds as slow as 28 kilobits per second. Sarnoff bases its technology on the latest industry standard for video compression, called MPEG 4, but uses its own proprietary algorithms to produce the best quality video for those demanding conditions.

The breakthrough came during a high-pressure couple of days in April 2005, when Parikh and the Bangalore crew teamed up to prove their concept. It was a successful attempt to win over their first customer—a large European cell-phone operator they wouldn't identify.

## Weekend Work

This started on the Thursday before Easter. Parikh was in India on a driving vacation with his family when he got a cell-phone call from the customer detailing the video quality levels they wanted to see. While his wife drove, Parikh worked up ideas on his laptop for how to tweak some of the algorithms to squeeze out extra performance.

He called Laddha, and the Bangalore engineers set to work. Over the next three days they took Parikh's ideas, improved on them, and tested the results until they were sure they got it right. By the time the boss returned to the office on the following Monday, the job was done.

To celebrate their victory, Mitchell treated all the employees to a day-long outing at a place on the outskirts of Bangalore called California Resort. They spent the day playing cricket, badminton, and volleyball.

## Tech Necessity

There could be some long-lasting rewards as well. The Bangalore team has filed five invention-disclosure reports on the work they did on this project—the first step toward filing U.S. patent applications. "We got some breakthroughs from the Indian engineers," says Parikh.

Over the coming years, that sentence could become a mantra for the many Western tech outfits that are counting on their Indian research operations to give them a competitive advantage. In fact, one day, having a brain trust in India may not be a luxury for the world's tech giants. It may become a necessity.

# 7

# The Financial Challenge

WEAK FINANCIAL SYSTEMS HAVE BEEN THE downfall of numerous other big developing nations that once seemed destined to economic greatness. India and China both have serious financial shortcomings. India, which suffered a financial crisis requiring International Monetary Fund intervention in 1991, still posts runaway public budget deficits at both the federal and state level. China's banking system is weighed down by mountains of bad debt to state corporations, while its private equity and debt markets remain remarkably underdeveloped for an economy its size. As a result, Beijing's ability to control excessive monetary growth and tame booms and busts is weak. Only currency and capital controls, many experts believe, immunized China from the contagion of the Asia financial crisis of 1997.

Modernization of the financial systems is a vital priority for India and China. "The Great Bank Overhaul" illustrates the challenge in China by offering an in-depth look at the challenges facing Newbridge Capital as it attempts to turn around one big Chinese bank. "Betting on China's Banks" explains the role that proposed public listings of China's state-owned banks could play in drastically altering the nation's banking system. Meanwhile, "China's Bourses: Stock Markets or Casinos?" shows how the underdeveloped stock exchanges in Shanghai and Shenzen largely remain short-term trading dens, rather than essential vehicles for China's best companies to raise capital. As economist Fan Gang explains in "China Is a Private-Sector Economy," however, a considerable but unofficial private lending system now is developing in China.

The challenges in India are different. The privately owned banking system is much healthier than China's, and India's stock market is among the biggest and most sophisticated in the developing world. Getting capital to the sectors in most need of funds—such as infrastructure, small businesses, and ordinary consumers—is a different matter. Heavy restrictions on foreign investment also have slowed industrialization. Progress is under way, however. "India: Who Wants to Build Some Roads?" explains how private institutional financing finally is starting to pour into public works such as highways. "Tiny Loans, High Finance" shows how savvy banks are learning to make money by making microloans to poor Indians who are starting small businesses, while "Private Equity Pours into India" explains how liberalization is opening lucrative new sectors to foreign investors.

---

# The Great Bank Overhaul

*Can a Chinese bank be a model for heroic reform?*

When Frank Newman paid a visit to Shenzhen Mayor Xu Zongheng in June 2005, it wasn't just to exchange pleasantries. Newman would soon be chairman of Shenzhen Development Bank (SDB), the first foreigner ever to hold such a post, and he needed Mayor Xu's help. The private bank, which is 18% owned by Newman's other employer, Fort Worth–based private-equity firm Newbridge Capital Group, is loaded with bad debt. Newman was there to explain his restructuring plan to the mayor and seek his help in collecting from some local deadbeats. Having seen an ornamental sword in the office of Shenzhen Vice-Mayor Chen Yingchun a week earlier, Newman said to Xu only half-jokingly, "Maybe you can use that sword on these guys." Xu smiled and assured Newman that "we will use the sword of the law."

Can China repair its mismanaged financial system—perhaps the most serious threat to sustained Chinese prosperity? Foreign investors, in hopes of finding the answer to that crucial question, are closely watching the unusual arrangement that gives Newman and his handpicked staff managerial control over SDB.

Newman, a bank turnaround artist who ran Bankers Trust Corp. in the mid-1990s, became SDB's chairman in 1995. But he had been scrutinizing the bank's operations for months before that, and he has observed plenty of the kind of trouble that is typical of Chinese banks—a backward information-technology system, a bloated staff, primitive credit controls, and a complete lack of cost consciousness. Branch managers around the country have made huge, risky loans without ever getting approval from headquarters. And there are hundreds of borrowers who were unable or unwilling to pay the money back. In the weeks before Newman was to take charge, the bank finally called in the Shenzhen police to speed up collection from at least one delinquent debtor.

The world has rightly marveled at China's dazzling growth, but the colossal waste of money involved in pushing that expansion has been less well publicized. It takes $5 to $7 of investment to generate a dollar's worth of gross domestic product in China, versus $1 to $2 in developed regions such as North America, Japan, and Western Europe. For now, China has both the enormous profits from its export trade and the captive savings of its citizens to invest recklessly. More than $3 trillion is stuffed inside Chinese banks, earning paltry interest, because the country's capital controls and undeveloped capital markets prevent savers from investing it elsewhere.

Unfortunately, much of that cash has been allocated so badly by China's four biggest banks and thousands of local lenders that most of them are limping financially—along with many of the state-controlled enterprises that were recipients of the banks' loans. Beijing to date has spent some $100 billion bailing out the Big Four—the Bank of China, China Construction Bank, the Industrial & Commercial Bank of China, and the Agricultural Bank of China. Standard & Poor's estimates the four will need an additional $190 billion later this decade to stay above water.

Why are China's banks in such terrible trouble? Because for most of their history they weren't banks in the Western sense at all; rather, they were financing arms of the Chinese government. "It used to be that local governments controlled the banks," says Fan Gang, president of the National Economic Research Institute.

## Big Steel, Little Steel

Consider the steel industry. China now has more than 200 steel plants, in part because every regional government felt it needed one to feed the hot-rolled stuff to local industries. The steelmakers were all built with big bank loans. But the largest 85 of the plants produce 90% of China's steel. The rest are marginal operations that wouldn't exist without the generosity of the banking system. At the same time, China's rail network is starved for money, but its managers don't have the political connections to garner bank loans. The result is massive railyard bottlenecks. In 2004, 25% of those seeking to ship goods by rail were turned away, according to Andy Rothman, a strategist with investment bank CLSA Asia-Pacific Markets in Shanghai.

China's financial managers know the country's growth engine is at risk if it can't allocate capital more shrewdly. That's why they've developed a plan for each of the Big Four—which together make 57% of all corporate loans—to link up with one or more foreign banks, as the banking system fully opens to foreign investors. The idea is that the foreign stakeholders will lend their expertise and, among other reforms, help straighten out the big Chinese banks' loan books. Bank of America Corp. bought a 9% stake in China Construction Bank for $3 billion, and in June 23, 2005, Switzerland's UBS announced it was in negotiations to make up to a $500 million investment in Bank of China.

Analysts note, however, that the Big Four and their government overseers are unlikely to let foreign partners have much real control over management. That's why Newbridge Capital's effective takeover of SDB is so important. SDB is one of a half-dozen younger, privately owned banks created in the late 1980s. These smaller banks are much more malleable reform vehicles, although Newbridge's Hong Kong–based managing partner, Weijian Shan, notes that, even in those banks, "you really need an experienced management team" willing to shake things up. Several of these "shareholding" banks have important foreign partners. Shanghai Pudong Development Bank is 5% owned by Citigroup, while Tianjin-based Bohai Bank is expected to get regulatory approval to sell a 20% stake to London-based Standard Chartered Bank.

Newbridge's investment in SDB, a commercial bank with $25 billion in assets, took two years to negotiate. The talks were led by Shan, a Beijing native whose family was relocated to the Gobi desert during the Cultural Revolution and who later went on to earn a doctorate in business at the University of California at Berkeley. The key sticking points were share price and managerial control. In the end, Newbridge paid $145 million for its 18% stake in the bank, making it the biggest single shareholder. It bought the shares from Chinese companies with the consent of the government. As part of the deal, Newman was appointed chairman. He has recruited other outsiders for top bank posts.

## A Banker's Banker

Newman is no stranger to salvage jobs. As chief financial officer of Bank of America in the late 1980s, he plugged gaping holes that appeared in the bank's balance sheet after a wave of credit card and consumer-loan defaults. In 1996 he took the top job at Bankers Trust after a scandal involving derivative contracts drove out a big chunk of senior management and sullied the bank's reputation. Newman "is a banker's banker," says friend Timothy C. Collins, CEO of Ripplewood Holdings LLC, the New York private-equity firm that acquired and turned around Shinsei Bank Ltd. in Japan.

Those turnaround skills will be sorely needed at SDB, where Newman has found that normal budget control mechanisms don't exist, and there is no system to measure which bank products are selling. When he arrived, Newman was shocked to find that loan officers didn't generate regular reports detailing which loans were being paid off and which were not. That matters greatly, since in 2004 the bank doubled its provisions for bad loans, which pushed SDB's profits down 21%, to $39.4 million. Bad loans now account for 11% of the bank's loan book. Also worrisome is SDB's capital adequacy ratio, which is 2.8%, well below the 4% mandated by Chinese regulators.

Newman, who doesn't speak Mandarin, is working with a team of experienced players who do. SDB President Jeffrey Williams is the former CEO of Standard Chartered Bank in Taiwan. Twenty years ago he opened Citibank's first mainland branch in Shenzhen. Other key players include Liu Baorui, head of retail banking, and NPL workout czar Wang Ji, both recruited from other Chinese banks. SDB's chief technology officer, mainlander Bruce Sun, is a former chairman of the Department of Information Systems at California State University. He worked for one of China's major banks before joining SDB.

Job No. 1 at SDB is to gain effective control over the bank's 230-odd branches in 18 major cities, including Shanghai, Beijing, and Chongqing. Newman says the branches have operated like "fiefdoms with their own emperors." And the little emperors have made bad loan decisions—for instance, lending millions of dollars to build little-used toll roads connecting coastal cities. Now all major branch loan officers report to headquarters, and a central credit committee clears major lending decisions. "You try to turn off the spigot," Newman says.

## Detective Work

A priority is doing triage on the bank's loan portfolio to decide which nonperforming loans it should attempt to collect. Newman says he has been surprised at the number of defaulted borrowers who suddenly come up with the money they owe when pressure is put on them. To go after the tougher cases, SDB has assembled a 130-person, specially trained loan collection department. "Collection has its own special set of techniques," says Newman. "You have to know how to work with lawyers, sometimes the local government, and sometimes you need to do a little detective work to see where people have assets hidden."

Another pressing issue is how SDB will raise the capital it needs to meet minimum capital requirements and upgrade its decrepit IT systems. Unless it can do that, senior executives won't be able to track costs and earnings in real time or invest in new businesses such as credit card and mortgage lending—a high priority for Newbridge. Newman says the bank likely will raise the cash it needs via a stock offering on the Shenzhen exchange, where it is already listed, perhaps in combination with a private placement of shares with another strategic foreign investor.

That's a tough strategy for the time being. China's markets are at an eight-year low, and stock prices will be held down for the foreseeable future by the government's promise to sell off a big portion of its shares in listed companies. SDB likely will try to raise $483 million, according to Hong Kong–based ABN-AMRO analyst Simon Ho, who is advising his clients to steer clear of the stock. Newman, however, is convinced he can put together a plan to raise the money he needs.

If he does, and if there isn't a huge increase in bad loans, SDB may have some interesting growth areas to exploit. First, Shenzhen (population: 10 million) is a major technology center, home to 100-plus major tech companies, including telecom networking equipment makers Huawei Technologies Co. and ZTE Corp. Newman wants to build up the bank's expertise in lending to them. He also intends to get into trade finance, raising and lending money in multiple currencies for the nation's exporters.

Then there's consumer lending. It represents only 11% of all loan assets in China, but it has doubled since 2000 as a middle class has emerged in the affluent coastal cities where the bank does most of its business. SDB has just a few hundred thousand credit card accounts at a time when 98 million cards are in circulation in China. Lending rates on cards are capped at 18%, but the cost of funding is only 3.6% or so. The risk is that China doesn't really have a system of independent credit bureaus that can help banks assess risk.

Just how long will it take to get SDB back on its feet? Well, Newbridge has made a commitment to hold its stake in the bank through the end of 2009. After that, it will probably sell to the highest bidder—and maybe make a bundle on the way out, as it did early in 2005 when it sold its stake in Korea First Bank to Standard Chartered. But there's more to this saga. If Newman & Co. can refashion SDB into a bank with a real credit culture, its success could have a ripple effect throughout the Chinese money system. For an old banking hand from the States, that would be quite a legacy.

# Betting on China's Banks

*The biggest IPO on earth may signal the start of a rich, new era of financial markets. No wonder Western institutions are lining up.*

Never accuse the Chinese of thinking small. The global public offering in late October 2005 of China Construction Bank, the mainland's third-largest bank, raised a head-turning $8 billion—the biggest IPO on the planet that year, and the biggest anywhere since Kraft Foods went public in 2001.

The offer was vastly oversubscribed, as investors lined up to buy a piece of a bank with $521.8 billion in assets, the first of China's Big Four state-owned banks to publicly list shares overseas. "We are well positioned to capitalize on the growth in China," says CCB Chairman Guo Shuqing. The Buy China syndrome has long gripped global investors entranced by the country's hypergrowth story. Some 117 Chinese companies have raised $45.5 billion in global equity markets in the past decade. In August 2005, Baidu.com, a Beijing search-engine outfit, blew away a five-year record on Nasdaq for best first-day trading performance as its share price jumped fivefold, to $154 per share.

## The Next Turn

Yet the China Construction deal was in a different realm. First, CCB already has the backing of Bank of America, which has committed

$3 billion for a minority stake. BofA is just one of several major banks, including Citigroup, HSBC Securities, Goldman Sachs, and American Express, that ponied up some $20 billion to buy into China's financial institutions, the biggest of which have plans to go public in the near future. Bank of America is sitting on a hefty profit.

Not bad. But what has BofA, Goldman, HSBC, and others excited is the prospect of winning a giant bet on China's next turn. The wager is that China's financial system, long one of the most dysfunctional anywhere, is finally getting fixed. It will blossom into one of the world's biggest profit machines as its banks make lucrative loans, the local bourses take off, a bond market develops, and consumers learn the joys of credit cards, mortgages, and personal finance. China, with more than $1.8 trillion in personal savings—and a savings rate of close to 50%—could become the financial market of the 21st century.

## Unreal Banks

That's the idea, at least. Beijing is in a titanic struggle to reinvent its financial system against considerable internal opposition. "The scale of what is happening has never been seen in the world," says U.S. Treasury Secretary John W. Snow.

Yet the great turnaround could still end up as the great flop, and global banks jumping into the fray could get hurt. A major economic slowdown could derail China's banks, some of which are hooked on real estate loans that sour easily. It will also be a struggle to escape the legacy of the past and forsake state-directed lending that almost brought the banks down.

Ever since the Great Helmsman Mao Zedong nationalized China's banks more than 50 years ago, they have served as massive employment agencies, money pots for pet projects, and key props for the party apparatus. They've done everything except act as real banks—institutions that gauge risk correctly, lend to the most promising businesses, and develop sophisticated services for consumers and companies alike.

## Waste Pile

Instead, China piled up half a trillion dollars in bad loans by the late 1990s. Huge bailouts courtesy of Beijing have lessened that load, but some analysts say a fresh crisis may be developing as the banks back too many new real estate projects and too many new factories.

Beijing's grand plan is to fix the main banks, inject foreign capital and expertise into the system, clean up the local bourses—and throw the financial markets virtually completely open to outside competition by December 6, 2006.

"It would be difficult to overstate the importance of this transformation," says Nicholas R. Lardy, a senior fellow and China watcher of the Institute for International Economics in Washington. "The financial sector is immense relative to China's GDP." Immense—and wasteful. It takes about three times as much investment to generate $1 of gross domestic product in China as it does in the U.S., Japan, and Western Europe. That's largely because the banks have been ineptly run.


## Still Fragile

So a lot is riding on the successful transformation of CCB from a plaything of state planners into a viable business. Since the late 1990s, the Chinese government has pumped $259 billion into CCB and the three other big state-owned banks—Bank of China, Industrial & Commercial Bank of China, and Agricultural Bank of China. With good reason: These Fantastic Four account for 57% of all lending, control $1.8 trillion in deposits, and have bounced back from near insolvency in the late 1990s.

The government's cash infusions have stabilized the banks, but the situation is still fragile. Neither China nor its banks have the managerial resources they need to build a better banking system. For that they are depending on investors like Bank of America. The Charlotte (N.C.) lender, the largest retail bank in the U.S., bought a 9% stake in CCB for $2.5 billion. It will spend an additional $500 million to buy equity during CCB's global offering of up to 30 million shares.

Although it will get only one seat on the board, BofA plans to send in a SWAT team of some 50 managers to help implement best practices in a Chinese context. If everything goes according to plan, Bank of America could exercise an option to raise its stake to 19.9% by March 2011.

## Shaping Up

Executives at BofA will train their local partners in such basics as due diligence on potential borrowers and fine-tuning loans to reflect borrowing costs and client risk. Construction Bank also desperately needs help in corporate governance and information technology. Of course, CCB officials may not be such quick studies. "There's a lot of work to be done when it comes to straightening up the bank sector in China," says banking analyst Andrew Collins at Piper Jaffray & Co. in New York. "You don't know how long this change in culture is going to take."

Yet as the new era of IPOs begins, the banks are in better shape than they have been in decades. Not only are the Big Four profitable, but thanks to the economy's white-hot growth and rising incomes, they saw 18% annualized growth in deposits from 2000 through 2004.

China Construction Bank is raking in profits. It says nonperforming loans are now 4% of its portfolio, down from 17% in 2002, although it has a much higher percentage of loans that need careful watching. Chairman Guo, a fluent English speaker, is a well-regarded former deputy governor of the country's central bank, the People's Bank of China. Better yet, CCB is earning a fat spread thanks to China's heavily regulated interest-rate regime. Banks can charge a 5.76% rate on one-year loans, but only need to pay out 2.23% on 12-month deposits.

## Embezzlement

True, former bank Chairman Zhang Enzhao was arrested in June 2005 for allegedly taking bribes, and the banks and authorities have disclosed precious little about who got the money. Also, the offering prospectus reveals more than 100 cases of theft and embezzlement at the bank between 2002 and 2004.

But CCB earned $6.07 billion in net income in 2004—and $3.5 billion during the first half of 2005, according to accounts audited by KPMG in Hong Kong. The bank has also acted to cut costs by trimming its branches from 21,391 in 2002 to 14,458 in 2005. Head count has been pruned 20%, to 311,000, over the same period. "CCB management is extremely focused on cost controls," says bank President Chang Zhenming.

What's in it for BofA? It's buying into a bank with a huge footprint and millions of potential customers for Bank of America products and services. China Construction already controls loans valued at about $293 billion, or 12% of the industry total. The bank enjoys dominant market positions in home loans (23.1%) and even credit cards (18.7%). Guo says CCB has a huge edge with blue-chip companies in growth industries such as power and telecoms.

## Lack of Leverage

With the Bank of China and Industrial & Commercial Bank of China expected to list in 2006 and investors already chomping at the bit to buy shares, it's clear that China will get all the Western help it wants to help it with bank reform. The question is whether that help will be enough. Beijing still insists the government retain a majority stake in its Big Four state banks. (Post-IPO, CCB will be 62.5% owned by the state.) China has refused, despite pressure from Washington, to lift its 25% cap on total equity held by outsiders and 20% for any single investor.

And while foreign investors may land a board seat or two at the banks, they won't be calling the shots on bank strategy or structure. If BofA CEO Kenneth D. Lewis or other foreign investors want to cut back on some of the banking industry's 1 million employees—CCB alone has 300,000-plus—they will have no leverage to do so. The American bank has also agreed to abandon any solo efforts on the mainland and any tie-ups with other Chinese lenders.

These rules don't appeal to some of its global competitors. Citigroup, for example, plans to expand its existing mainland retail network—although it has hedged that by taking a 4.6% stake in Shanghai Pudong Development Bank. Analysts say Citi officials are actively scouting for branch locations in urban areas throughout China.

## What If It Flops?

Beijing, meanwhile, is still keeping as tight a grip on bank reform as it has on its broader economic opening—despite a weeklong visit by U.S. Treasury Secretary Snow and Securities & Exchange Commission Chairman Christopher Cox. In meetings with PBOC Governor Zhou Xiaochuan and China Securities Regulatory Commission Chairman Shang Fulin, Cox says he heard a lot of talk about gradual steps, not quick leaps. As Cox puts it: "If you take nothing but half-steps to reach the wall, will you ever reach it?"

Given all the hoopla, it could prove embarrassing for Chinese leaders if CCB flops as a listed bank. For starters, about 25% of its loan portfolio is tied to the highly volatile residential mortgage and property-development markets at a time when many worry about a possible housing bust in big cities such as Shanghai.

"Its exposure to China's red-hot property sector is higher than many of its peers, but the asset quality of CCB's property portfolio is slightly better," says May Yan, vice-president and a senior analyst with Moody's Investors Service in Hong Kong.

## Growing Pains

The other issue with CCB is the quality of its numbers. Although the books have been examined by Western auditors, the possibility of unpleasant surprises is still there. Moody's notes the disturbing existence of "special mention" loans on CCB books that represent almost 17% of borrowing activity. Moody's is monitoring them closely, since a portion of these credits could eventually tip into the bad loan column.

Chinese officials urge the critics to be patient. After all, they say, just a few years ago there was no financial system to speak of that a Western banker would recognize. "China's capital markets were created out of nothing," says securities regulator Shang. Now they have to grow up.

## Tiny Loans, High Finance

On a foggy September morning at dawn more than two dozen women wearing colorful saris, little green books in hand, are sitting in rows on the terrace of a private home in Pothaipalli village— a poor rural area in the central Indian state of Andhra Pradesh. A young man patiently collects cash from each woman, who then makes a notation in her loan book. The women are paying back tiny loans from Share Microfin Ltd., a Hyderabad microfinance institution that serves 415,000 households in four Indian states.

This kind of small–lot lending to the impoverished has been around since the 1980s. Time and again it has been proved that just $50 can make a huge difference for an entrepreneurial villager, who can build a business around a new cow, a sewing machine, or a chicken coop. Development economists have also long remarked on the near-zero default rates of these credits.

Now the women of Pothaipalli are linking up with global capital markets. Their loans are being bundled with thousands of others and sold off as part of a $5 million securitization deal. The microloans' move into the world of high finance is designed to raise money for more microcredit while at the same time parceling out risk and pro-viding investors with a stable, income–generating security.

It works like this: The income stream from thousands of microloans is repackaged into an asset that mutual funds and insurance companies such as Life Insurance Corp. of India buy in the form of interest-bearing notes. If it takes off, the formula could revolutionize the world's estimated $10 billion microcredit market by bringing in new and cheaper funding derived from the sale of this paper. Securitizing microfinance loans "is the most effective way of getting market capital to the rural poor and pulling them out of poverty," says Subir V. Gokarn, chief economist of top Indian rating agency Crisil Ltd. "India's efforts could take microfinance to the next level."

India's pioneering program falls under the country's Securitization Act of 2002, which has not been fully implemented but has already spawned 221 deals worth $7.7 billion. The new legal structure and involvement of private banks lends India's model credibility that could help it spread throughout the developing world, says Priya Basu, a senior economist at the World Bank in New Delhi.

In Share Microfin's case, India's biggest private financial institution, ICICI Bank, securitized $4.3 million from the microloan portfolio and wrapped it up with $1 million in crop loans from Basix, India's oldest microfinance institution. Two other banks snapped up 60% of the April 2004 offering. With the money from ICICI, which used the deal to meet part of its state-mandated rural-lending quota, Share was able to add $4.3 million to its $137 million microcredit budget. ICICI is currently working with 30 different microfinance groups to securitize their loans. The upshot: Capital markets get access to the entrepreneurial spirit of rural India, and villagers get more loans to generate wealth. Twenty-nine-year-old Lata Dayala, for example, borrowed $435 in 2003 and now earns $87 a month from the little provision store she has set up in Pothaipalli—enough to send her three children to private school. She has even been able to repay two-thirds of her loan. "And now," she says shyly, "my husband treats me more like an equal."

Of course, $4.3 million does not a market make. And not all microcredit gurus are so sure securitization will take off. "Securitizing microfinance portfolios is beginning to develop, but you don't have a large enough portfolio in any given country that you can bundle it and put it out in the international capital markets," says Maria Otero, president of Accion International, a Boston nongovernmental organization that provides technical assistance to microcredit banks worldwide.

India's banks are mandated to extend 40% of their lending to rural areas, but because few actually meet that obligation they're interested in ICICI's program. Basix, for example, covers 4,000 villages and has

**Spreading the Wealth**

Securitizing microloans means everybody wins:

- Microcredit banks can immediately raise cash to lend by selling future revenues from repayment of existing loans.

- Investors get access to low-default loan portfolios that are repackaged into liquid, interest-bearing bonds.

- Intermediary banks can earn fees charged to investors for repackaging the loans.

- Low-income borrowers get more loans from the increased pool of capital at microcredit lenders.

500 representatives, most of whom live in the villages they serve. "Basix is integrated into the lives of the villages. Regular banks simply don't have those structures," says Rupa Kudwa, chief rating officer of Crisil.

At the same time, ICICI's role has lent greater credibility to micro-financiers such as Basix, which has eased their access to capital. That's a far cry from the days when bankers wouldn't even give Share's founder, Udaia Kumar, a hearing. Now Kumar has big plans. "Over the next five years, I need $150 million to serve 1.1 million more customers," he says. With global investors pumping in new money through securitization, that goal may be within reach.

---

# India: Who Wants to Build Some Roads?

*To remake its creaky infrastructure, India is banking on public-private partnerships*

When the skies opened up on July 26, 2005, dumping more than three feet of water on Bombay and the surrounding area, the creaking infrastructure of India's financial center collapsed under the strain. The aging suburban train service froze, the airport halted flights, and waterlogged roads forced commuters to abandon cars and buses. "It was as if someone had turned off the switch; everything just stopped," says Ann Iype, a teacher at downtown Cathedral and John Connon School who waded four hours in waist-deep water before she was given refuge in a friendly stranger's apartment.

It was a disaster, but one that woke up the markets to India's acute need to upgrade its infrastructure. So it is no surprise that when a new company called the Infrastructure Development Finance Co. Ltd. went public in an initial public offering, the event was lustily cheered by investors. The share price of IDFC, which will lend to builders of roads, ports, airports, energy, and telecom projects, doubled on its first day of trading two weeks later. "Investors realize the huge investment potential in Indian infrastructure," said Partha Bardhan, a New Delhi–based executive director at consultant KPMG. "The Bombay rains are the trigger that will get governments to act."

If India's state and national governments do accelerate their plans to rebuild the country, it will be in close partnership with private contractors and finance outfits like IDFC. The biggest, and most visible, such public-private enterprise is the massive $38 billion project to rehabilitate India's roads. Companies now build highways with government assistance, then operate them for profit by charging tolls. Competition is stiff to bag the contracts. A fifth of the planned 30,000-mile road network is complete, with the rest scheduled to be finished by 2012.

## Chinese Example

Roads are just the biggest of India's public-private infrastructure projects. The government is also inviting private investors and contractors to build airports and ports, water systems, and electricity distribution networks. The idea is to match China, which is leagues ahead of India. "Compared with China's infrastructure spending of 20% of its gross domestic product," says Chetan Ahya, an economist at Morgan

Stanley's Bombay offices, "India spends just 6%. It needs to increase that to at least 10% to prime economic growth further."

How do the public-private partnerships work? One variation is a "build-operate-transfer" arrangement in which the private company operates a toll road or other facility until it has recovered its investment and made a profit, then turns it over to the government. In other cases, the builder gets a partial capital subsidy from New Delhi. That's true of a new 62-mile, six-lane expressway that replaced a potholed stretch of National Highway 8 from Jaipur in the Rajasthan desert to Bombay. The project, led by Indian engineering giant Larsen & Toubro Ltd. and Hyderabad's GVK Industries, cost $141 million, with $49 million provided by New Delhi. Operated as a private road, the four-month-old length of new highway collected $62,000 in July 2005.

Sometimes the government acts as an investor in a private project. That's the plan for the New Delhi and Bombay airports. The government is now accepting bids for expansion and renovation of the two facilities, at a price of about $1 billion each. The airports will then be owned and operated by the bidder who agrees to pay the biggest slice of landing fees and other revenues to New Delhi as royalties. Construction will be financed through bank loans, vendor financing, and by selling shares in the airport corporations. Suitors from Australia to France have put in bids together with local partners. Whoever wins, New Delhi will retain a 26% stake in the airports and maintain regulatory authority. In the south, new airports being built at Hyderabad and Bangalore will also be owned by public-private consortiums and operated privately.

If India is to be a manufacturing and export power, nothing is more important than efficient ports. To get dilapidated shipping facilities in shape, the government has sold the right to operate several ports and terminals, with the private operators collecting shipping fees and paying the government royalties. Private port and terminal managers now handle more than a third of the country's cargo. On private docks, the loading or unloading of a cargo shipment that might have taken three days a few years ago now takes 10 to 12 hours. The Netherlands' P&O

Nedlloyd, a global shipping company, runs one terminal in Bombay's Nhava Sheva Port and another in Madras. And in 2003 it paid $212 million to buy an entire small port at Mundra in Gujarat on the Indian Ocean. Danish shipping giant A.P. Möller-Maersk Group runs a terminal at Bombay together with state-run Container Corporation of India Ltd. Port investors paid the federal Shipping Ministry $107 million in royalties over a three-year period.

Novel projects are being attempted in the public-private sphere by local governments too. The city of Tirupur (population: 900,000) in the southern state of Tamil Nadu is India's knitwear capital, exporting over $1 billion worth of garments a year. But the city's mills are hampered by an inadequate water supply. So the local state government has formed a joint venture with Bombay financial firm IL&FS to build a $220 million water system that includes a pipeline to Tirupur from the Cauvery River 43 miles away, plus pumps and a purification plant. The system will be owned and operated for profit by the private New Tirupur Area Development Corp., in which the state government, the Asian Development Bank, IL&FS, and other private companies are all investors. An added benefit: The project includes installation of a sewer system and new municipal pipes that will provide clean water to 60% of Tirupur's households.

Despite the government's efforts to clear the way for private operators, India can still be a frustrating place. Ashok Kheny is an engineer-builder who ran a successful business in Philadelphia, then returned to India in 1994 to build a 106-mile, $525 million expressway between Bangalore and Mysore. In the decade since, Kheny's Nandi Infrastructure Corridor Enterprises Ltd. has been harried by no fewer than 336 lawsuits from farmers, other landowners, and government allies trying to prevent the builders from gobbling up their land. The expressway, now eight years behind schedule, is expected to be completed by December 2007.

New Delhi is working hard to make sure Kheny's experience is not repeated. The federal Planning Commission is consulting with World Bank experts to finish a set of watertight contracts for private-sector infrastructure projects. "The main bottleneck is the lack of predictable regulation and standardized systems," says Montek Singh Ahluwalia, the commission's deputy chairman and a key architect of India's economic reforms. The contracts won't stop all the lawsuits, but they could help India reach the next level in its quest to build the infrastructure it needs.

## Private Equity Pours into India

*A lucrative Warburg Pincus deal sends a signal to other firms:*
*There's big money to be made in India*

When private equity fund Warburg Pincus LLC announced on Mar. 14, 2005, that it had sold the latest chunk of its stake in India's top cellular player, Bharti Tele-Ventures Ltd., it was the biggest sensation of the year for India's markets. Not only was the $560 million sum huge—the largest stock trade in India's history—but the deal was completed seamlessly in just 26 minutes. "No one realized the Indian market had so much depth or maturity," says Manisha Girotra, chairman and managing director of UBS India, which executed the trade for Warburg. "Or that there was such an appetite for India."

Warburg Pincus has now made $1.1 billion by selling off two-thirds of its 18% share in Bharti—not a bad payoff on a $300 million investment made in stages between 1999 and 2001. "It was one of the very best deals in the firm's history," says Dalip Pathak, a London partner at Warburg Pincus in charge of Europe and India and the man who led the Bharti investment. "We were willing to take certain risks when we backed the management, and the risks paid off."

Warburg's painless and profitable exit sent an important signal to the private equity community: India is finally open for business. Private equity investors from around the world are increasing their bets on Indian corporates or making new ones. That includes big-name U.S. firms like Blackstone Group, Carlyle Group, and General Atlantic Partners, as well as Britain's Actis Partners. Local firms such as ICICI Venture Funds Management Ltd. and Kotak are also step-ping up investments. In 2004 these firms poured an estimated $1.3 billion into private equity deals in India, according to *Asian Venture Capital Journal*.

New foreign buyout firms are arriving monthly, snapping up experi-enced local staff and setting up shop in Bombay, Bangalore, and New Delhi at a rapid pace—often hitting the ground running by operating from five-star hotel rooms until they find suitable office space. For the first half of 2005, there were 32 deals worth $420 million. And also $1.2 billion in divestments, or exits, as they are known in the private equity business. In 2004, the largest investment came when Greenwich (Conn.)-based General Atlantic and New York's Oak Hill Capital bought 60% of New Delhi outsourcing company GE Capital International Services (GECIS) from General Electric Co. for $500 million.

While the traditional route for private equity firms is to buy a con-trolling stake in struggling, mature corporations and then try to turn them around, in an emerging economy such as India these firms act more like venture capitalists. They look for promising companies in industries ranging from tech to textiles and seek to give them a boost, doing everything from injecting more capital for expansion to holding the hand of management and providing strategic guidance. "Develop-ing countries like India offer [private equity] opportunities that devel-oped countries don't," says Ash Lilani, head of global markets for Silicon Valley Bank in Santa Clara, Calif., which funds the private equity and venture industry. "With the right capital and professional management, private equity players in India can invest early, expand companies, and make an impact on entire industry segments."

Of course, there is also a great deal of money to be made. That's why Blackstone Group elevated India to one of its key strategic hubs in Asia. Early in 2005, Blackstone hired several consulting firms, including McKinsey & Co., and looked at investing in various emerging markets. It chose India as the place to set up its next in-country office and intends to invest $1 billion in local companies, says Akhil Gupta, head of Black-stone in India.

India's chief advantage over countries such as China is that it offers investors better trained managers and more corporate transparency in the private sector. It also boasts the oldest stock market in Asia—the 130-year-old Bombay Stock Exchange—and the largest number of listed stocks, over 7,000. Most important, the courts are a fairly reliable arbiter of investors' rights. "India is more sophisticated than other Asian markets because of its more developed jurisprudence and relative sanctity of contracts," says Donald Peck, a managing partner in charge of the India office for Britain's Actis, which has successfully enforced a disputed contract.

True, there are significant downsides that still give foreigners pause. For all of its recent financial and regulatory reforms, the country remains mired in bureaucratic red tape and bedeviled by poor infrastructure. Plus, there are limits to foreign ownership in industries such as defense, news media, retail, and some forms of banking. A much-ballyhooed privatization process of state-run firms has been stalled by the current government, so big Indian and foreign private investors cannot exercise control over the juiciest public sector companies.

## Bubble Worries

At the same time, there are plenty of players in emerging industries such as software, tech outsourcing, and pharmaceuticals. And opportunities are expanding in newly deregulating industries such as cellular telecom and broadband, airlines, and port infrastructure. All require not only funding but also outside management and strategic help. While many Indian companies have global ambitions, they are often "not properly channeled," says Shankar Narayanan, head of India operations for Carlyle Group, which has invested $50 million in India since 2003. Players like Carlyle help local companies "scale up and get access to the knowledge and markets they seek," he says.

But all this enthusiasm is new. Warburg's 1999 wager on Bharti, for instance, was initially mocked by those who thought the country would never emerge from the strictures of the license raj. Today, India is the fastest-growing cellular market in the world. Bharti was the first to aggressively expand across India, increasing its customer base to 10 million last year. Bharti's management credits Warburg for supporting its bold plans. "They believed in us a little more than we believed in ourselves," says joint managing director Akhil Gupta (no relation to the Blackstone chief).

Some have placed bets on more traditional businesses. In 2003, for instance, Actis paid $60 million for a 29% stake in state-owned Punjab Tractors, India's most profitable maker of farm tractors and forklifts. Investors expect more opportunities as India develops. "In the next five years the roads will get fixed, the ports sorted out, there will be 200 million mobile subscribers and a huge increase in productivity," says Warburg's Pathak.

Is the Indian market ready to handle such dramatic change? Most dealmakers say yes, noting that the size of their investments has grown steadily larger over the past six years—from tiny $1 million bets to $500 million buyouts. All that cash sloshing around has some observers worrying about a bubble in Corporate India. But the smart money, according to investors like Pathak, is betting that the best deals are still to be had.

---

# China's Bourses: Stock Markets or Casinos?

*They're still roller coasters of instability—and change may take some time*

When shares of Han's Laser Technology Co. began trading on June 26, 2004, it was a red-letter day for the Shenzhen Stock Exchange, which hadn't seen an initial public offering since October 2000. But the joy was short-lived for any investors who had been hoping for more than a speculative pop from the stock. After soaring 367% on its opening day of trading, shares of the Shenzhen maker of laser markers deflated by the maximum 10% limit the next day—and the next, and the next. By July 7, 2004, Han's Laser was nearly 50% off its high and, though still above its offering price, showed no signs of stabilizing. Such volatility "doesn't have any meaning at all," says a Han's Laser spokesman. "It only reveals speculation." To experts, the stock was acting just like the market in which it trades. "It's like a casino," says Zhang Qi, analyst at Haitong Securities Co. in Shenzhen. "Everybody's speculating."

Indeed, Shenzhen and the larger Shanghai Stock Exchange both have a reputation for being little more than short-term trading dens that scare away serious investors. That's a problem, because China has a pressing need for stock markets capable of efficiently allocating capital to its fast-growing industrial base. As in the 1990's dot-com boom in the West, nothing exposes the instability of China's markets better than IPOs. Seven other companies made their debut on the Shenzhen market the same day as Han's Laser. Each rose an average of 130% before beginning a downward spiral.

The stock-flipping behind these gyrations, by both brokers and retail punters, even has a name: *chao gu*, which translates roughly as "stir-fried shares." Fundamentals? Some companies have them, some don't. (Han's Laser, for its part, is profitable, boasting net income of $4.44 million in 2003.) No matter: In the 16-year history of the mainland bourses, the initial success rate of IPOs has been almost 100%. In 2003 the average first-day gain among the 64 new listings in Shanghai was an eye-popping 72%—and 2003 was a bear market. Most quickly lose altitude. One exception: China Yangtze Power Co., whose shares have climbed steadily since it debuted in November 2003. But trading in new stocks is typically purely speculative. Almost no one in these markets thinks of buying and holding stocks—a sure sign of an immature market.

## Bring On the Foreigners

What can be done to create authentic market conditions? The China Securities Regulatory Commission has been declaring its good intentions since it was created in 1992. But the agency has been hampered by its inexperience and lack of independence—it is basically an arm of the State Council, China's all-powerful Cabinet. Plus, the markets were established solely as a way for state-owned companies to privatize, not as a way to raise money for deserving companies.

One strategy authorities are pursuing to strengthen Chinese bourses is to allow in foreign investors. The theory is that with foreigners demanding higher standards for listed companies, trading will become more regular and IPOs more thoroughly vetted, and the reputation of the exchanges will improve, making them competitive with rival Hong Kong. Thus, under the Qualified Foreign Institutional Investors program, which began in May 2003, foreign institutions may now invest directly in the $500 billion A-share markets of Shanghai and Shenzhen, which were previously off-limits.

But things are off to a slow start. According to the State Administration of Foreign Exchange, out of $1.8 billion in foreign investment capital approved at the end of March 2004 and earmarked for financial investments, only 63% has gone into securities and convertible bonds. The rest is parked in bank deposits. Most foreign fund managers find slim pickings among mainland equities and have concentrated on 50 to 100 stocks from the 1,300 available. "There's certainly nothing like HSBC or General Electric or IBM," says Mandy Yang, general manager of China International Fund Management Co. in Shanghai, JPMorgan Fleming's joint venture with Shanghai International Trust and Investment.

The IPO practices on the Shenzhen and Shanghai exchanges are especially exasperating. For one thing, the shares are priced according to a rigid formula dictated by the government, so that IPO prices bear little or no relation to the underlying fundamentals of the company. Strict rules on who can subscribe to an IPO also create a false scarcity that drives demand—for a short time. "The IPO market is not really market-driven, it's more regulation-driven," says Nicole Yuen, head of China equities at UBS in Hong Kong, and a member of the CSRC listing committee.

An even bigger problem with China's stock markets stems from the government's reluctance to relinquish control over state-owned enterprises when they list. About two-thirds of all listed companies' shares are nontradable blocks held by state agencies and other state-owned companies. This makes for thinly traded shares, which increases volatility. It also deters investors from taking a buy-and-hold approach, for fear the government will one day dilute their holdings by releasing its shares. One solution under consideration: allow existing shareholders to buy untradable shares at a discount.

Yet the government, despite its vow to fix the system, remains reluctant to unleash real market forces. "I don't think the capital markets have anything to do with risk; they have everything to do with funneling money to state-owned enterprises," says Carl E. Walter, chief operating officer for JPMorgan Chase & Co. in China. This in turn provides little incentive for local underwriters to conduct thorough due diligence on the stocks they bring to market. "It's a joke," says Walter.

With such structural problems, it's hard to see how the mainland exchanges will rapidly mature. But fund managers are quietly exerting more discipline on the market by buying stocks of well-run companies, to which they make regular visits. The number of funds has grown to about 135 since 1998, with some $30 billion under management, representing 5% of the market. Beginning in 2003, a number of foreign houses, including ABN Amro, ING Group, and JPMorgan Fleming Asset Management have set up joint-venture fund companies. "Mutual funds and more transparent institutional investors have brought some sense to the market," says Joon Lü, deputy chief investment officer at China International Fund Management.

The presence of long-term investors hasn't put a stop to the IPO wildness, but some brakes are being applied. On June 29, 2004, for example, Jinan Iron & Steel Group's debut fizzled, closing just marginally above its 76 cents IPO price, reflecting investor concern that a Beijing-imposed slowdown in the steel industry would hurt earnings. A flat IPO? That may be a sign that one day mainland exchanges may behave like real stock markets.

# China Is a Private-Sector Economy

*Economist Fan Gang points to a 70% share of GDP now in private hands, but he acknowledges that much improvement is still needed*

Fan Gang is one of China's best-known economists. He directs the National Economic Research Institute, a Beijing think tank affiliated with the China Reform Foundation. He's an advisor to the Chinese government and has been a consultant to the World Bank, U.N. Development Program, and other international agencies.

Fan has published eight books and more than 100 academic papers. He has been an advocate of tight monetary policy coupled with expansionist macroeconomic policy to compensate for still-inadequate private investment in areas like infrastructure. He recently discussed his views on China's economic future with *BusinessWeek*. Edited excerpts of the conversation follow:

**Q: What is China's basic challenge?**
**A:** China has two big issues. First, it is an emerging economy, and second it is an economy in transition. The first challenge requires development. The second requires reform at the same time. Plus, it has the world's biggest population. And China is the only really large country with only one coastline. That translates into big regional disparity. This is why China is full of problems.

**Q: What's the role of the state sector, versus the private sector?**
**A:** The major reform achievement has been in privatizing state enterprises. The private sector accounts for 70% of gross domestic product. There are 200 large state companies—basically, they are in utilities, some in heavy industries, some in resource industries. Traditionally, this is where governments have invested.

China Mobil and China Telecom are huge, but these are natural monopolies. Even France and Britain had those large state companies for a long time. If you take these away, China is a private-sector economy. In the financial sector, reform has been much delayed. Banking is still a state monopoly, and a concentrated monopoly.

In heavy industries, there are many private steel companies and chemical companies. Private companies have been behind the recent boom in capacity. They hired managers from state companies, then started up in a very efficient, competitive way. In terms of competitiveness, they are better than Taiwanese companies. They have the newest equipment, along with some local equipment. However, the private sector is hard to document. There is a lot that is not on the table.

**Q: How would you characterize China's financial markets?**
**A:** The capital markets and securities markets still are underdeveloped, because 70% of shares of almost all listed companies are not tradable. So there can't be takeovers—only when the management wants to sell, which is usually when the business is nothing to them. Just a few months ago, an experimental program was announced to make the nontradable shares tradable. This should be good news in the long run.

**Q: What about bank reform?**
**A:** There has been some progress in the banking sector. There still is political interference, but control of the banks has been centralized [away from local governments]. As a result, the whole system is more independent of the local politicians. The managements of local branches aren't appointed by local governments any more.

The reform has started—but maybe too late. The government has injected money into the banks to float shares. To improve the capital market, 20% to 30% of their shares have to be sold to the public. But more state injections are likely.

**Q: Will foreign banks be able to compete in China?**
**A:** The government still controls the pace of liberalization. By the end of 2006, the market will open. But banks still need licenses.

The real issue is that when foreign banks come into the Chinese market, they will find it is very difficult to compete with the retail networks of the state banks. Chinese banks have thousands and thousands of branches to collect local deposits. It will take years for foreign banks to make an impact. To do business in yuan, [foreign banks] will have to borrow from the Chinese banks.

Also, Chinese deposit rates have not been liberalized. So the banks' margins are big. They can invest a lot in ATMs, bank cards, the Internet, and so on. And they don't charge depositors for these services.

**Q: Will China's current-account surplus abate?**
**A:** Trade has essentially been in balance, except recently. The current account is high basically because of capital inflows. But how much is Chinese money? Many companies are just moving funds in commercial bank foreign currency accounts, [and those funds] don't count in reserves.

Before, the market speculated that the yuan would devalue. Now, companies are moving their money back into China through trade channels. They can wait, and they know the loopholes.

**Q: What should China do with the yuan?**
**A:** I believe that it is a good idea to let the yuan trade in a bigger range. Small steps will invite speculation. My main argument is that this is a global issue. What worries me most is the fiscal deficit of the U.S. That is the whole reason for these imbalances. The U.S. dollar is international money, and the real problems will be borne by everybody. A dollar devaluation will become our revaluation problem.

# The Education Challenge

ENORMOUS POOLS OF LITERATE PRODUCTION WORKERS and university-trained professionals have been crucial to India's and China's ascent in manufacturing, engineering, and services. But the education systems of both India and China still face daunting challenges. These challenges must be overcome in order for development to reach the hundreds of millions of Chinese and Indians still living in poverty—and for these nations to be considered truly industrialized.

India has made great strides in boosting public school enrollment to 90% of children aged 6 to 14. But poor teachers, underfunded schools, a politicized bureaucracy, outdated learning methods, and family financial pressures translate into low-quality public education and high absentee and dropout rates. Private school enrollment is growing rapidly, but tuition is beyond the means of most Indians. "Trying to Tame the Blackboard Jungle" examines the broad issues by getting inside a struggling school program in a densely populated Bombay slum district.

India's elite schools are world-class. The Indian Institutes of Technology, for example, have drawn worldwide fame for their remarkable success in graduating brilliant engineers and world-class technology entrepreneurs. "India's Whiz Kids," published in 1998 well before the nation drew worldwide attention as an outsourcing mecca, remains an excellent primer on the secrets of the IITs' success. "India: Big Brains on Campus" explains why the Indian Institutes of Management, meanwhile, produce some of the world's best managerial talent.

The quality of the higher education system for the vast majority of Indians is inconsistent, however. That could leave India short of the professionals needed to meet the escalating demands of domestic and foreign employers. Modern new schools are on the way. The Manipal Institute of Technology, profiled in "The Other MIT," illustrates a new breed of privately run second-tier colleges and institutes that are borrowing from Western methods to provide modern education to the nation's next generation of talent. "The Seeds of the Next Silicon Valley" shows how the IITs are starting to help engineering students incubate their own business start-ups.

"No Peasant Left Behind" explains China's efforts to overhaul public education to sustain the next stage of growth. Literacy has improved from 60% in the late 1970s to 85%, but high school and university enrollment are low. Poor funding of rural schools means millions of rural Chinese youth are being left behind. Efforts also are underway to shift from the emphasis on rote learning and exam-based grades and put more emphasis on in-class discussion and experimentation. "A Whole New School of Thought" profiles Shantou University, whose Western-inspired curriculum is regarded as a blueprint for national reform. "Making Waves in Guangdong" interviews Shantou official Julia Hsiao, who also is an assistant vice-chancellor at the University of California at Berkeley.

---

# Trying to Tame the Blackboard Jungle

*As more Indian children flood into schools, educators struggle to boost quality*

To understand the educational challenges facing India, pay a visit to Dharavi, a poor and densely populated Bombay neighborhood. Its lanes are so small and winding that no vehicles can traverse them. Open drains run outside the crudely built brick and corrugated metal homes, and garbage is piled high every few yards. The area, where 1 million of Bombay's poorer migrants live, is Asia's largest slum.

This is the home of the Dharavi Transit Camp School, one of two in the neighborhood run by the municipal corporation. Outside the high school gates, ragged, half-naked children play amid scattered garbage. Some run in and out of the gates, but nobody stops them. There is no school guard, and the teachers who pass through don't bother. The school, four stories high, is shorn of paint and looks grim under the monsoon clouds.

It's past noon, and schoolchildren are starting to straggle in for the afternoon shift of classes. The girls wear blue pinafores, the boys blue shorts and shirts. Many are barefoot. Like most state-run schools in Bombay, the Transit Camp School runs classes up to seventh grade, in two shifts, with each floor teaching classes in a different language, reflecting the regional origins of its 6,000 students. Blackboards, tables, and benches crowd the 12 classrooms on each floor. With 100 students per class, the sessions sometimes spill into the corridors.

On this day, Gautam Dandage, a cement spreader, has brought his 8-year-old daughter, Ujwala, to school. She is doing OK in class but his older son, he complains, has lost his motivation. "My son failed because of the class master. He never showed up for class all year," Dandage gripes. The deputy head teacher, Sampat Bhandare, tries to shush the worried father, explaining that the teacher in question was sick and the school could not find a replacement. Dandage isn't convinced.

A day at school in Dharavi is a vivid lesson in India's education gap. In a nation striving to be a global leader in brainpower, the Transit Camp School underscores the enormous scale of India's struggle to provide adequate education for its youth. India has the world's youngest, potentially most productive population. Nearly 500 million Indians are under age 19. In primary school alone, some 202 million students are taught by 5.5 million teachers in 1 million schools.

Yet while free and compulsory primary education became law in 2001, the quality of learning is poor and the failure rate is high. Even in fifth grade, some 35% of Indian children cannot read or write, according to Pratham, India's largest education nonprofit group. According to government statistics, just a quarter of students make it past eighth grade, and only 15% get to high school. Of the 202 million who start school, only about 7%, or 14 million, graduate. And without a fully literate population, India won't easily sustain the demands and aspirations of its people or become a global power. "The government is failing our youth," says Vimala Ramachandran, an education specialist and author of *Getting Children Back to School.*

Increasingly, Indian parents want their children educated, particularly in English and computing. That's not only critical for youth but it is also key to India's development. Education is a "ticket out of poverty," says New Delhi economist Surjit Bhalla. Parents understand that when India began to grow in the 1980s and 1990s, the educated got better jobs— "even if it meant going to the Gulf states and achieving blue-collar success," Bhalla notes.

But India's state system just isn't meeting people's aspirations. "It's two decades behind the population's needs," says Madhav Chavan, founder and program director of Pratham. Poor-quality teachers, a politicized education department, outdated learning methods, and the pressures Indian children face at home are just some of the roots of India's education gap. Many girls drop out of school after fourth grade, for example, to do household chores while their parents work. Just half of India's girls are literate, versus nearly three-fourths of boys.

## Teacher Troubles

Indians can't blame the government for not trying to improve the situation. The Ministry of Human Resource Development has thousands of schemes aimed at enhancing educational opportunities. The most ambitious is the 2001 Sarva Shiksha Abhiyan, or universal education incentive program. Its $2.4 billion annual budget provides students with a meal a day, free textbooks, medical care, and remedial classes. The Congress Party, which returned to power in New Delhi in 2004, is pushing the agenda even further. The government's spending on education has gone from 3% of gross domestic product in 2004 to 4% in 2005 and is expected to rise to 6% soon.

These efforts are making an impact. Almost 90% of all children are now enrolled in school—up from 75% in 2000. Yet the growth is a strain for some schools. In the poorer regions of Uttar Pradesh and Bihar, class sizes are now "too large to manage," says Venita Kaul, who oversees World Bank education projects in India. The Bank is providing $500 million for the Sarva Shiksha Abhiyan budget over three years until 2007.

Despite increased enrollments, graduation ratios are falling—even in top states such as Maharashtra, where Bombay is located. This year, 57% of the 10th-grade students in Maharashtra passed their final exams—a big drop from 2004 when 67% cleared the exam. "We aim for a zero dropout and failure rate," says Abasaheb Jadav, who is project director for the federal government's Sarva Shiksha Abhiyan in Bombay. Good intentions aside, the experts say India's educational system faces its most serious challenges at the classroom level.

Start with the teachers. State-employed teachers earn up to $300 a month and often four times as much as private school teachers. But they are poorly trained, unmotivated, and often commandeered for other government services like election duty or overseeing polio vaccination drives. Consequently, teacher—and hence student—absenteeism is high. At the same time, increased enrollments—thanks to the midday meal now required in all schools—have caused a teacher shortage. As a result, in many schools, teachers have to handle up to four different grades at once, another blow to the quality of schooling.

Another issue is infrastructure. The government is boosting spending on schools, books, and classroom equipment, but the funding often doesn't reach the remote rural areas. In Bihar, India's poorest state, schools are crumbling and buildings lack roofs, windows, or blackboards. In Behrampur, a village about three hours away from the capital of Patna, the broken-down single-room school serves as a playground for the village's 200 children. Locals say the schoolmaster comes by every three or four days. Devbali Rai, a 30-year-old farmer, is near despair. "We want schooling. Our children must study," he says.

## Curriculum Crisis

Adding to the cauldron of problems is a curriculum crisis fueled by political rivalries. In 1998, when the right-wing Bharatiya Janata Party won the national elections, education became the first target of revisionist historians. School textbooks were rewritten to reflect the BJP's ultra-nationalist ideology. Then the Congress government reverted to the original facts when its party defeated the BJP in national elections in 2004. Now parents and teachers worry that another election will mean more tinkering with the school syllabi and textbooks. "This oscillating between the orthodoxies of the right and the left, the yo-yo-like swings in curricula, is driving parents and teachers mad," says Kanti Bajpai, headmaster of the Doon School, the country's most elite school.

All these difficulties are accelerating the rush to India's 100,000-plus private schools. For decades private schools such as the Doon School, modeled after Britain's Eton, have catered to the elite. Now even poor students are enrolling in private schools, where the tuition can range from $24 a year in remote villages to $15,000 at the top end. In underdeveloped states many private schools are just single rooms in village homes. But even in cramped surroundings students learn enough to take a school-graduating exam.

Despite the proliferation of private schools, few experts believe they are the solution to India's educational challenges. True, they tend to be better than their state counterparts. But many are unregulated, and they still serve just a fraction of the population. Privatizing education, while often suggested by experts, isn't the answer either. India is too large, and many of its poorest parts are so remote that few private educators would want to teach there.

Yet some experiments are taking place that could provide models for education reform. ICICI Bank has invested in organizations such as Vidya Bhavan Society that are experimenting with alternate teaching systems to replace rote memorization. One of its projects is in the state of Chattisgarh, which three years ago was carved out of the large and poor state of Madhya Pradesh with the idea that smaller states could be governed more easily. "We were new and inexperienced, we needed everyone's help," recalls Sanjay Kumar Ojha, an official whom New Delhi sent to help the state's Education Dept. Ojha and team have readied a new set of textbooks, plus teacher recruiting and training programs, in just two years. If successful, Chattisgarh could become a model.

Encouraged by such efforts, Pratham's Chavan confidently predicts "a major change in the provision of education" in the coming years. The driving force will be parents who desperately want to educate their children in English. In Kashmir, the government has already switched to an English-language-based school education from the first grade. Even in conservative, Hindi-dominated Rajasthan, English as a language is now taught from the first grade. The state of Kerala, which stood alone in India for its 99% literacy rate, is now joined by Mizoram and Himachal Pradesh in the north. Such efforts could one day help India close its education gap.

# No Peasant Left Behind

*China has made great strides. Now can it fix its
backward rural schools?*

At South China Normal University's primary school, the walls at the campus gate are painted bright red, blue, and yellow. Inside, students in their colorful uniforms scurry past giant posters telling the story of Snow White and the Seven Dwarfs. The leafy campus has three basketball courts, a track, and the latest in child-safe playground equipment. A new computer lab is packed with 30 Lenovo PCs and liquid-crystal display monitors, and there's a school Web site.

These are just some of the ample resources the government of Guangdong is lavishing on one of its pet educational projects. Because

Beijing now considers overhaul of the school system to be critical to economic growth, public schools like South China Normal are being turned into laboratories where new pedagogical approaches are tried. The best methods will then be seeded across the nation's vast network of schools.

For one thing, educators are shifting away from lecturing and exam-based grades—just as the U.S. is embracing more standardized metrics. In China, education czars are putting less emphasis on tests and more on in-class experiments and discussions. "Students cram and recite," says Shen Baiyu, director of curriculum development at the Education Ministry in Beijing. "They remember, but they don't understand." The lack of creativity, says Shen, is "a fatal disadvantage of Chinese education."

That educators are focused on such questions is testament, in a way, to how far China has come educationally. The country has achieved enough of the basics that planners can focus on the next level of pedagogical quality. Consider that China has a literacy rate of 85%, compared with just 60% at the end of the Cultural Revolution, the decade of radical upheaval that ended after Mao Zedong's death in 1976. Moreover, thanks to a mid-1980s policy to provide universal education for grades one through nine by 2000, the literacy rate among people between the ages of 12 and 40 is now 96%. "Almost every child can have a basic education," says Wei Yu, former Education Vice-Minister who is now a vice-president of the Chinese Association for Science & Technology. "That's a big achievement if you think how large our country is."

## Stark Disparities

The scale of the educational challenge is indeed daunting. China has 218 million children in grade school through high school, more than the total populations of Japan and South Korea combined. There are over 10 million teachers and more than 500,000 schools in all, about 75% of which are scattered across the vast countryside, far from the coastal boomtowns. Elite schools like South China Normal may be well off, but overall spending is low: China spends just 3.2% of its gross domestic product on education, versus 5% for the U.S., though that's more than ever before. "There is little doubt that China's leaders have done extremely well," says Gerard Postiglione, a professor of education at the University of Hong Kong.

Today's big worry is that the system can't accommodate the next stage of growth. Beijing has prepared an ambitious road map for the country's educators, part of a broader goal for China to become a developed nation capable of competing with the U.S., Japan, South Korea, and Taiwan in science and technology. Plenty of stellar grad students from China attend top U.S. universities, but the government wants to get more Chinese into the ranks of the highly educated at home. To do so, they have set a goal to push high school enrollment, now at 40%, up to 70% by 2010; university enrollment is to reach 20%, versus 13% today. By 2020, the government wants 85% in high school, and it's aiming for university enrollment to exceed 40%. (In the U.S., the high school enrollment rate is about 93%, and university enrollment is about 60%.)

## Technology Gap

China's elite also worries that the school system favors wealthy areas along the coast at the expense of poor inland provinces. The disparities are stark in places like Pucheng, a rural county in north-central Shaanxi Province about 60 miles from Xian, the ancient capital of the Han Dynasty. Unlike Guangzhou's cheerful schoolyards, Pucheng's schools are covered with grime. The students sit at backless wooden benches, two to a desk, in classrooms where the lights are turned off to save power. Puddles of water stain the cement floors.

Another rural feature: Boys far outnumber girls in many classes. Peasants traditionally favor boys and often keep their daughters out of school. In recent years, the one-child policy has led to a preponderance of boys nationally, since some families are suspected of aborting female fetuses to make way for male children. The male-female discrepancy can be extreme: 9 girls to 21 boys in one class.

Pucheng schools don't have deluxe new computer labs either. Administrators are happy to have one PC with a satellite dish for downloading education programs beamed to them from Beijing, part of a program for rural schools run by the Education Ministry. Sun Chengli, a 24-year-old Pucheng native, is in charge of training teachers how to use the equipment. It's not much compared with the largesse at Guangzhou schools, but it's a start. Training "is not very difficult," says Sun. "The teachers are all very motivated."

## Ease the Burden

Closing the rich-poor gap has become a hot issue, especially since President Hu Jintao and Premier Wen Jiabao took office in 2003. Both often talk about the need to alleviate poverty in interior provinces by encouraging more investment and infrastructure there. The overriding worry is that sharp inequality could lead to social unrest, which would in turn spook foreign investors, threaten economic development, and weaken Beijing's rule. "The lack of equality has caused serious concern," says Wang Rong, head of the department of education economics and administration at Peking University. "If you don't solve this problem, then you can really have trouble. Education is a starting point."

So Beijing has been working to ease the burden on families and governments in poor regions. A few years back it capped the amount schools can charge families for textbooks and miscellaneous fees to supplement meager school budgets. In 2003 the central government followed up by launching a $96 million-a-year program to subsidize the costs of textbooks in poor areas. Working with the charitable foundation of Hong Kong billionaire Li Ka-shing, who funds many educational initiatives, the government has provided satellite dishes and PCs to 70,000 schools in the countryside, at a cost of $1.2 billion, with plans to double that amount by 2007. "There are lots of smart students in the villages, but they're not exposed to information and knowledge," says Wang Zhuzhu, deputy director of the national center for educational technology at the Education Ministry. "It's important to change the mindset."

Like the U.S., though, China has a decentralized education system in which local governments foot much of the bill. Funding can vary widely, depending on a province's fortunes. Shaanxi is one of China's poorest, with a per capita income of just $170, versus $1,800 in Guangzhou. The provincial government spent just $72 million on education in 2004 for 10 million students in all grades. In a new program, officials plan to exempt 1.6 million students from some school fees. But given widespread poverty, Lu Mingkai, deputy director general of the provincial education bureau, says there are limits to what the province can do. "People's desire for good, quality education has significantly increased; everybody wants their child to go to the best school," he says. "But there's a gap."

Even wealthy cities have their problems, namely legions of migrant workers who arrive in search of jobs. The size of the "floating population" is estimated at 120 million, about 8 million of them school-age children. In Beijing alone, there are 340,000 migrant children, many of whom aren't permitted to attend the city's schools. So they enter schools set up by the migrants themselves that are unlicensed and often located in run-down neighborhoods. Even so, migrant families, which make about $900 a year, pay more than $100 per child to attend. There are more than 200 such schools in the capital, estimates Han Jialing, professor at the Institute of Sociology of the Beijing Academy of Social Sciences. Responding to the government's prodding on inequality, Beijing has let about 240,000 migrant children attend official schools, up from 80,000 in 2003.

The new measures should help some of China's poor families. But even as educators talk about addressing educational inequality and revamping curriculums, scoring well on entrance exams remains the key to upward mobility in the Chinese school system. And unlike poor families in Shaanxi, the wealthy residents of cities like Guangzhou have the cash to help their children do well. Chen Xuqi, a 13-year-old student at South China Normal's primary school, says she and her friends spend weekends at cram seminars to study English and math. They're getting ready to enter junior high school and want to ace the entrance exams. "We always talk about this," says Chen in near-perfect English. "All the people want to get into a good school." For China's education reformers, coming up with the money is just the start.

---

# India's Whiz Kids

*Inside the Indian Institutes of Technology's star factory*

In 1998, Victor J. Menezes, the 49-year-old newly appointed co-CEO at Citigroup's corporate and investment banking branch, vividly remembers his grueling college years in India—and Professor M. S. Kamath's electrical engineering class in particular. Menezes recalls Kamath as "the most dreaded professor" on campus 30 years ago at the Indian Institute of Technology–Bombay. His class was the hardest to get into.

And once in, students wondered what hit them. Kamath's grading system was a punch in the nose for students who fancied themselves as the best and brightest in India. Often, only one student per test got an A—the top scorer. The second-best score got a B. Everyone else got Cs, Ds, or Fs. But Kamath had his reasons. Now retired and living outside Bombay, he brushes off his legendary reputation as a campus terror: "I used to tell my students, 'IIT is a center of excellence. I don't want you to be third-rate products.' "

Far from it. Some of the most prominent chief executives, presidents, entrepreneurs, and inventors in the world are graduates of IIT, India's elite institution of higher learning. Its impossibly high standards, compelling the mostly male student body to average fewer than five hours of sleep a night, produce numerous graduates who are masters at problem-solving. Familiar with Western ways due to India's colonial past, they have spent their academic years studying in English, which gives them an edge over other Asians competing for jobs in global corporations.

While IIT has been producing talented engineers, scientists, and managers for four decades, the school has taken on a new prominence lately. With Menezes' ascension at Citigroup and the appointment of

45-year-old Rakesh Gangwal as US Airways Group's new CEO, IIT counts two more alums among the highest ranks of global business. They join Rajat Gupta, who has led McKinsey & Co. for four years, Vinod Khosla, the co-founder of Sun Microsystems Inc., and hundreds of others now working in the top ranks of U.S. corporations and Silicon Valley powerhouses. (*BusinessWeek* has an IIT connection. Graduate Vasant Prabhu is president of the Information and Media Services unit of The McGraw-Hill Companies, *BusinessWeek*'s parent.)

## Former Prison

Wall Street firms rely on Institute grads to devise the complex algorithms behind their derivatives strategies while big multinationals call on them to solve problems in new ways. When recruiting from colleges for its annual crop of consultants, McKinsey hires a significant number of the school's graduates every year. Many more write the software and design the chips and peripherals that Silicon Valley sells to the world. One example: The founders of Internet browser Junglee.com— all IIT grads—made fortunes in August 1998 by selling their company to Amazon.com, the online bookseller, for $180 million.

The rise of IITians, as they are known, is a telling example of how global capitalism works today. The best companies draw on the best brains from around the world, and the result is a global class of worker: the highly educated, intensely ambitious college grad who seeks out a challenging career, even if it is thousands of miles from home. By rising to the top of Corporate America, these alumni lead all other Asians in their ability to reach the upper echelons of world-class companies.

It's not just that entrepreneurs have forged a path through high-tech arenas; corporate executives have proven proficient at managing companies too. Cost-cutting by US Airways' Gangwal, for example, helped pull the airline back from the brink of bankruptcy and increased revenues fourfold.

In that regard, the story of these Indians provides a model for other Asians to emulate—and an example for U.S. companies and universities to ponder. For India has created, out of limited resources, a class of executives and entrepreneurs who manage to combine technical brilliance with great management skills. And the Indian government, to its credit, has not tried to keep these first-class students at home. In many ways, the IIT grad is the hottest export India has ever produced.

To mold them, the schools put these 18-year-olds through an experience akin to boot camp. Theories learned by rote—a key element of Japanese education—are only part of the experience. "Students should see the problem and conjure up a solution, not only memorize a theory," says Deepak Phatak, professor of computer science at IIT–Bombay in 1998. The focus is on hands-on learning. IIT maintains workshops where students even learn how to make machine tools and operate rotation motors, the kinds of crafts relegated to trade schools in the U.S.

When he helped found IIT in 1951, Jawaharlal Nehru, India's first Prime Minister, wanted an elite that could build the great state-sponsored power plants, dams, and bridges so badly needed in the newly independent country. The planners drew on Massachusetts Institute of Technology as a model and on UNESCO for funds to build the first campus, in Kharagpur, near Calcutta, in a former British prison for Indian political detainees. Five other campuses followed, in Kanpur, Delhi, Bombay, Madras, and Guwahati. At various times, the U.S., Britain, the former Soviet Union, and Germany have all provided backing.

## Free Rein

The schools have kept their edge by staying out of India's partisan politics. "It is the most uncorrupt institution in India today," says Kartik Kilachand, a New York–based consultant and IIT alumnus. IIT has an autonomous board that doesn't have to kowtow to state bureaucracies. The Indian government pays most of the $3,000 it costs annually to educate each student. Famous alumni in India include B. K. Syngal, chairman of Reliance Telecom; Nirmal Jain, managing director of Tata Infotech; N. R. Narayanamurthy, founder of software developer Infosys; and Yogi Deveshwar, CEO of Indian Tobacco.

IIT's huge campuses are vastly superior to other Indian universities but spartan compared with Western counterparts. Many of the faculty have U.S. degrees and are stars in their fields, such as V. Rajaraman, who has helped New Delhi formulate its software policy. Professors double as administrators, limiting India's notorious bureaucratic malaise.

More than 100,000 Indians aspire to enter IIT each year, sitting for the grueling entrance exams every May. Students typically spend two years in preparation. Of those, just 2,500 are admitted to the network of campuses. Fewer than 2,000 make it to graduation each year. "The process of selection is absolutely draconian," says McKinsey head Gupta.

Once in, it gets tougher. Aman Parhar, 22, a biochemistry major at IIT–Delhi, was a high school star. "But here, everyone is as smart or smarter than you are," he says. Textbooks are so expensive that an entire class of 25 often has to share a single book. Students routinely stay up until 3 a.m. to study—or, in IIT lingo, "mug." But they get plenty of attention. Faculty-student ratios, at 1:6 or 1:8, are among the world's lowest. MIT's is 1:11.

## Technobrats?

Tales abound of the secrecy and ritual of IIT's dorm life. Students have their own exclusive slang, where "crack" means a job well done, and "fundoo," short for "fundamental," means great. The jobs and salaries grads command make them highly prized in India's contractual marriage market.

While some of the swagger gets beaten out of them by the rigors of the system, these students retain high expectations for their careers. Below the surface of being "well mannered and polite," according to Rukmini Bhaya Nair's book on IIT, *Technobrat*, students are "ruthlessly competitive and have an annoying complacency at having 'arrived' at age 19."

This attitude often leads to disappointment with the opportunities India has to offer. Thousands of graduates have emigrated to the U.S., causing the Indian government anxiety over the brain drain of its brightest. A full 30% of the graduating class—over 500 students—headed to the U.S. for graduate degrees and better job opportunities in 1998. In the more popular computer-science programs, nearly 80% leave for Silicon Valley. So routine is the exodus that at IIT–Madras, the local campus postman and bank clerk provide unsolicited advice on the best U.S. schools to attend. When acceptance letters arrive, the postman waits outside the student's door for a tip—a large one if it's from a highly regarded university such as Stanford. While IIT does offer graduate programs, students know that an advanced degree from a U.S. institution is the entry ticket to an American or global corporation—and big bucks.

The U.S. also benefits enormously from the influx. AnnaLee Saxenian, an associate professor at the University of California at Berkeley, conducted a 1998 study of Silicon Valley's new immigrant entrepreneurs. According to Saxenian, of an estimated 2,000 start-ups in Silicon Valley, 40% are Indian-spawned, and of those, half are by IIT grads.

The influx began in earnest in the 1970s as Indian students graduated from such schools as Stanford, MIT, and Carnegie Mellon and became a vital source of brainpower in the research labs of Hewlett-Packard, Intel, IBM, and Texas Instruments. They then played founding roles in Sun Microsystems, Cirrus Logic, and numerous other high-tech powers.

Yogen Dalal, an IIT alumnus and partner with prominent venture-capital firm Mayfield, says the Valley has "a critical mass of IIT alums who can finance and guide the new generation." Suhas Patil, who founded chip-design innovator Cirrus Logic in 1984, is now a prominent "angel" investor who provides early capital and business connections for Indian-owned start-ups. Another angel is Kanwal Rekhi, who founded and sold add-on board maker Excelan and who served as chief technology officer for Novell Inc. Among the dozen or so start-ups Rekhi helped launch are Ambit Design Systems, a developer of chip-design software, and info-tech consulting firm CyberMedia.

## Schoolyard Lessons

U.S. graduate schools actively seek out the institute's grads. California Institute of Technology "writes to us regularly, asking us to recommend students for scholarships they have available," says Kharagpur campus Professor Badriprasad Gupta, who is vice-chairman of the entrance-exam committee. Amitabha Ghosh, director of IIT–Kharagpur, recalls the dean of the University of Maryland at College Park, entreating him to "send his entire graduating class to Maryland" and promising them all financial assistance. Even the French and German governments, faced with declining numbers of engineers, are trying to attract grads through exchange programs. IIT graduates frequently find U.S. graduate schools a breeze by comparison.

India's math-focused education gives students a leg up on American students, who depend heavily on calculators in the learning process. India has a long tradition of conceptual mathematics, and schoolchildren are forced to master multiplication tables early on. The math advantage helps: Gangwal of US Airways, renowned in the aviation industry for his speedy mental calculations, says "people always pegged me as being this terribly analytical guy who can run numbers in his head." Yet it was Gangwal's number-crunching that helped cut through the morass at the airline.

Another factor of campus life is India's diversity of languages, ethnic groups, and castes. "You learn how to manage across them," says Citigroup's Menezes, who managed to thrive in Citibank's cutthroat environment. "You couldn't survive any Indian schoolyard unless you figured out how different people think and behave."

Recently, IIT grads in the U.S. have been formalizing their powerful network. Two years ago, Indians and Pakistanis in the San Francisco area formed The Indus Entrepreneurs. Easily half its 1,000 members are IIT grads. "We help each other and provide role models," says Desh Deshpande, an IIT–Madras alumnus whose computer-networking company, Cascade, was sold to Ascend Communications Inc. for $3.7 billion.

Now that they have the means, alums also want to help their alma mater. Rekhi, in 1997, donated $2 million to the school and urged fellow alumni to follow suit. Says Mayfield's Dalal, who has given $10,000 to kick off an alumni-sponsored endowment fund: "We want to make it right for the next generation."

## Government Cutbacks

Their help could not have come at a better time. New Delhi has been reducing funding to institutions of higher learning such as the IITs by 25% since 1993. Alumni help is taking its place: Vinod Gupta, for example, founder of Nebraska-based database American Business Information, built a $3 million school of management for IIT–Kharagpur in the late 1990s. McKinsey's Gupta was active in setting up a business school in Hyderabad in conjunction with the Wharton School at the University of Pennsylvania and Northwestern University's Kellogg School.

The IITs have also been teaming up with industry on development. IIT–Kharagpur patents a dozen new products each year. Companies such as Intel and Philips Electronics, which are big recruiters at the IITs, have funded endowments and scholarships. They have even bankrolled computer and electronics laboratories in order to keep IIT grads up to snuff on the latest technology.

The bottom line for students and grads is that India has produced a world-class university at surprisingly little cost. By nurturing the schools, the government stands to reap huge rewards as these grads invest in India and draw it further into the circle of global trade and prosperity. Much like Taiwan-born engineers in the U.S., IIT grads are well positioned to set up ventures in their native country. "These Indians will play a key role in the resurgence of India," says Vijay Sahni, country head for Arthur Andersen's India operations. It's not quite how Nehru thought it would be. But this school is vital to India's place in the world.

---

# India: Big Brains on Campus

*Its select Institutes of Management draw recruiters from top companies, but national job prospects are up too*

In the leafy, open-air cafeteria at the Indian Institute of Management in Ahmedabad, a group of students discuss their career options over a breakfast of eggs and *uttapams*—spicy rice pancakes. Ranjith Roy, 25, will be joining Goldman, Sachs & Co. in New York. Naman Vidyarthi, also 25, an engineer who worked with telecom giant BT Group PLC in London before going for his MBA in India, will try to make his way in India as an entrepreneur. Shashwat Sharma, 23, will look for a spot in one of the booming India-based consumer-products companies.

All of these students were at the top of their class as undergraduates and could have gone for their MBAs at prestigious U.S. or European business schools. Just a few years ago they certainly would have, despite the high cost. That they chose to study in India says something about both the country and its business schools. India is booming—in technology, in manufacturing, and in consumer products—providing plenty of relatively high-paying jobs for business graduates. At the same time, the cream of India's business schools—the half dozen Indian Institutes of Management—have gained a reputation as among the world's best. Proof is abundant at the end of each year, when recruiters from top multinational companies such as Goldman, J.P. Morgan, Boston Consulting Group, and Procter & Gamble come to India looking for junior executives for their global operations. Goldman Sachs has been hiring from IIM–Ahmedabad since 2001. Calum Forrest, who heads recruitment for Goldman in Europe, says that Indian IIM grads are as well prepared as any MBAs in the world. And he appreciates their work ethic. "They are very keen to work as hard as necessary to get the job done," Forrest says. "India is at the upper end of the scale here."

What this means for India is that the brain drain of the past has been turned into a "brain gain," with Indian students both remaining in India to stay close to family and returning to the homeland to manage businesses after doing apprenticeships in London and New York. "Earlier, going overseas was a discovery, everything was new, and India had scarcity and restraints," says Indira Parekh, dean of IIM–Ahmedabad. "Now what's available there is available here, so the attraction of going West has diminished."

Some argue that the best of Indian business education is the equal of Yale, Stanford, or France's INSEAD. Certainly students at IIM–Ahmedabad, India's top school, had the choice to go or stay and chose to remain in India. They sat with 127,000 of India's brightest students who every year take a common MBA entrance exam. Only those in the 99th percentile qualify for one of the IIMs, which have a total of 1,100 seats. The schools accept just 1 of every 115 applicants, while the best of the rest are scattered among a dozen other top-ranked schools. Even though India has more than 1,000 business schools, many bright undergraduates don't get accepted at any of their top picks. "They don't have a choice but to go overseas," says Vaidehi Asar, who was among the top students in her class at Bombay's St. Xavier's college but didn't make the cut for an IIM. "India's so competitive; everyone wants to do an MBA." Asar is now pursuing a master's in economics and finance at Britain's Warrick University.

## Luring Its Own Foreign Students

India's IIMs—located in Ahmedabad, Bangalore, Calcutta, Lucknow, Indore, and Khozikode—have gained such a reputation for excellence that they attract their own foreign students. A typical 250-student class at Ahmedabad will host 35 foreigners. Johannes Suikkanan, 26, a second-year student at Copenhagen Business School, chose IIM–Ahmedabad when he was given the chance to take a semester abroad. "India challenges me at every level, spiritually and intellectually," he says. There's one Ahmedabad option that a student at, say, Berkeley, won't encounter—coursework on the Indian socio-political environment that includes spending a week in India's remote regions living with nomads and villagers. Rural poverty "is a problem of Indian life, and as a manager, you should be aware of it," says Sriram Vaidyanathan, a second-year student who is of Indian parentage but has lived most of his life in Saudi Arabia. He gave up a place at Carnegie Mellon University to come to Ahmedabad.

The Indian schools do have drawbacks. The IIMs lack the funds to attract the high-priced and Nobel Prize–winning faculty who teach at the best U.S. schools. And they are government-funded, which means that while tuition is relatively cheap—$7,000 for two years—they can't accept private funds to do research or endow chairs without permission from New Delhi. As a result, though many young Indians will now pick a local school over a prestigious school abroad, others still heed the siren call of the best of the U.S. B-schools. Aparna Piramal, 28, whose family runs Asia's largest luggage company in Bombay, first went to Oxford, then chose Harvard over an IIM. Though she recognizes that the Indian schools are now considered excellent, she says Harvard gave her "exposure to the latest management thinking, to international business and a diverse peer group, which India can't offer to the same extent."

The fact that they are state schools also makes the IIMs subject to political wrangling. For instance, in February 2004, India's then-Education Minister decided to cut tuition at the IIMs, declaring them to be too elite. An alum challenged the tuition proposal in court, charging that it infringed on the autonomy of the school and would make it overly dependent on government funding. In the end, the Education Minister lost his job along with the rest of the Bharatiya Janata Party–led government in May elections, and the new Congress leadership dropped the matter.

## Start-Ups, Anyone?

Critics of the IIMs also charge that their student bodies are heavily weighted toward quantitative skills. That's in part because many of those enrolled have degrees in engineering. Recruiters find that IIM students sometimes disappoint when it comes to management and marketing expertise. Ahmedabad student Ranjit Roy did an internship at Goldman Sachs in New York last summer and says he found that the Goldman interns from U.S. schools had far better skills in marketing and branding than he did.

In addition, there is a need for more emphasis on entrepreneurship, says Anil Gupta, who teaches a course on agribusiness management and runs a well-regarded center for rural innovation at IIM–Ahmedabad. He notes that India's history of state control of business means that salaried jobs remain the most prestigious. "We are producing followers, not leaders," Gupta says. "Indian society makes people fit into a groove." Indeed, surveys have shown that just 1 in 10 IIM students want to start their own business.

As India becomes more globalized and business school education grows more international, the Indian schools will likely overcome these limitations. Many of their graduates are already part of the new generation of tycoons, both in India and abroad. In the future, hopefully more and more of India's best and brightest will go to business school at home, not just to please their families or because it's cheaper but because Indian B-schools provide the kind of education that will turn their students into creators of wealth—both for themselves and for India.

# The Other MIT

*Manipal Institute of Technology and other second-tier schools like it are India's real tech secrets*

Rajendra Kumar Nayak considers himself a lucky guy. Sipping his favorite 60-cent milkshake at a trendy coffee shop in Manipal, India, he's rejoicing about the job he'll start soon, following his recent graduation from the Manipal Institute of Technology (MIT). Nayak will work as an industrial engineer at Wipro Fluid Power in Bangalore for $390 a month—a lucrative salary by Indian standards. But Nayak, 22, isn't simply lucky. He's gutsy and smart. The son of a steelworker, he gambled in 2001 by taking out a $7,000 loan and heading to Manipal. Four years later he's graduating first in his class. "MIT was expensive, but worth it," he says.

Nayak is an example of the breed of ambitious young engineers who will power the next phase of India's tech and industrial boom. And Manipal Institute of Technology is one of the leading Indian colleges educating this next generation. For decades the famed campuses of the Indian Institutes of Technology were just about all the world knew of the country's technological genius. But lesser-known colleges such as MIT will be playing a key role as India continues on its fast-growth path. This second tier of some 2,240 engineering schools—55% of them public institutions, the others privately run—aren't nearly as exclusive as the IITs, which snap up just 2% of the 200,000 candidates who take its demanding entrance exam every year. Graduates of IIT's seven campuses rarely top 3,000 annually. The second-tier institutes educate far more Indian engineers—some 207,000 graduated in 2005—and fill an important need.

## A Young Nation

To keep up its 30%-plus annual growth in tech services, India requires more than 65,000 newly graduated engineers a year, according to software trade body NASSCOM. New Delhi's Institute of Applied Manpower Research figures the country also needs about 10,000 engineers annually to fuel growth in other industries, including autos, chemicals, construction, metals, and energy. Moreover, since 35% of India's 1 billion people are under age 15, national demand for everything from roads to power grids to PCs will skyrocket, making the need for engineering skills urgent. NASSCOM predicts enrollment in Indian tech schools will jump by 70%, to 600,000, by 2008.

Of the second-tier institutions, MIT is one of the most prestigious. It's part of a sprawling network of 53 private professional colleges called the Manipal Academy of Higher Education, located on India's southwestern coast. Founded in 1953 as a medical school by Dr. Tonse Madhava Anantha Pai, the academy trains its 30,000-strong student body in everything from hotel management to software development. "We have to give our people skills if India is to be a global power. We can't depend on the government alone to do that," says Ramdas Madhav Pai, the academy's chancellor and the son of its founder.

Like other top-notch engineering schools such as PSG College of Engineering in Tamil Nadu and Pune Institute of Advanced Technologies, MIT goes out of its way to ensure that graduates are prepared to move straight into jobs. Companies such as Motorola Inc. and network-storage outfit EMC Corp. often recruit Manipal students in the final weeks of their penultimate year. Once a student accepts an offer, the college creates final-year electives geared to his or her prospective job.

Infosys, Tata Consultancy, Wipro, and Satyam Computer Services, which together hired more than 40,000 engineers in 2004, take such cooperation a step further. They provide course material and train lecturers on developments in areas such as chip design, radio frequency identification, and network management. The collaboration pays off in shorter in-house training once graduates become employees. "We've brought down our training program to 52 days from 76 days," says S. Ramadorai, chief executive of Tata Consultancy.

Although it's not as exclusive as IIT, Manipal is not easy to get into. Some 12,000 candidates applied for the 600 seats up for grabs in 2004. Compared with subsidized "IITians," who cost the federal government $18,500 each by the time they complete their four-year degree, MIT students must pay $9,000 tuition for four years. That can be tough in India, where a typical urban middle-class household earns $800 monthly. With some 100,000 Indians heading to the country's 975 private engineering colleges, the student loan market is beginning to show signs of life. A 2005 mechanical engineering graduate from PSG College, Ramu Lakkumanan, is the fourth child of a paddy farmer in coastal Tamil Nadu. He took out a $700 loan to ease finances at home. The first graduate in his family, he is training to join Tata Consultancy.

Manipal Academy's Pai is striving to give students value for their money. His goal is to build an IIT-like campus that would cost students a fraction of what an IIT education costs the government. Currently the institute is working on a project to build a $7.6 million innovation and incubation center to house labs of Hewlett-Packard, Philips Electronics, EMC, and Infosys. All told, Manipal Academy is investing $23 million over three years in new facilities. Part of the funds for expansion come from the Academy's 9,000 foreign students, who pay two to four times what Indians pay.

Other private institutions are experimenting too. At PSG College, the faculty is planning a new "play-and-learn" approach, in which classes are broken into 20 minutes of lecture and 30 minutes of hands-on training. "To simulate real-life situations, we want students to meet customers, and we want faculty to spend two summer months with companies to solve their problems," says P. V. Mohanram, dean of PSG's mechanical engineering department.

India needs more cutting-edge educational institutions if it is to keep advancing as a technology-service provider and make the big shift to high-value manufacturing for global companies. Experts worry that only a third of India's second-tier engineering institutes provide an education that meets the benchmarks of major global corporations, forcing employers to spend big bucks training fresh graduates. One reason is underpaid faculty. A professor with 15 years' teaching experience in a second-tier engineering school takes home $575 a month, less than one-eighth the salary of a software designer with similar experience. "The divergence between industry and academia is getting so acute that faculty recruitment is getting extremely tough," says S. Vijayarangan, principal of PSG.

All these issues explain why India must keep striving to raise its engineering education standards. One way to do that would be to encourage more cooperation between the IITs and other institutions. A first experiment in such collaboration—between three local colleges and IIT–Bombay—will begin soon in Maharashtra. The colleges will follow the IIT syllabus and work together on research projects. "India needs 10 times more graduates of IIT quality. Only then will we be globally competitive," says P. Rama Rao, a former vice-chancellor of Hyderabad University. Rao is coordinating the project and pushing bureaucrats to replicate the model with IITs and colleges in Madras, Kharagpur, New Delhi, and Kanpur. If such efforts succeed, India's brainpower is likely to keep surprising the world.

---

# The Seeds of the Next Silicon Valley

*How Indian tech companies are helping to incubate start-ups*

At the Indian Institute of Technology (IIT) campus in Kharagpur, near Calcutta, a small team of engineers is beavering away on what they hope will prove a killer competitor to the BlackBerry. At

IIT–Bombay, an earth sciences professor is about to launch a company that will tap the vapor of geothermal springs to drive turbines, generators, and power stations—the first company to do so in India. Across the country, at IIT–Madras, students and professors have spun off a start-up that's working on a no-frills network computer aimed at the Asian corporate and government markets that will sell for just $100. "We dream of building billion-dollar-product companies here," says Ashok Jhunjhunwala, an electrical engineering professor at IIT–Madras. "We believe we have laid the foundation for them."

No one knows how many of these products will take off. But the odds are that some of the fledgling companies will make real money. Dozens of such projects are now taking shape at India's elite IITs. In the same way that Stanford University and Massachusetts Institute of Technology helped spawn Silicon Valley and Route 128 in the 1970s and 1980s, Indian institutions are encouraging professors and students with business ideas to take the plunge. The schools are providing initial office space, labs, and seed money to "incubate" start-up companies. Some are also building tech parks to attract companies willing to collaborate. Since India began opening its economy in the early 1990s, the seven IITs have created some 50 new companies. The pace has accelerated.

That's a big change from the early days. When they were conceived in the 1950s, the IITs churned out top-notch engineers to meet an almost insatiable appetite from the country's steel, construction, power, chemical, defense, and textile industries. The schools so excelled at the task that they became a world-famous source of engineers, particularly for the U.S. But actual involvement by the schools in start-ups was almost nonexistent. Now students and professors alike are busy trying to become entrepreneurs in commercially applicable areas where IITs are strong, such as telecom, microelectronics, computer sciences and software, heat transfer, and, of late, biochemistry and biotechnology.

The big challenge is finding funding. IIT–Kanpur, for example, has a budget of just $1.15 million to sprinkle around a half dozen projects. IIT–Madras has teamed up with institutions such as ICICI Bank Ltd.,

State Bank of India, and other local state-run sources to raise up to $230,000 for each of its 16 companies. And IIT–Kharagpur is creating its own fund. "We have plans for a $230 million venture fund that we will raise from our alumni, investors, financial institutions, and the government," says Partha Pratim Chakrabarti, dean of sponsored research and industrial consultancy at IIT–Kharagpur. All these efforts are necessary because Indian start-ups aren't much on the radar screens of American venture capitalists, who invested only $240 million in Indian companies in 2004. They invested $20.4 billion in the U.S.

Funds are rarely available for companies that don't have a track record of sales and customers. For example, Midas Communications Technologies Ltd., an IIT–Madras spin-off that makes broadband and wireless telecom equipment, finally raised $10 million from American venture capitalists Argonaut Private Equity in July 2004, seven years after it was founded. Midas's sales topped $104 million in 2005, 50% higher than 2004. Its success is a boon for IIT–Madras, where the electrical engineering department helped develop the technology for Midas products. Midas and other licensees of the technology paid the IIT $3.5 million in royalties in 2004.

Of course, applied research and business incubation at India's top technology institutes remain a far cry from their U.S. peers. But dozens of IIT spin-offs are a start. If India's software and tech stars can start to attract more venture funding, the breakthroughs of the future may come just as much from Bombay and Madras as Silicon Valley and Boston.

---

# A Whole New School of Thought

*Shantou University offers a blueprint for education reform*

Julia Hsiao, an assistant vice-chancellor at the University of California at Berkeley, has participated in countless commencements over the years, and this one had all the usual trappings: students in caps and gowns, proud parents snapping photos, a marching band playing *Pomp & Circumstance*. But the ceremony in June 2005 was different in one key respect. The graduates were from Shantou University, an upstart school deep in China's Guangdong Province.

Staging a U.S.-style graduation was the latest accomplishment for Hsiao, who as vice-president for student and academic affairs at Shantou since 2001 has been trying to transform the school into a show-case for Chinese education reform. Although it is a public university, Shantou gets most of its funds from one of the world's richest men, Hong Kong billionaire Li Ka-shing. Li tapped Berkeley's Hsiao, who in turn recruited other ethnic Chinese academics, some of whom travel back and forth between their home universities and Shantou.

This star-studded corps of American-trained educators wants to ditch tradition and remake Shantou in the image of a U.S. university. They're introducing new teaching methods, overhauling the curriculum, and giving Shantou's 8,000 students more responsibility for their own education. Instead of a set of required courses, Shantou now has a credit system, the first of its kind in China. Almost nothing is sacred. Hsiao and her colleagues are shaking up departments from engineering to medicine to the arts and journalism. Architects from Hong Kong, Taiwan, and Europe are redesigning the campus of drab white buildings. PricewaterhouseCoopers is modernizing the school's accounting.

Above all, the reformers are focused on educational quality. The goal is to replace rote learning, a tradition that dates back to the Han Dynasty, when rulers introduced exams for would-be mandarins, and instead emphasize creativity. In the past, students crammed only to spit back the information on tests. The Chinese call this pedagogical style *tianya*, the word for force-feeding a duck. Now, says Hsiao, Shantou is hoping to nurture students to "really be inspired to be creative, inquisitive learners."

The Shantou experience could serve as a model for other Chinese schools. Political leaders are setting their sights on higher education and aim to boost university enrollment sharply. Still, since elite schools in Beijing and Shanghai won't be able to absorb so many new students, universities in second- and third-tier cities like Shantou will be thrust into important roles. "There is huge demand that has been left neglected," says He Jin, program officer at the Ford Foundation in Beijing who has helped develop U.S.-style community colleges in China. "That's where the future is."

With a population of 1.2 million, a mere speck in a country of 1.3 billion, Shantou is an unlikely place for bold experiments. In the late 1970s, when Deng Xiaoping first opened China to the world, Shantou was one of a handful of southern cities named as special economic zones. But it was too isolated and never boomed. Today there's just one flight a day to Hong Kong, and China's intellectual hubs are far to the north in Beijing and Shanghai. Shantou may never be the Athens of China, but its university reformers are determined to try.

---

# Making Waves in Guangdong

*Berkeley's Julia Hsiao discusses educational reforms being pioneered at Shantou University. "We are creating a ripple effect," she says.*

Shantou, a small city in southern China's Guangdong Province, is an isolated place. It's far from the bustle of more prosperous Guangdong cities, which have benefited from their proximity to Hong Kong. Yet Julia Hsiao, assistant vice-chancellor for international affairs at the University of California at Berkeley, has made Shantou her second home.

In addition to her job at the flagship of the University of California, Hsiao is also vice-president for student and academic affairs at Shantou University, a government-backed school that Hong Kong billionaire Li Ka-shing is supporting. Li hired her in 2001 to turn the university into a hotbed of education reform.

Hsiao frequently travels between Berkeley and Shantou, and she has led an effort to recruit Western-trained academics willing to put up with the frustration of working at a provincial school in order to turn it into an American-style university. In 2005, Hsiao talked to

*BusinessWeek* about the work that she and her colleagues have been doing at Shantou. Edited excerpts of their conversation follow:

**Q: Compared to bigger and wealthier cities in China, Shantou is small and quite isolated. This isn't the most obvious place to do this type of work, is it?**

A: In some ways, one would ask, why Shantou? It would be so much easier to do what we're trying to do in Shanghai or Beijing. But the notion is access. People in this region should have access to quality higher education. Traditionally, the southern part of China hasn't had its fair share of universities.

**Q: What's your goal?**

A: Shantou is filled with people who really believe in the need to have quality education, taking the experience and best practices they've learned in the States to participate in an environment that will allow change to take place. What we are trying to do is build a platform for the talented pool of academics and scholars to come and share their expertise.

**Q: Why do you think it's important to do that?**

A: We like to see ourselves in some ways as an oasis, where inquisitive learners can come and really be nurtured, revitalized, inspired to be creative, and become part of a population that understands the role of global citizenship.

Unless China's people are educated in the language of global citizenship, it will be difficult for them to speak the cross-cultural language and compete. [So, at Shantou,] we are moving beyond rote learning and setting them up to learn for life, how to make critical decisions, and how to be open—open to new things, to change.

**Q: Is it necessary to bring in U.S.-trained people to do that?**

A: As much as it looks like we have been parachuted in, what we are trying to do is capacity-building. You need to jumpstart this with people with expertise and experience, but at the same time bring up the capacity of colleagues.

**Q: One of your first changes was to introduce a U.S.-style credit system. Why is that significant?**

**A:** In America, it sounds so common, a credit system. But in China, to build a credit system that's flexible you really have to dismantle the old system. You have to change the philosophy, from the top down. It's about options and self-responsibility. Instead of being told to learn, you have to want to learn. You have to design your own learning process.

**Q: The university is planning a major overhaul of the campus. Why pay so much attention to architecture?**

**A:** We want students to take notice, have impressions, and talk [about the campus]. If everything looks the same, it doesn't encourage varied and diverse opinion. Unless you build a community you don't have a thriving intellectual environment.

It's really about building that community and networking them together. The architecture will help us get to our end goal. It's not for vanity; it's to provide that kind of reflective environment that's necessary for an intellectual community.

**Q: Is Shantou's governing structure different from that of other schools?**

**A:** Only four universities in China have governing structure with boards—Jinan University, Shantou University, Huaqiao University in Xiamen, and Ningbo University. The four don't have to follow the rules of how education is set up.

Typically, the president is accountable to the Party secretary. Here, there's a board, the Shantou University council of 20 members. Li Ka-shing is the honorary chairman, and the chairman is the vice-governor of Guangdong. The president of the university reports to the board.

**Q: What impact do you think Shantou's changes will have on education in China?**

**A:** Mr. Li wants to be a catalyst for greater change. We are a little rock, a pebble, thrown into the pond. We are creating a ripple effect. We are trying to move fast. There is so much work to be done.

# 9

# The Social Agenda

THE BIGGEST THREATS TO LONG-TERM prosperity in India and China are internal. Even though both nations have managed remarkably well given their enormous, ethnically diverse populations, the gap between rich and poor is widening fast. Basic social services such as health care are insufficient. And disenfranchised masses, from once-isolated villagers to oppressed factory workers, are waking up to their rights. If leaders in China and India do not address these inequities and find ways to spread the benefits of growth more broadly, economic progress could become unsustainable.

China's mounting social pressures are becoming clear in the workplace. Although conditions remain harsh by Western standards, "Waking Up to Their Rights" shows how factory workers are starting to press their demands for better pay and benefits as labor shortages begin to surface and more opportunities open up in rural areas. In "A Black-listed Labor Leader Speaks Out," Lee Cheuk Yan of the Hong Kong Federation of Trade Unions, who has been prevented from entering China since participating in the 1989 Tiananmen Square protest, explains why he believes workers are finally making gains in asserting their rights. In "Hard Labor in Guangdong," a labor official in the industrial boomtown of Dongguan explains the challenges facing South China's manufacturing sector posed by labor shortages and workplace conditions.

Chinese leaders also must confront a seriously inadequate health-care system at a time when the nation's population is rapidly aging. "Breakdown" and the "The Great Wail of China" explain the dimensions of these problems.

India's more urgent challenge is to spread the fruits of economic growth to the vast majority of its population living in serious poverty. As recent Indian elections have proved, the frustrations of poor citizens can present serious political obstacles to continued reform. "India's Untold Story" profiles some of the encouraging gains in addressing the root causes of poverty in one rural village. "The Digital Village" explains how Indian technology professionals are beginning to use their talents and energy to develop creative solutions to poverty.

---

# Waking Up to Their Rights

*A grassroots movement of activists and lawyers is helping increasingly assertive workers get their due*

Luo Guangfu, a serious 27-year-old from the city of Chongqing, spends long nights at the weaving and dyeing machines of a textile factory in the industrial suburb of Panyu just outside Guangzhou. When he finishes his 12-hour shift at 7 a.m., you might expect him to sleep the day away. Instead, he usually grabs just a few hours of shut-eye, then heads for a run-down building surrounded by electronics, toy, and textile factories.

Once there, Luo climbs the stairs to the Panyu Migrant Worker Culture Center, joining dozens of other migrants in a stuffy room on the second floor. Though the center offers Ping-Pong, movies, and well-thumbed comic books in its small library, Luo usually opts for classes taught by the center's small volunteer staff—most of them workers themselves. His favorite is a seminar on his rights at the factory. "If a worker doesn't know China's labor law, then he's in big trouble," Luo says.

Luo has put his knowledge to good use. In April 2005 he and 300 other workers sent a letter to their factory manager demanding that wages be raised from less than $60 per month to the legal minimum of $69. At an earlier job, he joined 1,000 workers in a six-day strike that also successfully led to a wage hike. "If bosses don't pay us enough money, we can use the law and confront them with it," he says.

Luo and migrant workers like him are at the vanguard of a new labor-rights revolution sweeping China. In 2004, some 3 million workers joined a total of 57,000 protests countrywide, according to China Labour Bulletin, a Hong Kong–based rights group. These legions made China a manufacturing powerhouse. Today they're harnessing the power of the Internet and communicating with each other via cell phones to make sure they get their due. Employees are no longer the docile hero workers of the Communist era. Nor are they any longer easily exploitable. From Guangzhou to Zhengzhou, training centers and legal aid clinics are giving workers support and helping them take thousands of their grievances to the courts each year. "It's a de facto labor movement happening in China," says Robin Munro, research director at China Labour Bulletin.

This surge of activism is part of the changing labor math of China. Worker shortages are popping up in the manufacturing strongholds of Guangdong, Fujian, and Zhejiang Provinces. Rising rural incomes mean fewer people are migrating in search of work. The one-child policy has cut population growth, which means there are fewer young people to staff factories. After years of wage stagnation, salaries are starting to creep up. "Workers have more choices than before," says Huang Huiping, deputy chief of the labor bureau in the Pearl River Delta city of Dongguan. She estimates the city's factories have 267,000 unfilled jobs.

If this labor movement is sustained, foreign investors will have to consider their China strategy in a whole new light. China's phenomenal growth has been based on an endless labor supply and wage rates a fraction of those in the West. But suddenly, China's pool of the willing doesn't look quite so vast. The country's 169 million manufacturing workers are more mobile, and those who are now migrating often do so in search of a specific job, not just whatever work they can round up. That means China's attraction for sweatshop investors will diminish. The country will begin trumpeting its other advantages: new highways, railroads, ports, phone and data networks, pools of hyperefficient suppliers of everything from hubcaps to hard drives, and perhaps most important, its huge domestic market.

## Social Compact

Growing activism has special significance for the coastal areas where multinational activity is most intense. There are clear signs that many foreign companies and their suppliers are entering into a new social compact with workers in these regions. At the same time, some of the most sophisticated players simply need fewer workers in any given factory. In General Motors Corp.'s most automated mainland plants, for example, labor accounts for less than 10% of the cost of a car produced—lower than in many factories in the U.S. and Europe. That means GM can more readily afford the wages and training needed to woo the best workers.

If other companies emulate GM, the low-wage model for China could slowly start to morph into one that depends on higher pay and greater productivity. Other factors—spiraling costs for construction, land, and housing on the coast, as well as the revalued yuan—could help speed this trend. China will have to compete more and more in areas where the stress is on delivering sophisticated, value-added products that depend on state-of-the-art factories and highly skilled labor. The increasing sophistication of Chinese consumers—who now want the best, most advanced products possible—will accelerate the demand for value-added manufacturing.

Employers in the lowest-tech industries, meanwhile, may shift away from China's coastal regions. Guangdong's "factories have been designed with the most cutthroat wage structure," says Judith Banister, a demographer with Beijing's Javelin Investments, a management consulting firm.

With wages creeping up, low-end "manufacturing is moving to other countries like Vietnam, India, and Pakistan."

These changes will take years to play out, of course. And for now, the activists are much less concerned about the macroeconomic implications of what they're doing than they are about the day-to-day battle for better wages and working conditions. "A high-growth economy shouldn't be based on violating workers' rights," says Jiang Junlu, a labor lawyer at King & Wood, China's largest law firm.

It's a slow struggle. There's still only sporadic enforcement of rules on everything from overtime pay to child labor and safe working conditions. In China's vast hinterlands you'll find no shortage of workers willing to toil long hours sewing shirts, cutting and polishing the rubies and jade sold in U.S. malls, or digging coal from some of the world's most dangerous mines. Last year more than 137,000 workers were killed on the job. And Western retailers and marketers that buy the bulk of China's exports apply relentless pressure on manufacturers to cut costs, so plant managers are loath to raise wages.

Even as workers on the coast demand better wages and benefits, the Rust Belt is being largely left behind. Nationwide unemployment is only 4.2%, but in the northeastern provinces focused on heavy industries, official joblessness runs up to 18%. "Look at the industrial history of England, Japan, and Germany," says Arthur Kroeber, editor of Hong Kong–based *China Economic Quarterly*. "It's a span of decades before workers are able to really organize for higher wages."

Nevertheless, what's happening in China these days is truly revolutionary. The epicenter of the revolution is Guangdong Province north of Hong Kong. China's export base, the region has thousands of factories making everything from motherboards to Barbie dolls. It's home to 7 million migrant workers—and provincial officials estimate local factories need another 2 million. "Anyplace in China that traditionally relies on migrant workers is now suffering shortages," says Wang Guanyu, director of the Guangdong labor and employment service and administration center. The shortfall has driven average wages up 30%, to roughly $97 per month, in one year.

Some factories are taking pains to make sure their laborers stick around. Apache Footwear employs 12,000 people to produce 1.1 million pairs of Adidas shoes a month in the city of Qingyan. With monthly turnover rates of nearly 10% at its original factory in nearby Guangzhou, Apache sought to make the five-year-old Qingyan plant a more inviting place. "Before, you just had to pay workers and that was enough," says Steve Chen, Apache's Taiwanese boss. "Now you really have to take care of them."

Apache started with the living quarters. Rather than house its staff in the concrete-and-steel high-rises that are the norm at most factories, it built a series of one-story, red-brick buildings. The company organizes Saturday night movies and dances. When it hires, Apache gives preference to its employees' relatives. And it is building apartments it plans to sell cheaply to workers with families—a rare benefit in a country where breadwinners often spend most of the year working hundreds of miles from home. Turnover in Qingyan is now about a third the level of the Guangzhou site. "The environment here is much better than at other factories," says 22-year-old Li Linli, who, in 2002, followed her older sister to Apache from their village in Hunan Province. "She told me the benefits were quite good and that they always pay on time," says Li.

In part, multinationals like Adidas have spurred such changes. Foreign companies face pressure from consumers and shareholders at home who are concerned about corporate social responsibility. The multinationals are targeted more often for workplace investigations by Chinese officials, so they're better at complying with China's labor law, say labor analysts. And as the multinationals compete for increasingly scarce workers, some of their labor practices are being picked up by Chinese rivals. Haier, for instance, has established a 24-hour phone hotline and a support group to help employees cope with emergencies.

The more important agents of change, though, are the workers themselves and the labor organizations that support them. The Migrant Workers Community College in Shenzhen's grubby Chegongmiao district—home to scores of garment and chemical factories and dorms housing 200,000 workers—provides free or nearly free training in everything from computers to AIDS prevention. The center works with the likes of Nokia, Adidas, and all their suppliers to ensure they meet Chinese labor standards. Now the center is in talks with domestic tech power Huawei. "We want to let companies learn how to expand their business through being responsible corporations," says former teacher and journalist Liu Kaiming, who founded the center.

Students, too, are playing a role. Law students from Tsinghua University in Beijing and Sun Yat-sen University in Guangzhou run seminars on factory floors, and some do much more. Wen He, a 23-year-old student at Sun Yat-sen, is representing four workers in Dongguan who caught a potentially fatal respiratory disease called silicosis after working long hours without protective face masks in a poorly ventilated jewelry factory. "I decided to go to law school because I saw how poorly migrant workers are treated," says Wen.

Even Beijing is lending a hand—up to a point. Under President Hu Jintao, the government has ordered local labor bureaus to ensure that work sites are safe and that migrants get paid fairly and on time. Migrant worker detention centers—de facto jails where authorities locked up migrants without residence papers—were banned in 2003. That's when Guangzhou-based daily *Nanfang Dushi Bao* wrote about a 27-year-old graphic designer who was beaten to death in such a center.

Beijing's tolerance, though, has its limits. The law requires companies to allow a union to organize if just 25 workers ask for one—but that only applies to the official All-China Federation of Trade Unions. Woe to those who try to set up their own unions or push too strongly for workers' rights. In 2002 two organizers of protests against unpaid wages and pensions at a ferro alloy plant in the northeast city of Liaoyang were sentenced to seven- and four-year sentences, respectively, on charges of "subversion." "The Chinese regime is very much worried about the Solidarity experience in Poland coming to China," says Lee Cheuk Yan, head of the Hong Kong Confederation of Trade Unions.

Chinese authorities will also let the press go only so far. Indeed, Hu's administration is proving less tolerant than its predecessor. The government routinely shuts down newspapers, magazines, and Web sites and currently has more than 40 reporters in jail for reporting on issues such as labor rights and corruption. Cheng Yizhong, the muckraking editor of *Nanfang Dushi Bao*, was arrested on trumped-up corruption charges last year. He was released but remains barred from working as an editor.

But the workers keep asserting themselves. Back in grimy Panyu, Luo Guangfu still isn't satisfied, even following the latest wage hike. He is considering farming rice and sweet corn as his parents have long done, a more attractive proposition after Beijing cut taxes and hiked subsidies for rural regions. With workers like Luo free to make such choices, China's factories will soon need to do far more to keep workers happy and on the job. The revolution is quiet, but it's real and growing. China's workers—as well as corporations and consumers worldwide—will be feeling its consequences.

---

# Hard Labor in Guangdong

*Not only must Huang Huiping find workers for local factories, she must defend their rights and conditions. That can be a tough brief.*

Dongguan, Guangdong, in the heart of the Pearl River Delta is ground zero for China's export-processing zone. It's also home to more than 3.6 million migrant workers toiling in the thousands of factories producing toys, plastics, and computer components.

Huang Huiping, 43, has worked at the Dongguan Labor Bureau for 13 years, rising to deputy chief and overseeing her bureau as it more than doubled in size, to some 800 employees. "We are continually adding staff as there are so many migrant workers to oversee," she told Beijing Bureau Chief Dexter Roberts in her office. Edited excerpts of their conversation follow:

**Q: Can you tell me about the labor shortages that have emerged?**
**A:** We expect the situation to be more serious this year. Shortages first emerged in 2003 and are especially serious in labor-intensive industries like

clothing, shoes, toys, and in electronic components. The shortages are happening because workers have more choices than they did before. There are new places they can find work, and new kinds of opportunities for them.

The rise of the Yangtze River Delta has opened a new destination for them to find factory work. And the government's policy of *sannong* [Beijing's preferential tax policies that focus on improving rural incomes] has made farmers' incomes go up and made staying on the farm more attractive. It's not like before, when a migrant worker's only choice was the Pearl River Delta. At the same time, Dongguan enterprises also continually need more labor.

**Q: What kind of workers are Dongguan factories looking for?**
**A:** That is also contributing to the shortages: Most factories are looking for young woman workers. For example, of those Dongguan enterprises that were facing shortages last year, 75% were looking for women, and 60% were trying to find women 18 to 25. The fact that they are being so selective also makes it very difficult for them to find workers.

Also, many of those enterprises now facing shortages are those that were first set up in the 1990s and are doing simple manufacturing or export processing. Traditionally, these kinds of factories pay salaries that are very low, and this is making it difficult for them now to attract workers.

**Q: How does your bureau ensure that Dongguan factories follow the labor law and treat migrant workers properly?**
**A:** We do inspections of all the factories in Dongguan. We send out more than 200 inspectors into the factories every year to check on labor conditions, including that working-hours regulations are being followed, and that wages are paid on time. We are trying to ensure that migrant workers have the same rights as local workers [those from Dongguan city].

Enterprises in Dongguan must follow the labor law. For example, workers should only work five days a week and eight hours a day. Employers must give them overtime pay if they need their workers to exceed that.

Migrant workers are coming from other provinces and cities across China, so the enterprises must also provide housing and canteens where they can eat, as well as some entertainment activities for their workers.

**Q: Where do you find that local enterprises are not meeting the law?**
A: Overtime pay is the biggest problem companies face when it comes to the labor law. Many factories also must do seasonal hiring, which creates problems. For example, in the months before Christmas many factories have a high season of producing toys. According to the labor law, if workers exceed 36 hours a week, then you must pay them one and a half times their salary, and double pay for Saturdays and Sundays, as well as triple pay for holidays.

But many factories don't obey China's labor law. There is a conflict between the labor law and the fact that many factories have peak hiring periods and off-peak times. There are also problems with companies withholding worker salaries.

So we have set up a minimum wage in Dongguan. That was raised from $57 a month to $69 a month [in 2004]. Our bureau then does inspections to make sure companies are paying full salaries according to the regulations, and doing so in a prompt fashion. We also check to see whether companies are meeting regulations on safety standards and factory cleanliness standards.

**Q: Does your bureau ever find it hard to balance the needs of protecting workers and ensuring that your factory investors are satisfied too?**
A: The labor bureau's job is not to attract investment but to enforce the law and regulations of China. Really, we have two roles: The first includes protecting the legal rights of both workers and of investors. Our labor bureau doesn't stand on either the workers' side or the investors' side. If workers break the laws of China, we won't support them.

Our second role is to supervise the implementation of the labor law. Our job is also to cooperate with other provinces, particularly those where migrant workers are from, to ensure we have a steady supply of labor for our factories.

# A Blacklisted Labor Leader Speaks Out

*Lee Cheuk Yan of the Hong Kong Federation of Trade Unions talks
about the challenges of protecting workers*

Hong Kong Legislative Councillor Lee Cheuk Yan, 48, hasn't been
in China since participating in the Tiananmen Square protests that
culminated in a bloody massacre on June 4, 1989. He is one of 10 to 20
Hong Kong residents blacklisted from entering the mainland for supporting the protesting students.

Yet rather than be cowed by that restriction, Lee has continued his
activism. As general secretary of the Hong Kong Confederation of
Trade Unions, he now works to improve the lives of Chinese workers.
*BusinessWeek* Beijing Bureau Chief Dexter Roberts recently met
with Lee in the historic former Supreme Court Building—now the
Legislative Council Building—in Hong Kong's Central District, where
they talked about the labor movement in China. Edited excerpts of
their conversation follow:

**Q: How much room do labor groups have to organize on the mainland
now?**
**A:** That's an interesting development in China. For the first time, labor
NGOs [nongovernmental organizations] seem to have some sort of space
to operate. As long as you don't get the workers organized it's OK.

You can serve workers as a labor lawyer, as a resource center, as a
research center, or as a service center. But still unions are very sensitive, as
are real workers' organizations. For example, lately there have been more
detentions of strikers in textile factories.

The government will allow some labor organizations to develop as long
as it is under Beijing's control. That's so that the grievances don't build up
to such a point that they cause social instability.

**Q: Why is Beijing being more tolerant toward labor now?**
**A:** It is because of the need to ensure that the transition toward a market
economy and further privatization and further foreign investment won't
lead to labor disputes and the rise of organized labor.

One safety valve is the labor NGOs. The other safety valve is to try to make the official union pretend to be a union. When you look at the recent amendments to the Trade Union Law, very clearly it is still controlled by the Communist Party—that hasn't changed.

But they have begun to allow a sort of union elections and are using the jargon that says they need to better represent workers' interests. And they are moving the union into private enterprises and into foreign enterprises especially. So there is new union formation going on in the private sector.

**Q: What role is played by the All-China Federation of Trade Unions, China's official government-controlled union?**
**A:** The ACFTU also wants to play the role of a safety valve. It wants to show the workers that there is an organization to represent them. But it still represents predominately the interest of the Communist Party. So this is more of a move toward the official union pretending to play the role of a real union.

**Q: How effective can the official union be?**
**A:** There have been some cases where within the union they have held elections where they have successfully gotten rid of ACFTU candidates and other worker candidates have won. So there are some cases where there has been more opening up of opportunity for ordinary workers. But even if through an election you get elected to the enterprise level, workers still cannot rise to the industrial level or to the provincial level of the official union.

Take the Liaoyang case where thousands of workers protested over unpaid salaries in 2002 [in the city of Liaoyang in northeastern China's Liaoning Province] with worker organizers Yao Fuxin and Xiao Yunliang. They were both arrested and even now are still in prison. They emerged out of this struggle [for worker rights], but even before they had formed an independent union, they were arrested.

**Q: How serious is the Chinese government about improving worker conditions in China? The Premier, Wen Jiabao, for example, publicly puts much emphasis on improving safety conditions for workers.**
**A:** Premier Wen Jiabao wept over a mining accident where 160 people were killed, but not long after that even more people died in another accident.

This regime is more concerned with stability. Of course they are also concerned about labor and peasant unrest. But what really triggers the anger of the working people is corruption. And mining accidents are always connected to corruption. It is either illegal mines that are allowed to operate by corrupt officials or official disrespect for safety conditions, which also occurs in state-owned mines.

So this regime is concerned about workers because they don't want to trigger instability. But in a way they are helpless. That's because the only way to fight corruption is if you have transparency and democracy. They always try to do it from the top down. But actually they need to allow bottom-up supervision.

And it is very clear that this regime is politically more controlling than even the Jiang Zemin regime. Look at the way they control the media and stifle the development of democracy on the Internet. The [regime] is sort of a benign dictator. I think that is the right word to describe them.

**Q: Are there signs that workers are becoming more knowledgeable of their rights and more demanding?**
**A:** Yes. First there is more publicity in the press about labor law. Secondly, there are more resources—labor lawyers, service centers, NGOs—devoted to legal education now. But everyone in China knows their limits. They know they cannot organize an independent union. And I think that is the main frustration of the workers in China now.

**Q: What is the role of your organization?**
**A:** We here in Hong Kong are trying to work with international unions and put pressure on China to open up in the area of freedom of association. We are an independent union in Hong Kong. We are representing 70 affiliates with 170,000 workers. Our constituency is just in Hong Kong. But of course we support workers' rights in China. And we have also established a liaison office to inform the international union movement about what is happening in Hong Kong and China.

We also monitor changes in labor conditions in China. We are doing research on the impact of the World Trade Organization on Chinese workers, and we have put out a guidebook for international unions that want to go into China. We are also thinking of using this strategy: putting pressure on foreign enterprises in China to allow their workers to elect their own representatives within the Chinese operations of their companies.

**Q: How optimistic are you that China will eventually have real independent unions?**
A: In a way I feel not really very optimistic. Because the overwhelming concern of the Chinese regime—even this new generation of leaders—is too much focused on political control. The Chinese regime is very much worried about the Solidarity experience in Poland coming to China. And they don't want the workers' movement to rock their power base.

With Hong Kong it is the same. We had a half-million people march for democracy. And at that outpouring of anger and discontent and in support for democracy here in Hong Kong, we have seen Beijing's reaction: to be even more hardline. They have ruled out the right to universal suffrage in the years 2007 and 2008. So I say if the people of Hong Kong have democracy, then the workers in China will have freedom of association. It is the same struggle against political control.

# Breakdown

*How China's decentralized health-care system is failing hundreds of millions, as diseases like SARS spread*

The doctor was polite but adamant. "I am not allowed to talk about my country's public health," the physician, from one of Beijing's premier hospitals, said to a reporter arriving for a scheduled interview. "I'm sorry, but the ministry has just informed me of this order."

Even as top Chinese officials scramble to assure the world of their new openness in facing severe acute respiratory syndrome (SARS), the doctor's refusal is a powerful reminder of how difficult it is for China's health system to change. That's not just a problem for the Chinese. It's a problem for the world. China's vast network of public hospitals, rural clinics, and private facilities is now so inequitable and inefficient that many public health professionals see the country as one of the weakest links in the global medical system. Already, more than 5 million Chinese suffer from tuberculosis, the second-highest number on the planet—and a large number of the cases are drug-resistant. Despite China's impressive growth in gross domestic product and per capita income, it is still plagued by diseases usually associated with much poorer countries, including rates of neonatal tetanus and hepatitis B that put it among the worst in Asia. China is also belatedly waking up to a crisis with AIDS, already estimated to affect more than 1 million people. That number could soar to 10 million or 20 million by 2010, making China one of the hardest hit countries in the world, says a report by the Center for Strategic & International Studies in Washington. "They don't have the infrastructure to deal with epidemics of this sort," says Bates Gill, a China expert at CSIS and co-author of the report. "This will have an increasing impact on the social and economic viability of China."

And now SARS, the disease that in 2003 spread from southern China. "As China becomes a much more mobile country, infectious diseases that hit one place can quickly become a national and international problem," says Yuanli Liu, an assistant professor of international health at Harvard University. "Out of the current crisis, we are all learning this lesson."

The larger question is what lessons the Chinese are learning. Sources say Vice-Minister Wu Yi has pledged $55 million to fight SARS. "We are setting up epidemic prevention divisions for railway, road, and airline transport across China," says one deputy director at the Chinese Center for Disease Control and Prevention. The Chinese are also showing a new level of candor: Premier Wen Jiabao said in 2003 that although progress against SARS had been made, "the overall situation remains grave."

But a partial lifting of the veil is only a start to what's needed. In many ways, China's health system has actually slid backward since the days of Chairman Mao Zedong, when the country developed one of the world's most comprehensive health-care systems. A pillar of the network was an army of "barefoot doctors," workers trained to serve basic health-care needs. With relatively low expenditures, the mainland was able to ensure basic health for 85% of its population, slashing infant and maternal mortality rates. "China used to be regarded as one of the great success stories" in public health, says Jagadish Upadhyay, a lead project officer for health in China at the World Bank in Washington. That quickly began to change, however, when Deng Xiaoping launched economic reforms in 1979 and carried out a massive decentralization that devolved responsibility and funding of public health to the provinces, cities, and even townships.

As a result, the portion of total health care funded by Beijing has fallen from 36% in 1980 to less than 20% in 2003. In principle, that's not bad: After all, China's total health expenditures have soared more than tenfold in that period, to $48 billion in 2003. But tremendous inequalities have emerged. A full quarter of health-care spending goes to the wealthy areas of Beijing, Shanghai, and Jiangsu and Zhejiang Provinces. The seven provinces and autonomous regions in the far west—a vast area home to China's poorest people—only get 5%. That inequity has ominous implications as SARS spreads to the countryside.

Huge inefficiencies also dog the system. Price limits set on basic procedures and services—a holdover from China's more socialistic past—force struggling clinics and hospitals to sell patients excessive amounts of pharmaceuticals, many of which are not subject to price caps. The result: Health-care costs have jumped 500% to 600% over the last 10 years. "There is massive overuse of drugs in order to subsidize the health system," says Dr. Ray Yip, a senior advisor to the UNICEF Office for China in Beijing. "This has undermined the relationship between the public and health-care workers and created an avoidance phenomenon [where people avoid seeking medical care]. The few that do show up for treatment get squeezed."

Not only is the care available markedly worse for China's 800 million rural inhabitants and migrant workers, but also the vast majority of the rural population, some 90%, are without any insurance at all. Urban residents are much better served under a medical social insurance program initiated in 1998 by former Premier Zhu Rongji or through other programs. But a full 45% who are self-employed, jobless, elderly, or work for private companies are uninsured. This inability to afford care contributes to the spread of diseases and pushes families into poverty as they struggle to pay bills.

The decentralization of the overall health sector has also badly weakened China's ability to respond to national health crises. "Before, surveillance, reporting, and research could be quickly mobilized," says Harvard's Liu. "Now, this is a major challenge."

To be sure, China is taking some steps. It wants to end the practice of the same doctors prescribing and selling medicine to patients. President Hu Jintao and Premier Wen appear more attuned to the needs of the poorest. In October 2002, a rural cooperative medical system was launched, with the central and provincial governments pledging to match funds contributed by rural workers. That may be a challenge. "So far, there is not enough funding to meet the expenditures of the localities," admits Gao Hongbin, deputy director of the State Council's poverty alleviation agency.

For many Chinese that is no longer acceptable. Take one 23-year-old Beijing tour guide, whose business has been badly hit by the SARS scare. Like millions of other Chinese who aren't part of the national health plan, she doesn't know what she would do if she faced a medical crisis. "For now I am young, so I probably don't have to worry," she says. "But later, when I am older, I'm not so confident about how I'd cope." For China's health-care network, business as usual looks increasingly like a dangerous choice.

## India's Untold Story

*For those at the bottom, standards of living are inching higher*

The road to the remote village of Kharonda winds around the gentle slopes of the Sahayadri hills in the western Indian state of

Maharashtra. Most of the road is well-paved, a black ribbon wrapped around hills washed a brilliant green. Along the way, other small hamlets peep out of the misty hillsides, their red-tiled roofs flashing in the sun. The people of Kharonda and the other villages have a lot invested in this road. Through the seasons, even during the fierce monsoons, they use it to send the mangoes, guavas, and cashews they grow into nearby towns and distant cities for sale. They've got a new commercial activity, too, selling grafts of their flourishing mango trees to other communities in Maharashtra and the neighboring state of Gujarat.

Just a few years ago, Kharonda and the Jawhar district of which it is part were typical of the rural villages where 650 million of India's 1 billion people live. There was no road, and there were no orchards. There was only grinding poverty. In one particularly bad year, 1993, 45 children in Jawhar died of malnutrition in one week. Today the district's transformation proves what can be done, even with limited funds, to combat the poverty that many have thought would always be the fate of most Indians.

Yes, poverty is still a scourge in India. At least 200 million people earn less than $1 a day, when they can find work. Their sense that their problems were being ignored helped the Congress Party and its allies unseat the center-right government of Prime Minister Atal Bihari Vajpayee in May 2004. Congress has since made poverty reduction a big focus, introducing a raft of programs aimed at the urban poor and rural areas like Jawhar. Yet a 2005 study by New Delhi economists Surjit Bhalla and Nirtha Das, who evaluated several anti-poverty programs over the last 30 years, found that less than 27 cents of every dollar allocated actually reaches the poor. The rest is misappropriated and misdirected by local politicians and bureaucrats, the study says.

## Sweet Harvest

Still, progress, often through self-help, has been made. Indian government census statistics show the number of those living on less than $1 a day dropped from 26% of the population in 1999 to an estimated 20%

in 2005. A combination of projects by nongovernmental organizations, local villagers' efforts, and grants from the government has made the difference, as has the beneficial effect of 7% annual economic growth in recent years. "The big unsung story about India is the rapid strides it has made in poverty reduction, though many challenges remain," Michael F. Carter, World Bank head for India, told an audience of Indian industrial leaders in 2004.

Dhavalu Mahale of Kharonda is one of those unsung heroes. A tall, wiry man, Mahale, like other Jawhar residents, was a textbook example of extreme poverty 10 years ago. He cultivated finger millet, a rough crop used by tribals for their daily bread, on a denuded hillside inherited from his father. When the growing season was over, he and his family moved to the shanties of Bombay, where he did building and road construction. "I didn't like it, but there was nothing in the village," he recalls. Even with construction work, the total annual income for the family of five was $80. Life was so hard that three of their five children died of malnutrition, and Mahale was desperate for a new chance. In 1995 he approached workers of BAIF Development Research Foundation, a private group in Pune.

The foundation had started a program in Gujarat, in which it worked with impoverished villagers to diversify their farming by combining agriculture with horticulture and forestry on fallow land. Maharashtra authorities had asked BAIF to replicate the program in the Jawhar district. It targeted 10 mountain villages, including Kharonda, where 1,000 families lived. The problems were enormous. There were no roads leading to the villages; deforestation and erosion were severe. And the locals were suspicious of the outsiders. But the staff persuaded some of the families to visit their projects in Gujarat. That helped, and in the first year, 67 families signed up.

BAIF workers found their way into the pathless mountains on motorcycles, carrying seed and fertilizer with them. They helped the farmers plant saplings and fruit grafts on the hillsides. They taught them to level the small patches of land and harvest rainwater by building small stone dams at the front edge of each patch. In the first year, 90% of the mango and other trees planted survived. Until the trees could bear fruit—it takes four years—the foundation taught farmers modern farming practices for the millet they were still sowing. When the trees finally bore fruit, each participating family netted an average of $35—way over the $7 savings they generally had upon returning from the city, recalls Sudhir Wagle, BAIF's chief program coordinator in Jawhar, who helped initiate the project.

## New Brick Homes
Mahale soon asked the BAIF workers for help. Wagle set Mahale to work planting fruit trees and developing land and water resources. And he planted high-value crops like watermelons until the mango trees bore fruit. His neighbors smirked. Who would buy the watermelons? How would they be transported? There were no roads. But Mahale persisted and managed to get his first crop to the nearest town. It earned him $115—more than he had ever earned in a year.

Meanwhile the government's Tribal Affairs Ministry pitched in. Jawhar is populated by "tribals"—indigenous people with special rights whose roots on their land go back millennia. The Ministry gave cash grants to individual farmers of $115 over five years to buy seeds and fertilizer, gave Kharonda a grant to repair and chlorinate the village well, and provided motors and pipes to help bring the water up the hillside to the land and into homes. Within five years, Kharonda and surrounding villages were producing tons of nuts, fruits, and other produce.

Today, villagers like Mahale are local role models. Mahale owns the largest house in the village of Kharonda: an eight-room structure with brick walls and a red-tiled roof. Inside, the house boasts electricity, running water drawn by motor from the local well, satellite TV, a sofa set, and a large bed in the master bedroom. Last month, Mahale bought himself a motorcycle with one of the consumer loans easily available in India these days. His wife, Sintar, a stately woman with a confident smile, helps her husband. Their income is now nearly $4,000 a year, the fruit of the 20 mango trees, 40 cashew trees, and a stand of eucalyptus, plus the 6,000 mango-sapling grafts they sell annually.

In fact, the income of the entire district has increased. The grass huts typical of less prosperous times are gradually being replaced by brick homes. Vans fly up and down the hill carrying sapling grafts, produce, and supplies. The successful program in Kharonda shows that, in its fight against poverty, "the government has kept space for human, social interventions—more in India than anywhere else," says BAIF Executive Vice-President Girish G. Sohani. The program "catapults people from poverty right into the market economy," he adds. It's a model that is giving the abject poor of India hope and could do the same for others who live in poverty around the world.

## The Digital Village

*India's high-tech dynamos are turning more attention to the needs of the nation's countless poor*

Among the grand gothic columns of Bangalore's colonial-era urban administration office, a couple dozen village dwellers neatly dressed in cotton shirts, sarongs, and turbans wait their turn at what looks like an automatic teller machine. But this machine isn't dispensing cash. Instead, farmers from nearby villages can use the terminal to see computerized copies of the deeds to the tiny patches of wheat, rice, and vegetables they till for a living. Once they've checked their information, they can get a printed copy of their records at a neighboring window for just 30 cents.

That's a big change. Until the records were computerized, the deeds were controlled by powerful village accountants. These men routinely charged poor farmers anywhere from $2 to $22 for a copy—which they typically need two or three times a year when they ask banks for loans to pay for fertilizer, seeds, and crop insurance. Worse, some accountants would even collude with upper-caste landlords to steal the land by writing over the original names and then tricking illiterate, lower-caste farmers into signing away their property by putting their thumbprints on the deeds.

In 1999, the Karnataka state government launched a program to computerize the land records of 6.7 million farmers in 30,000 villages. Two years later, all 20 million deeds had been digitized and filed along with information such as the land's productive capacity and any loans that use the property as collateral. Today, the information is available in Kannada, the local language, through 200 government-owned computer kiosks in administrative offices across the state. Muniratnama, a cheerful 45-year-old farmer, traveled 15 kilometers from her village to Bangalore for a copy of her land record so she could get a loan to replant her 1.6 hectares. The new system, she says, is far better than the old way. "The village accountant was corrupt," she says with disgust. "He'd delay making any changes, and he made mistakes too."

Computerizing land records may not seem like much of an achievement; most developed countries did it years ago. But in rural India, where the majority of people are semi-literate and live in remote communities unconnected by road or phone, it's almost a revolution. "With equal access to information, a lower-caste person now has the same privileges as an upper-caste person," says Rajiv Chawla, who oversaw the $3.7 million program, called Bhoomi—which means "land" in both Hindi and Kannada. In Karnataka alone, for instance, deed fraud once cost poor farmers $20 million a year; today, the problem has been virtually wiped out, according to the World Bank. With all the information digitized, land reform—which had slowed because limited access to records made it hard to prove ownership—could now be restarted. And the data can be mined for commercial information: A tractor maker, aiming to better target its marketing efforts, recently asked for the names of communities where most farms are larger than four hectares. Soon, says Chawla, the government will begin charging for that sort of information. Even now, though, the Bhoomi program earns $2.6 million a year from the 30-cent fees.

Such initiatives add up to a digital turning point for India. For the past decade, the country's high-tech sector has boomed, with outsourcing companies and software shops popping up like mushrooms in tech capitals such as Bangalore and Hyderabad. But that growth has largely left

India's 700 million impoverished villagers, slum dwellers, and tenant farmers just as poor as their forefathers were for centuries. Jobs are scarce, cash is scarcer, and simply getting water is an immense daily challenge. This huge gulf between India's thriving elite and its vast hinterland is one reason the ruling Bharatiya Janata Party lost the general election in the spring of 2004. The victorious Congress Party has pledged to deliver prosperity to the masses—a stupendously difficult task in India. Although the BJP planned to shell out $3 billion by 2007 to computerize government services across the nation, it will now fall to Congress to implement the plan and see that it improves the lives of ordinary Indians. "The government's challenge is to leverage India's technological and manpower potential to solve our problems of poverty and actually deliver services to the masses," says R. Chandrashekar, who oversees e-governance programs at India's Information Technology Ministry.

In the fight against poverty, the policymakers of Congress may find natural allies among the more altruistic of India's digital generation. Even before the BJP lost the election, many of the educated elite responsible for the success of India's tech and software houses—or who have helped U.S. multinationals prosper—decided to turn their energies to helping India's poor. NASSCOM, the trade group for India's software houses, estimates that there are hundreds of such programs across India, many of them private initiatives, connected by a common theme: to find cheap, digital solutions to the problems pressing on the poor. They range from a "smart chip" payment card for the working poor to a diagnostic kit for isolated health clinics to a successful e-commerce initiative that lets farmers buy supplies and get market information online. "It can act as a bridge between the rapidly growing new India and the lagging old India," says NASSCOM President Kiran Karnik. "We have to figure a way to take these sparks and turn them into a prairie fire."

For a decade, such efforts were merely experiments—small-scale, splintered acts of charity and attempts at business creation. And many have been hindered by government inertia or regulation. But some have become successful and are starting to look like valid business opportunities. Now, the entrepreneurs are starting to discover one another: In

2004, India served as host to three conferences on the use of technology for development in rural societies. So far, most of these ventures have been funded with entrepreneurs' savings because venture capitalists see few prospects of early returns. With the number of success stories growing, though, NASSCOM and the World Bank are planning a fund of up to $1 billion to support promising ideas. And other developing nations such as South Africa, Brazil, and Sri Lanka are closely watching India's progress to see whether the projects can be successfully replicated. "India could lead the world in creating the grassroots social experiments that could teach both India and other nations how to use technology for the common good," says Kenneth Keniston, a professor at the Massachusetts Institute of Technology who follows such experiments globally.

## Stretching Resources

Many of these efforts are driven by the urge to profit: If a fraction of India's poor logged in or dialed up just once a day—and paid a minuscule fee to a service provider for the privilege—then the sheer mass could create a viable business. "If you can conceptualize the world's 4 billion poor as a market, rather than as a burden, they must be considered the biggest source of growth left in the world," says University of Michigan management theorist C. K. Prahalad, who profiled several such grassroots efforts in his influential book *The Fortune at the Bottom of the Pyramid*. Other pioneers are purely altruistic—they want to break India's millennia-long curse of poverty.

It's an awesome curse, and at first look, it's hard to see how digital technology cooked up by some entrepreneurial do-gooders can relieve hunger or thirst or guarantee a better crop. No laptop, however cheap or durable, can compensate for India's lack of a nationwide power grid, or a comprehensive network of highways. But digital technology can deliver information—information the rural poor desperately need—about crop conditions, fertilizer prices, health care, and more. Reliable information can help India's poor stretch their resources—to plant the right crops, deal with bureaucrats more effectively, and operate on a level playing field with customers and merchants. The digital revolution in India is largely an information revolution.

Computer kiosks are at the center of all this. These are typically in the front room of an entrepreneur's home, with one or two PCs linked to the Internet via a satellite, phone, or wireless link. The country already has some 7,000 such kiosks, and more than 100 new ones pop up each week. By 2007 there could be as many as 300,000, estimates NASSCOM. The giant Indian Tobacco Co. has taken the lead in this movement: The company has funded more than 4,000 kiosks so far, giving them to farmers in a bid to boost sales of everything from seeds to soap via its Web site, e-Choupal. But new players are emerging, offering eager entrepreneurs a chance to open kiosks as a business. N-Logue Communications, for instance, has adopted something of a franchise model. The company arranges a low-interest loan of $1,000 to buy a computer and install a wireless link to the Internet. Then it teaches the kiosk owner its possibilities: Net-based education, computer training for local children, videoconferencing, photo work, and more.

These kiosks often become the hub of village activity. Take the one operated by Mahesh Patel, a soybean and cotton farmer from Korgala, a speck of a village in the central state of Madhya Pradesh. Although the only place Patel had ever seen a computer was in Bollywood blockbusters screened at the cinema in a nearby town, he jumped at the chance when Indian Tobacco offered him the Korgala kiosk in 2001. Since he gets a small cut of every sale ITC makes via his computer, Patel's monthly income has jumped to $380 from $220 before he got the kiosk. His three-room home is now often crowded with villagers: Early in the morning, Patel and fellow farmers gather to check soy oil prices in Kuala Lumpur and Chicago via the machine's satellite Internet connection before looking into the going rate on local markets. In the afternoon, village children hone their computer skills on the machine. And since the e-Choupal site offers all kinds of goods for sale, Patel's house has become a virtual village store. "I'm just a farmer, but I get a lot of respect in my village now," he says.

Today, entrepreneurs in India are looking to capitalize on the kiosk boom. Many are working on projects that could make kiosks more useful to villagers, or extend their reach to more isolated locales. "India is no longer just a laboratory for these experiments," says Allen Hammond, vice-president for innovation at the World Resources Institute in Washington. "It's out of the pilot stage and ready to scale up."

Some believe kiosks can help ordinary Indians get better access to health care. Already, a handful of rural clinics has satellite video and data links to city hospitals. But Sameer Sawarkar believes the kiosks can serve as part-time clinics as well. The 31-year-old engineering grad from the Indian Institute of Science in Bangalore remembered the lack of medical care in his home village. So in 2002 the former Motorola Inc. researcher joined some friends to develop a portable $200 diagnostic kit the size of a boombox that can check blood pressure, temperature, and pulse; take an electrocardiogram; and work as an electronic stethoscope. The machine can be plugged into kiosk computers to transfer diagnostic information to a city hospital. Sawarkar now has a deal with N-Logue to install them in some of its locations.

## Handhelds and Wi-Fi

Others believe that handheld computers offer a way to extend the benefits of technology beyond the reach of typical desktops, or even laptops. Microsoft, for instance, is exploring the possibility of a $150 handheld device for the Bhoomi land records program, and the government of Andhra Pradesh has bought palmtops from Casio for school officials to keep attendance records. A high-profile Indian initiative is the Simputer, a simple, robust handheld computer that even illiterate farmers can use to pay bills, send e-mail, and keep records of their businesses using symbols or any of the 17 official Indian languages. It even has education programs in five languages and can turn text into speech. The device was developed under a public license not unlike the Linux operating system it uses. The professors at Bangalore's Indian Institute of Science who came up with the idea have posted the machine's plans on the Internet for anyone to use and charge only $25,000 for a manufacturing license in India. One company, Bangalore-based Pico Peta, is selling the machines for $200 to $450. Simputers haven't exactly been jumping off the shelves. Since 2002, the Karnataka government has given Simputers to 200 village accountants and farmers to maintain its Bhoomi land record program. About 25 governments around the world have shown interest in the machines, and inside India Pico Peta has sold 200 more in a four-month period. But the promoters are optimistic, keeping their eye on a potential order for 9,000 more handhelds from the Karnataka government, as well as the possibility of sales to other Indian states that are computerizing their land records. "When we developed the Simputer, our aim was to bridge the digital divide," says Vinay Deshpande, a co-creator of the device. "Other [Western] companies did it for commercial purposes."

Anurag Gupta, meanwhile, has developed a payment card that can plug into either a handheld or a kiosk—and make it easier for the poor to establish a credit history. It can be tough for many Indians to get loans because they use cash to buy virtually everything, and few have bank accounts. Under Gupta's plan, poor Indians could establish a bank account linked to the card, which contains a smart chip with personal information. Gupta hopes to install card readers in public phone booths and distribute the readers to kiosk owners, who would accept the card as a form of payment for computer time. Cardholders could also use it to pay bills or buy goods online. Banks could then monitor the user's spending patterns and decide whether he or she is a good credit risk. Gupta, a slight, intense man who studied architecture, has been working on the idea since 2000. It finally launched commercially under the name "Zero" in 2004 in Andhra Pradesh with the backing of ICICI Bank. Says Gupta: "It's been a long slog, but we've finally got the support that'll bring success."

At the same time, Praveen Bhagwat wants to extend the reach of kiosks with Wi-Fi. Bhagwat, a former wireless researcher for IBM and Bell Laboratories in the U.S., returned to his native India to adapt the wireless standard for rural use. By rewriting some software and redesigning antennae, he made a system that could send signals some 23 kilometers rather than the 100 meters typical for standard

Wi-Fi—meaning that it could provide Internet and phone service to several adjoining villages or a large town. "It's just not economic for large companies to do this. They wouldn't make any money on it," says 35-year-old Bhagwat. "We have to do it for ourselves."

Unfortunately, innovators often spend more time struggling against India's bureaucracy than they do coming up with products. Bhagwat, for instance, needed just a month to create his first Wi-Fi system. But then it took nine months to get permission to build six 12-meter towers between the city of Kanpur and neighboring Lucknow. And P. G. Ponappa, N-Logue's chief executive, says getting permission to put government services such as income and birth certificates online routinely takes a year. The government's "intentions are good, but they're just too slow," he says.

Can these projects transform India? Not by themselves. But if, bit by bit, they can make India's poor a little healthier, a little richer, and a little more literate, the cumulative effect on the country's fortunes could be enormous. The poor are eager for a wave of digital change. Young people across the country—even in many villages—are familiar with computers and keen to learn how to use them. These days, education and computers are primary items in every rural family's budget. In the poor, dusty village of Shahpur in Uttar Pradesh, for instance, impoverished farmers save their rupees to send their children to school in the neighboring town of Barabanki. There they can study English and computers, which are considered key to prosperity. Among India's poor, there's no shortage of ambition to learn them both. And no shortage of ideas on how to harness technology to give the poor a fighting chance to improve themselves.

## The Great Wail of China

Mrs. Wang, a 51-year-old native of the small city of Houma, in the province of Shanxi, retired last year after more than two decades of teaching in the country's primary schools. Although her former employer, the No. 5 Bureau of the Railways Ministry, pays her a pension of $60 a month, she's far from happy. Her pension is based on 14 years of employment, not the 24 years she actually worked, because she doesn't have documents from a previous teaching job. The money is barely enough to pay for food, never mind medicines for the occasional cold or other illness. "I'm not satisfied," says Wang, who declined to give her full name.

Wang's pension predicament is just one example of the tremendous challenges facing a rapidly aging but still relatively poor China. The one-child policy, which prohibits most families from having more than one child, is one of the main causes of the problem. Many Chinese families today face what is popularly known as the "4-2-1 phenomenon." That is, four grandparents and two parents, both from single-child families, must be supported by a single child. Already about 14% of the mainland's population is over 60—a percentage that will grow to about a quarter in 25 years, saddling China with the world's oldest population.

The peak of the crisis will come in 2030, when the number of workers per each retiree will fall to two, down from three today. That's a worrying prospect in a country where per capita income is just $1,000 a year. Most other countries have reached comparable levels of aging with average incomes three times that, says He Ping, director of the National Institute of Social Insurance in Beijing. "China is still not a rich country even as our population ages. This is a serious problem," says He.

The Chinese government isn't sitting still. In 2000 it began to reform its pay-as-you-go pension system, which covered primarily civil servants and state-enterprise workers, in favor of what it hopes will be a more sustainable program of individual accounts. But only 20% of all workers are now covered, and that's primarily those in the cities. And there isn't enough money. The national pension system has a shortfall of $6.2 billion, which could reach $53.3 billion by 2033, according to the Asian Development Bank. Most provincial pension plans are also in deficit.

China's increasingly mobile population further exacerbates the problem. An estimated 100 million migrant workers are unable to tap their pension funds when they transfer to new jobs. China must move to a system of portable pensions, says Social Insurance Institute's He, who is advising the Labor & Social Security Ministry on this. Other analysts suggest that national pensions—now funded by contributions from employers, employees, and the Finance Ministry, and by proceeds from a national lottery—be allowed to invest in a larger pool of assets, including overseas stocks and local infrastructure companies. Most of the money is currently tied up in Treasury bonds and low-yield bank deposits.

More radical moves are under consideration. China is likely to boost gradually the retirement age, now 55 for women and 60 for men, to 65 by 2030. And it might further loosen the one-child policy. Meanwhile, even those with two children, like Ms. Wang, are still worried about their future. Both her children work at the same No. 5 Bureau of the Railways Ministry where she and many other family members toiled. But the ailing employer is several months behind in paying salaries, she reports. "I'm considering finding another job," says Wang. "I might work as a cook for construction workers, but I know that will be very tiring," she says. For now, too many of China's wannabe retirees may have to labor on into their golden years.

10

# The Ecological and Energy Challenge

RAPID INDUSTRIALIZATION IS MAKING CHINA AND India the fastest-growing consumers of energy and minerals. As a result, both nations now are competing against developed nations in the chase for access to the world's resources. But industrialization also is coming at enormous environmental cost in India and China. Already, air and water pollution prematurely take the lives of millions each year in both nations. Meanwhile, forests are disappearing fast and fresh water supplies are drying up. As industry, personal automobile use, and the population continue to expand in the coming decades, the ecological fallout will affect the entire planet if leaders do not act to adopt greener technologies and practices.

India has serious environmental challenges, but the most urgent problems now are in China because of its heavy-industry emphasis, inefficient energy use, and lax enforcement of environmental regulations. "A Big, Dirty Growth Engine" and "The Greening of China" lay out the harrowing extent of China's environmental crisis and the government's belated efforts to impose tougher regulations on industry.

Many promising efforts to make use of cleaner energy are under way in China, however, and could point to important future opportunities for foreign investors. "A Big Green Opportunity in China" profiles French company Veolia Environment that has invested $800 million in

10 water-treatment projects and power-generation plants fueled with methane gas from solid waste. "Winds of Change in Inner Mongolia" looks at a promising windfarm project. "A Courageous Voice for a Greener China" profiles Pan Yue, a rare government official who has been a leading crusader for environmental protection.

Nevertheless, the need for fossil fuels will continue to expand dramatically in both nations. "Asia's Great Oil Hunt" argues that China's quest to secure oil and gas to fuel its economy is destined to change prices and resource supplies worldwide. "How a Thirst for Energy Led to a Thaw" explains how a recent pipeline deal with Pakistan is part of India's own aggressive new push to obtain foreign resource reserves.

---

# A Big, Dirty Growth Engine

*Pollution still chokes China, but green technology is starting to emerge*

The 2008 Beijing Olympics don't look like much today. At most of the sites around the city, ground has barely been broken. But look a little closer and you'll find that the games have already had a dramatic impact in the form of a thorough pollution cleanup.

China's leadership knows the Olympics may define the country's international image for decades. So officials have spared nothing in their efforts to show how green they can be. On clear days it's now possible to look down Changan Avenue and see the peaks of the Western Hills, which had been obscured for years. Most homes and businesses have converted from coal heat to natural gas, many diesel-belching tractors and trucks have been banned from city streets, and 58% of sewage is treated. Beijing has moved nearly 130 factories out of the city and is building cleaner, gas-fueled power stations while installing scrubbers in older ones. It's even putting up wind turbines to help power the Olympic village. When the games start two years from now, the city and its residents will have spent $13 billion on the transformation. By the time the Olympic torch is passed, a sparkling Beijing may well wow the world.

And the world will be misled. The reality is that despite all the effort spent on cleaning up the capital and a handful of other big cities, China is at best at a standstill in its fight against environmental degradation. For all its efforts, China's unrestrained growth makes it one of the world's worst polluters. Most of the nation is still reeling from the devastation wrought by three decades of communist industrial development and the subsequent 25 years of quasi-capitalism. In 2025, China will consume 14.2% of the world's energy, compared with 9.8% in 2001. Because most of China's electricity comes from power plants that burn high-sulphur coal but lack effective emissions controls, acid rain falls on one-third of the country. And 70% of its lakes and rivers are heavily polluted, largely because more than 80% of China's sewage flows untreated into waterways. Six of the world's 10 most-polluted cities are in China, according to the World Bank, which estimates that pollution costs China more than $54 billion a year in environmental damage and health problems.

China's soaring energy use and resulting pollution are a serious threat to the country's continued prosperity and growth, not to mention the well-being of its citizens. China has spent more than $85 billion on environmental cleanup since 2000 and could shell out $380 billion—4% of gross domestic product—between now and 2010. But even those outlays aren't enough to offset the pollution generated by the country's annual growth rate of more than 8%. The problems are compounded by China's inefficient use of electricity, oil, and coal. China consumes nearly five times as much energy as the U.S. to produce each dollar of GDP—and almost 12 times as much as Japan. Alarmingly, the nation is getting less efficient, not more. After making steady progress in energy efficiency for two decades, China has been consuming energy at a rate faster than its GDP growth since 2002.

## Painfully Understaffed

In most of the country, enforcement of environmental regulations is lax. The State Environmental Protection Administration (SEPA), which oversees the environment nationally, is woefully understaffed, with a workforce of just 300 in Beijing and only 100 more for the rest of the country. That means monitoring and enforcement generally fall to local officials, or even factory managers—whose first priority is to create jobs, whatever the environmental cost. A chromium factory was ordered to close in May 2004, after dumping toxins into a river for five years. But just two months later the local environmental protection bureau let the plant begin producing again even though no new environmental protection measures had been installed, the state-controlled *China Youth Daily* reported. "The environmental bureaus of local governments would rather develop GDP than perform their role" as pollution watchdog, says Zhao Jian Ping, senior energy specialist at the World Bank in Beijing.

What's more, even where waste-treatment gear is installed, some Chinese companies opt to pay fines rather than operate expensive equipment. The cost of cleaning up wastewater from a yeast plant can reach $610 per 1,000 cubic meters, while the penalties are just $490 per 1,000 cubic meters. Furthermore, noncompliance is preferred by local officials, since fines shore up budgets. SEPA says that while most major industrial plants have water-treatment facilities, one-third don't operate them at all and another third only use them occasionally.

## Cheap and Sooty

Coal may be the biggest culprit. China has tens of thousands of small mines that pay scant attention to environmental concerns or safety. Such neglect helps keep costs down, making coal the preferred source of energy. Even though the price of Chinese coal has jumped 29% from 2002 to 2005, that's far below the 79% increase globally. So coal-based electricity generation costs a fraction of alternative energy sources. In Inner Mongolia, for example, wind power costs about 6 cents per kilowatt hour, more than twice the price of coal power.

The good news is that plenty of companies selling green technology are sensing an opportunity in China. Chinese enterprises are buying everything from scrubbers for coal-fired power plants to alternative power sources such as wind turbines and methane gas from decomposing solid waste. China will invest $61 billion in city wastewater treatment facilities between now and 2010. Scrubber sales could reach $1 billion a year. "China is at a crossroads, shifting from a focus on buildup of capacity to more environment-friendly and energy-conserving technologies," says Steven Fludder, chief executive of GE Power China, which has sold more than $1 billion worth of natural gas and wind turbines to the country since 2003.

GE isn't the only foreigner helping out. Some 400 non-Chinese companies now sell pollution-control equipment in the country. A joint venture between Westport Innovations of Vancouver, B.C., and Cummins Inc. has equipped more than 2,500 buses in Beijing with engines powered by natural gas at a total cost of $26 million. Veolia Environment of France has invested $800 million in 10 water-treatment projects—some under contracts that stretch to 20 and 50 years and offer a 12% rate of return—and two facilities that generate power with methane gas released from solid waste. Sweden's Purac Environmental System has sold equipment to dozens of companies in China. Its biggest customer, state-owned Huatai Paper in Shandong Province, has spent nearly $7 million to clean up effluent that looked like "thick, cloudy Guinness beer" flowing into the river, says Purac China chief Lennart Huss.

Those foreigners are facing increased local competition. Beijing Monitor Environment Technology Co. sold $3.1 million in emissions-monitoring equipment in 2004 to power and petrochemical plants. Beijing-based Golden State Environment Corp. had sales of $60 million that same year and has worked on more than 2,000 water-treatment plants and landfills in some 250 cities. And Anhui Guozhen Environmental Protection Science & Technology Co. says it has won five contracts worth $13 million annually to build and operate water-treatment plants for cities around the country.

One promising development occurred on Feb. 1, 2005, when the Kyoto Protocol on greenhouse gases took effect. The accord allows companies in developed countries to purchase gas emission "credits" from enterprises in developing nations. Effectively, corporations in Japan and the West buy the right to keep emitting carbon dioxide pollution. But under the terms of the protocol, the companies that sell their emission credits then have to reduce their pollution levels, the cost of which is presumably covered by the proceeds of the trade.

Such deals in essence subsidize the sale of pollution-control equipment in the developing world, where it's often cheaper to make bigger gains in emissions reduction. Three Chinese projects are benefiting from the trade in credits: a windfarm on the grasslands of Inner Mongolia, a power station fueled by methane released during coal mining in Shanxi Province, and a power-generation project using methane produced by solid waste in Anding, south of Beijing. "This is the beginning of a market that has vast potential," says Andres Liebenthal, head of environment and social development for China at the World Bank's Beijing office. Clean air is a commodity China desperately needs.

---

# The Greening of China

*As the economy has grown, so have waste and pollution. But there's big money in repairing the environment.*

By rights, the city of Xining ought to be a pretty nice place to live. A remote provincial capital of 22 million people, it's perched 2,275 meters up, right on the edge of the Qinghai-Tibet Plateau. It's flanked by the 4,000-meter-plus peaks of the Daban Mountains and sits astride the Huangshui River, coursing down from the plateau. But Xining is hardly an alpine idyll. In fact, it often looks more like an industrial nightmare. Thick smoke pouring from its 10 smelters blocks the view of the mountains, while the city's five chemical plants have long fouled the river with their waste. Outside the city, loggers have denuded the mountain slopes of their thick forests, and millions of sheep, goats, and yaks have left lush pastures rutted and barren. As if that weren't enough, the deforestation and overgrazing have rendered thousands of square kilometers of once-fertile grassland parched and unproductive.

China has won lots of praise lately for high-visibility cleanup campaigns in showcase cities such as Beijing and Shanghai. But much of the rest of the country is paying the price of rapid economic expansion. From Xining through the farmland of Hubei Province and on to the northeastern Rust Belt, much of China is an environmental disaster. More than half of China's main waterways have excessive levels of chemical and biological pollutants. And one recent survey found that nearly a third of China's largest cities have air that's barely fit to breathe. That has given China the world's highest rate of chronic respiratory disease, with a mortality rate five times that of the U.S. "It is very clear that, with pollution, China still faces very critical challenges," says Jostein Nygard, a China specialist at the World Bank.

This is plenty distressing for those who have to drink China's water and breathe its air, of course, but it's also quite simply bad for business. At some point, pollution is going to get in the way of China's ultrafast development. Factories—especially high-tech ones—need clean water to aid manufacturing, and farmers need fresh water for their fields. Workers who suffer chronic lung infections are less productive than healthy ones. Children with high levels of lead in their blood or nagging intestinal ailments can't study and learn. Inefficient factories waste precious energy and water. Deforestation and overgrazing destroy productive land, while acid rain damages crops. Economists estimate that the financial toll on China from the constant bombardment of environmental insults ranges as high as 7% of gross domestic product every year.

In short, China cannot afford to stand by and watch its environment collapse. That's why the mainland's Communist leaders have taken their cleanup effort beyond the biggest cities. The government spent $85 billion in a two-year period on environmental protection across the vast nation. Of that, some $68 billion went to major projects such as installing scrubbers on more than 50 large coal-fired power plants, building hundreds of sewage-treatment facilities, and putting emissions monitors on industry smokestacks. An additional $11 billion funded construction of scores of hazardous-waste treatment and disposal plants. Much of the remainder was spent to plant trees on deforested land and to enforce new regulations.

## Olympic Incentive

But while the cleanup campaign across China is serious, Beijing will continue to be the star. One big reason: To win its bid to host the Olympics in 2008, the capital had to promise huge improvements in air and water quality. The city plans to build new sewage-treatment plants, convert furnaces to gas, and introduce strict new limits on vehicle emissions. "It puts heavy pressure on us, but we will try our hardest to achieve our targets," says Pei Chenghu, deputy director of the Beijing Municipal Bureau of Environmental Protection, which has pledged to spend 4% of the city's gross domestic product—some $1.5 billion annually—on environmental protection.

All that money means lots of potential profits for companies that can help in the cleanup. Already, pollution fighting in China has become a $20 billion annual industry, and it's growing by roughly 20% a year, according to the China Association of Environmental Protection Industry, a Beijing trade group and consulting firm. Companies from around the world are rushing in to sell China smokestack scrubbers that cut emissions from power plants, build sewage-treatment and water-purification facilities, and clean up the country's gritty cement factories. "The next several years will be a golden era for environmental protection in China," predicts Li Baojuan, deputy director of the industry association.

One area that's seeing plenty of investment is water. In 1998, Britain's Thames Water PLC sank $23 million into China's first privately funded water-treatment project. Today, that facility provides clean water to 2 million residents of the Dachang district of Shanghai. In 2002, Thames spent $70 million to buy a 49% stake in China Water Co., which treats drinking and wastewater in seven Chinese cities. "China has the potential to become one of the top countries we work in," says Kyeong Choi, China country director for Thames Water. "I don't think any serious player could afford to ignore this opportunity." Another crucial part of China's cleanup is a drastic reduction in coal consumption. Most houses in the country are heated by coal, and this fuel powers most of China's industrial and energy infrastructure. The preferred substitute is clean-burning natural gas, and the switch can yield dramatic results. By 2003, Beijing finished refitting more than 40,000 small boilers and 10,000 large coal boilers with gas systems in the capital city's four central districts. The plan is to convert all eight districts of Beijing as well as the city's four suburban areas entirely to gas before the Olympics start in 2008. The shift has already doubled the capital's annual clear days. "You wouldn't have thought Beijing had any mountains around it before," says the World Bank's Nygard.

But for now, there isn't enough affordable gas to come even close to meeting China's needs. That's why PetroChina Co. is negotiating with international oil giants Royal Dutch/Shell Group, ExxonMobil, and Russia's Gazprom to develop gas fields jointly in China's west. If the companies can reach a deal, the foreigners will join PetroChina in building and operating a 4,200-kilometer pipeline to deliver the gas from the Xinjiang region to Shanghai.

Plenty of corporations are already profiting from China's big cleanup. Energy-hungry fertilizer plants are licensing Shell technology for turning coal into gas. Indiana-based Cummins Inc. has invested $140 million in factories making low-emission diesel engines for bulldozers, excavators, and buses. Nearly a dozen cities in China have bought machines that monitor auto emissions from Mustang Dynamometer of Twinsburg, Ohio. "Companies are becoming more and more conscious of the importance of the environmental protection industry in China," says Huang Jianghua, Mustang's chief representative in the country.

The government is also doing its part, even in far-flung places such as Xining. There, officials in 2002 launched a project they call "blue sky, clean water, quiet environment." The city spent $31 million to convert 357 boilers used in heating apartment and office buildings from coal to natural gas. And in 2001, the city invested $20 million in a wastewater treatment plant, so that the Huangshui River is now running cleaner.

To keep automobile fumes in check, scores of emissions-testing centers have been set up across Beijing and in other large cities. Since 2004, cars in the capital are required to meet the tough emissions standards in place in the European Union. And since 1999, Beijing has deployed more than 1,900 buses running on compressed natural gas, the largest such fleet in the world. By 2008, the city hopes to have 18,000 electric and natural gas–powered buses on the streets.

New laws and regulations are helping too. "There has been an enormous amount of environmental legislation passed in China," says Husayn A. Anwar, managing director of Sinosphere Corp., a Beijing environmental consultancy. Leaded gasoline is now banned in Beijing, Shanghai, Guangzhou, and Chengdu. A 2003 clean production law requires polluting companies to report on their emissions and recycle some products. This measure also grants preferential loans and tax exemptions to clean producers. And a law requiring that all infrastructure projects include an assessment of environmental impact also went into effect in 2003.

## Weak Environmental Cops

All those laws, though, won't do anything if they can't be enforced. The ministries of Construction, Land & Resources and Agriculture regularly overrule the less-powerful State Environmental Protection Administration when projects are slowed by land use and emissions regulations. Even though the laws outline sweeping goals for the cleanup of air and water, penalties for polluters often amount to slaps on the wrist. Furthermore, laws are often vaguely worded and difficult to implement. "Even the enforcement agencies often aren't sure how to apply legislation," says Anwar.

There's a bigger problem related to the growing chasm between rich and poor China. Factories facing burdensome regulations in wealthy regions often pick up and move to poorer areas, where authorities are more concerned about jobs and tax revenues than they are about the environment. For example, faced with stiff new local antipollution laws, paper and chemical plants in the rich coastal province of Jiangsu have shifted their manufacturing to landlocked Jiangxi in recent years. "It's one thing to have regulations, but another to enforce them," says Bruce Murray, the Asian Development Bank's representative in China.

Worse, for every step forward, China often seems to be taking two steps back. Even as pollution in big state-controlled factories is beginning to be addressed, smaller, less easily regulated private enterprises are causing environmental headaches. That includes everything from unregulated coal mines spread across the mainland to paper mills and dye plants along the flood-prone Huai River in Anhui Province. In addition, China's farmers are using ever more pesticides and fertilizers on their fields. The runoff from these toxins—as well as untreated sewage—too often leaches into drinking water.

And as consumers get richer, they pollute more. There is more auto traffic and car exhaust, more trash from the purchase of consumer goods, more sewage from rapidly growing cities. As a result, there has been an explosion of toxic waste from the factories proliferating in the Pearl River Delta and elsewhere.

But, as in much of the rest of the world, the rise in living standards is also leading to calls among members of the new middle class for greater attention to the environment. Newspapers are writing about the problem more often, and independent environmental groups are springing up. As Beijing's leaders try to balance the needs of development with the imperative to clean up, it may well be the citizens who lead the way.

---

# Winds of Change in Inner Mongolia

*The windfarm at Huitengxile can't compete with coal-fired generators, but a global market in emission rights could change that*

In many ways, the landscape of the barren steppes of Inner Mongolia hasn't changed much since the days when Genghis Khan and his warriors set off to plunder most of the known world. Nomads still herd their sheep on horseback and flocks of wild horses graze the vast rolling grasslands. But in recent years, several windfarms have sprung up on the gusty hills of this northeastern province, with hundreds of turbines toiling in the wind dotting the horizon.

At the Huitengxile windfarm, located 90 minutes east of the Inner Mongolian capital of Hohhot, 98 wind turbines, some as high as 65 meters, tower over the landscape. Their 20-meter-long blades make a gentle "whop whop" sound as they slice through the air against an azure sky dotted with puffy white clouds.

## Tourist Attraction

The elegant towers look distinctly futuristic in contrast with the squat cylindrical cement white *gers* (or yurts), the modern equivalent of the traditional felt tents still used by the nomads.

Dong Shao, 67, who raises horses and grows barley, looks on at the windfarm with bemusement. "It's better looking than before. All we had was cows and horses," he says, his two silver teeth glinting in the afternoon sun. The windfarm has also meant a better life for him in his nearby village, Chao Duo Shan. Now he can make $1.25 an hour leading tourists on horseback. Yes, they come to see the windmills in action.

During a 2005 visit, there were no tourists to be found, but there were plenty of locals like Chao with horses for rent. Although they've had electricity since 1972, the first TVs only came to the district in 1997 and refrigerators in 2002. But the wind turbines have made the locals more aware of something they still don't have. "There's no water pollution, no air pollution," says Dong, pointing to the intensely blue sky.

## Coal Is King

Run by state-owned power company Long Yuan Wind Power Development Company, the windfarm operates turbines made by GE Power, Micron of Denmark, and even one made by a local company.

The farm has a capacity of 68 megawatts, and there are plans to invest in an additional 163 megawatts by 2010.

That capacity doesn't come cheap, however. For example, a 1.5 megawatt turbine costs about $60,000, and after adding the cost of cables and power lines hooked up to the grid, the cost is upward of $100,000.

But conversion to cleaner power is complicated by the low cost of coal in China. In Inner Mongolia, for example, wind-produced power costs about six cents per kilowatt hour, more than twice that of conventional coal power. More than two-thirds of China's energy needs are met by coal, oil 25%, hydro 4% to 5%, and natural gas 3%.

## "Huge" Potential

Although the government has ambitious targets to increase its usage of renewable energy sources and cleaner burning fuels, it will remain dependent on dirty coal for many years to come. "Whatever you do in the next 15 years, coal will be the primary source of energy," says Zhao Jian Ping, senior energy specialist in Beijing at the World Bank.

"So that's why we are saying we have no objection to develop other energies," says Ping, "but we still need a major effort to improve the efficiency and environmental performance of coal, where the potential for improvement is huge."

But thanks to the Kyoto Protocol on carbon emissions reduction, renewable energy projects like Huitengxile can still be economical. The accord allows developed countries to purchase greenhouse gas–emission reduction credits from less developed countries, thereby subsidizing them to engage in greener technologies.

## More to Come

For example, Chinese companies will receive $4 to $5 per ton of $CO_2$ reduction, enough to encourage green investments that would otherwise be uneconomical.

And as the second-largest producer of greenhouse gases in the world after the U.S. (which did not sign the Kyoto Accord), China could reap huge benefits from the trade in emission rights. "This is the beginning of a market that has vast potential," says Andreas Leibenthal, head of Environment & Social Development for China at the World Bank in Beijing. That could mean that Inner Mongolians like Dong can expect to see a lot more wind turbines.

---

# A Big Green Opportunity in China

*Where some see pollution, Veolia's Jorge Mora sees $800 million worth of environmental projects, with lots more to come*

Jorge Mora, chief executive officer of Veolia Environment China, has been working in the Middle Kingdom for 10 years. The French company has invested $800 million in 10 water-treatment projects and two facilities that generate power with methane gas released from solid waste.

He spoke to *BusinessWeek*'s Asia correspondent, Frederik Balfour, about China's commitment to clean up its environment and the business opportunities the effort provides. Edited excerpts of their conversation follow:

**Q: Some foreign businesses have told me it's difficult to crack the environmental market in China. What do you think?**
**A:** I don't agree it's difficult to do business here. What is difficult is to get a clear understanding of the Chinese culture.

**Q: How much potential does the China market have for Veolia?**
**A:** It's more than potential—it's already a [real market] for us. When it comes to the environment, I must say that the [local] governments and central government have a very good understanding now about the difficulties China will face in the future without a proper environment assessment.

We see a lot of real opportunities for our business, whether it's water, energy, public transportation, or waste treatment. China probably offers more opportunities than any other country or region in the world because it's very much polluted and because of its high population.

**Q: What model of investment do you prefer in China?**
**A:** Build-operate-and-transfer [BOT] projects consume a lot of capital. We have to find financial partners to share the risk. The guarantee may be from Veolia or the project itself. The banks decide on the merits of the project. We don't necessarily incur a big debt, because we find partners who will take the financing risk. We are mainly the operators, designers, and builders, not the financial investors.

**Q: How much of your business is tied to soft loans to China?**
**A:** Very little, not enough, although the World Bank is helping us on a big project in China, on the Carbon Distribution Mechanism scheme [under the Kyoto Protocol for emissions trading]. We believe we have a real future here and could be very helpful setting up some projects in some cities that are not rich enough [to purchase green technologies].

One project in which the World Bank is very involved is the Laogan project in Guangdong Province, where we process 6,000 tons of waste daily, including energy recovery. This is a whole concept of landfill, treating fields by leach, and energy recovery.

**Q: How much energy can be recovered from solid waste?**
**A:** About 150 cubic meters of gas [released by decomposing waste] would generate 160 kilowatts of electricity. And 200 acres can produce about 140,000 cubic meters of gas. But of course we can't, say, produce enough energy for a city from waste. But still we're protecting the environment.

**Q: How much competition do you face from local companies?**
**A:** We are competing with local companies in all sectors, though we have no real presence in energy and public transportation divisions yet. We have

a lot of local competitors in the water and waste cleanup markets. But it's not yet very well organized, not like in other industries.

There are lots of newcomers who don't really know the industry but were told there was opportunity here. They're not as prepared as we and the rest of the Western companies are.

**Q: Is there demand for your services in second-tier cities?**
**A:** It's starting, but we must be very creative if we want to help them build up good environmental facilities. We have already invested in them but haven't seen revenues yet.

**Q: How much have you invested in China?**
**A:** About $800 million in the past 10 years, and our managed revenue [not consolidated revenue] was $400 million in 2005. We're expecting growth of 20% to 25% per year.

**Q: What kind of returns can you expect in China?**
**A:** A good internal rate of return is around 12%, so we expect to get that in China as we do in the U.S. and Europe and other parts of the world.

**Q: What share of your business will come from governments, versus the private sector?**
**A:** In the future, our share of the market will be balanced between local governments and the industrial sector, whether it's foreign direct investment or locally invested.

---

# A Courageous Voice for a Greener China

*Pan Yue, Vice-Minister, State Environmental Protection Administration, China*

It is perhaps the greatest challenge facing China: the runaway environmental degradation that is poisoning the country's skies, leveling its forests, and fouling its rivers. And until recently, there were few strong voices advocating a clean, green China, especially among Beijing's pro-growth, damn-the-consequences bureaucrats. But over the past few years one government official has stood up to the polluters. He is 45-year-old Pan Yue, vice-minister of the State Environmental Protection Administration (SEPA). Pan has taken on some of China's biggest industries because of their pollution records and forced them to clean up.

Early in 2005, Pan surprised much of China when he ordered 30 projects—with $14 billion in investment, ranging from thermal power to hydroelectric plants—shut down for not filing proper environmental-impact statements. The projects included several under construction by Three Gorges Development Corp., the politically powerful company that is building the controversial Three Gorges Dam. At the same time, SEPA publicly scolded 46 power plants for not installing required desulphurization equipment; some have since complied. Meanwhile, Pan has called for public hearings so that citizens affected by big development projects can discuss their environmental consequences—an unusual level of openness in China. And to take into account the negative impact of environmental damage when calculating China's gross domestic product, Pan has advocated the adoption of a "green GDP."

Born in Jiangsu Province, outside Shanghai, Pan is the son of a military engineer. He worked as a journalist for years before becoming a government official—and he has long been known for sticking his neck out. Several years ago Pan published an essay questioning the future of the Communist Party if it failed to reform. He acknowledges that his crusade for a greener China will attract opposition from powerful economic and political interests. Indeed, most of the 30 projects he targeted have since resumed construction after paying small fines.

But Pan can take credit for igniting an important national debate on whether China is sacrificing its environment to its runaway growth. At an environmental conference in Beijing in June 2005, he publicly questioned whether China should be proud of its reputation as the world's factory and called for a "green rise" of more environmental activism.

"The pollution load of China will quadruple by 2020, when the country's GDP quadruples, if the pace of pollution remains unchanged," he warned at the conference.

Pan's may be a lone voice in the wilderness, but his message is one that other Chinese officials would do well to heed before it's too late.

---

# Asia's Great Oil Hunt

*China needs energy more than ever. Its quest to secure enough oil and gas to keep its economy humming will change the world.*

For a sense of just how vast China's energy needs are, take in the night views from the observation deck of Shanghai's Oriental Pearl Tower. From that perch 263 meters above the city's streets, you'll see a spaghetti jumble of bright neon illuminating the colonial-era buildings of the waterfront Bund and the swarms of shoppers on Nanjing Road. Closer at hand, the shiny skyscrapers of Pudong are lit into the night. Across the city, long lines of trucks, buses, and cars clog narrow lanes, broad boulevards, and new elevated expressways. And farther afield, the smokestacks of Shanghai Baosteel Group belch smoke from the tons of coal the forges consume daily, while oil tankers in the harbor unload yet more fuel to keep the city of 20 million humming.

As China's economy expands, so does its thirst for oil, gas, coal, and electricity. In 2004, China accounted for 12.1% of the world's energy consumption. That's second only to the U.S., at 24%, and up from 9% a decade ago. China's whole modernization strategy is based on access to abundant supplies of energy. Its hungry basic industries such as steel, aluminum, and chemicals devour electricity and coal. A mushrooming middle class consumes growing quantities of heating oil and gasoline. By 2010 analysts expect some 56 million cars, minivans, and sport-utility vehicles to be rolling on China's highways—more than twice the number today. By 2020 the country's demand for oil will nearly double, to 11 million barrels a day, natural gas consumption will more than triple, to 3.6 trillion cubic feet annually, and coal use will grow by 76%, to 2.4 billion tons a year, according to a U.S. Energy Dept. forecast.

That means China will play a key role in influencing global oil prices and energy investment flows—not to mention climate-destabilizing carbon dioxide emissions. "There is going to be a huge increase in consumption across the region, and especially in China," says Edu Hassing, an energy analyst at the Asian Development Bank.

With China consuming ever more oil, it risks developing an ever-greater dependency on foreign vendors of crude. For the security-obsessed Chinese, that's pretty scary. Right now, though, it's hard to see how the Chinese will avoid the same fate as the U.S., which is uncomfortably dependent on oil states such as Nigeria, Saudi Arabia, and Venezuela. Just a decade ago, China was a net exporter of oil, but now it imports 40% of its crude as output declines at the big northeastern fields near Daqing and Liaohe. What about developing new sources at home? China is sitting on potentially rich reserves in the high, dry deserts of the far west, but gas and oil there lie much deeper than in the northeast and will cost far more to get out of the ground. And given the country's primitive pipeline and transportation networks, moving it to the coastal cities that need it will be a challenge.

## Colossal Waste

Meanwhile, China's power supply and grid haven't kept pace with demand, compounding the problems created by rising dependency on foreign oil. While power shortages and rationing have been common during recent summers, for the first time ever nine provinces in China expect outages during winters. "Energy could be an Achilles' heel of the government," says Scott Roberts, director of the China operations of Cambridge Energy Research Associates in Beijing. Adding to the burden—and increasing the need for oil—is a colossal amount of energy waste, thanks to primitive coal-mining techniques, loose building construction codes, and inefficient factories. "The Chinese spend three times as much as the world average on energy to produce $1 of gross domestic product," says Wenran Jiang, an associate professor at the University of Alberta.

The Chinese know they have a problem, and Premier Wen Jiabao and former Shanghai Mayor Xu Kuangdi, who now heads the Chinese Academy of Engineering, have taken the lead. In November 2003, the all-powerful State Council issued the broad outlines of a new energy policy through 2020 that called for a "leapfrog strategy in the energy field." The aims include securing more supplies abroad, shifting away from China's fixation with coal, dramatically increasing the use of natural gas, building more hydro generators on the mainland's vast river networks, upgrading the electricity grid, and pushing for more solar and wind power resources.

The plan even calls for a major ramp-up in nuclear energy. Beijing wants to have nearly 40 reactors by 2020. In late 2004, China accepted bids for building four 1,000-megawatt pressurized water nuclear reactors. Foreign companies such as Westinghouse Electric of the U.S., Areva and Alstom of France, Mitsubishi of Japan, and Atomic Energy of Canada were all in hot pursuit. China is also handing out fat contracts for conventional power-plant deals, cleaner coal-burning technologies, and wind power. "Growth is happening in all fuel types," says John Rice, chief executive of GE Energy, which nailed about $900 million in contracts in 2003 to build turbines in China.

What comes through most clearly in this energy scramble, though, is a mounting Chinese obsession with securing—and safeguarding—sufficient oil supplies from around the world. Coal is too polluting to rely on exclusively, and even nuclear energy won't come to the rescue. The 30 new reactors, when up and running, will kick in only about 4% of the juice the country needs. Oil, meanwhile, fuels China's cars, buses, and trucks and keeps many of its industrial plants churning out goods.

So the clock is ticking on locking in an oil lifeline that will keep the nation's supergrowth on track. By 2025, China will probably import 75% of its crude—nearly twice the percentage today—and consume 10.6% of the world's oil, the U.S. Energy Dept. estimates. Experts expect Chinese demand will help prop up prices for years to come. And the Chinese know just how vulnerable a country can be when its oil comes from somewhere else. In fact, the military has published a book, called *Liberating Taiwan*, that imagines Chinese warships seizing sea routes to the Persian Gulf and imposing an oil embargo on Taipei, Tokyo, and Washington.

Beijing wants no such energy cutoff for the mainland. So the Chinese are grabbing what they can—and fending off anyone with a rival claim. The result is a very muscular petrodiplomacy. Look at what's happening to the Chunxiao natural gas field, which lies largely in Chinese territorial waters on a continental shelf in the East China Sea. Japan says part of the shelf juts into its maritime border extending from the southern island of Okinawa, so Tokyo—also eager for energy—wants its share of the bounty. Too bad: Beijing argues it controls the whole thing. A Chinese exploration group has started drilling there, and plans are being drawn up for a pipeline to spirit the stuff back to the mainland. The two sides attempted to smooth things over in meetings in Beijing in October 2004, but got nowhere. "I don't know why these talks were even held," fumed Japan's Economic Trade & Industry Minister, Shoichi Nakagawa.

Japan and China are also clashing over the route of a pipeline across the dark forests and frozen steppes of Siberia. Tokyo wants Russia to build a pipeline costing as much as $16 billion to the Pacific port of Nakhodka, where the oil could be transferred to tankers and shipped to Japan and other markets. Beijing is seeking a shorter route that would terminate in the Chinese oil town of Daqing. Chinese leaders have bent over backward to outfox Japan, and in October 2004 even settled a long-standing border dispute with Moscow and promised some $12 billion in business investment in Russia. Yet Japan will likely triumph because a security-obsessed China insists on having full control of the end of the pipeline, and thus Russian oil supplies, within its borders. This Chinese solution would give the Russians zero flexibility in selling their oil to other customers. "It's like being tied to someone during a knife-fight," says Ronald Smith, an oil-and-gas analyst at

Renaissance Capital in Moscow. Beijing might ultimately accept a pipeline to Nakhodka with a spur to China. That would be far costlier, though, and there are questions whether Russia can produce enough oil to make such a plan viable.

China is looking elsewhere. Chinese companies have signed oil or natural gas exploration deals in Australia, Indonesia, Iran, Kazakhstan, Nigeria, Papua New Guinea, and Sudan. So far, these deals represent just 10% of China's oil imports. Even so, China says they're important. "China has to look at supply security," says Mark Qiu, former chief financial officer of offshore exploration company CNOOC Ltd., "and the name of the game in energy security is diversification."

Can Western companies profit from China's oil obsession? Beijing has for several years pushed for listings of its big oil companies on international markets in order to cement tie-ins with overseas energy producers. The 2000 initial public offering of PetroChina Co., a unit of China National Petroleum Corp., raised about $3 billion globally, and BP PLC quickly snapped up 20% of the shares offered—though it sold its stake in 2004. In later offerings, ExxonMobil and Royal Dutch/Shell bought pieces of Sinopec, the nation's refining and distribution giant, and Shell took a stake in CNOOC Ltd.

## Iffy Reserves

Initially, the deals looked like a win for both sides. Chinese players would get foreign capital and exploration know-how to nail new energy reserves, while the Western petromajors would get a foothold in the world's fastest-growing energy market. It hasn't worked out that way. In 2004, Western companies pulled out of two projects that are critical to China's energy security: the Chunxiao gas development and the West-East pipeline, a $6 billion project running from the western province of Xinjiang to Shanghai. Part of the problem is that the reserves in both Xinjiang and the East Sea are iffy, something even Chinese oil executives concede.

Another is that there is little economic incentive for the Western oil majors to foot big up-front investments when Beijing has been slow in handing out domestic contracts to foreign players. True, there has been some progress: BP is a 30% partner in a Chinese joint venture to build a $665 million liquid natural gas terminal and storage facility in Guangdong Province and runs several hundred gas stations there, while Shell has set up a joint venture with Sinopec to build and operate 500 service stations in Jiangsu Province. But Shell was an early participant in the West-East pipeline, only to pull out later. The company says that was for commercial reasons, but others say the benefits of the project would have flown to PetroChina, and that Shell had been denied access to the Chinese market for its own imported gas, as it had hoped when it signed on. "All these firms looked at the West-East gas pipeline as a gateway project," says Cambridge Energy's Roberts. "They wanted to leverage the project for political capital that would win them access to other deals."

To its credit, China is allowing foreigners into the crucial field of controlling pollution. Coal continues to be the source of 70% of the nation's energy. Many homes still heat with coal, and the mainland's inefficient power industry is a major polluter and often burns unwashed, high-sulphur coal that spews tons of sulphur dioxide into the atmosphere. China is years behind in adopting cleaner coal-burning technologies such as scrubbers that trap pollutants before they can escape into the air. In 2003, the Asian Development Bank found that just 5% of China's power plants had any serious pollution controls at all.

So China is letting foreign companies that specialize in cleaner-burning techniques, such as turning coal into gas or liquid fuel, start the cleanup. It's a vast project. China leads the global league tables in sulphur dioxide emission and is home to 16 of the 20 most polluted cities in the world, while cases of respiratory disease are surging. The World Bank estimates that pollution costs China about $170 billion a year, or 12% of gross domestic product, in lost productivity and health-care costs.

Beijing leaders acknowledge such problems, although they argue they are an inevitable side effect of rapid industrialization that once also bedeviled other regional economies, such as Japan. But the Chinese have begun experimenting with an emissions-trading market similar to those in the U.S. and Europe, in which permissible levels of pollution are established and enterprises that can't meet those targets can buy credits from greener companies. China also surprised critics in July 2004 by mandating some of the toughest auto-emission standards going.

That's encouraging, but it's only one part of the puzzle. It will take a sustained campaign of conservation, improved energy technologies, more enlightened treatment of Western oil partners, billions in investment, and loads of exploration luck at home and abroad for China to be truly energy secure. For the sake of its future prosperity, China needs to start getting a lot of things right—and quickly.

# How a Thirst for Energy Led to a Thaw

On the sidelines at the U.N. General Assembly meetings in New York in September 2004, Indian Prime Minister Manmohan Singh and Pakistani President Pervez Musharraf held an historic meeting in which they agreed to seriously negotiate on economic cooperation. One tangible expression of that cooperation would be a 2,700-kilometer natural-gas pipeline from southern Iran to Rajasthan in central India, with Pakistan allowing the pipe to pass through its territory in exchange for a yearly transit fee of as much as $330 million, plus some of the gas for its own use.

Funny how a thirst for energy can make the oldest of foes suddenly eager to cooperate. As India's economy undergoes a dramatic expansion, it finds itself desperate for new supplies of oil, gas, and electricity. And diplomacy—even with fierce rival Pakistan—is one way of getting them. Indeed, India is conducting petroleum diplomacy throughout the region and beyond. In October 2004, Burmese head of state General Than Shwe visited India following a deal with Indian oil major Oil & Natural Gas Corp. (ONGC) that would open up Burma to oil and gas exploration. And India is negotiating with Bangladesh to buy some of its gas and to allow the Burmese pipeline to pass through its territory.

According to India's Planning Commission, India needs to triple its power generation over the next two decades to feed its fast-growing technology and manufacturing industries. Beyond that, it needs lots of oil and gas for its autos and household cooking needs. But India is even shorter on energy resources than neighboring China. It imports 73% of its oil, largely from the Middle East, spending about $21 billion a year, or 4% of its gross domestic product. Those imports will only increase: Research by Bombay's Strategic Foresight Group predicts that by 2030, 90% of India's oil and gas will be imported. So India is reaching out to its neighbors. "Finally, India has recognized the need to engage in larger energy diplomacy," says Leena Srivastava, director of The Energy & Resources Institute (TERI), an energy think tank in New Delhi.

Leading the charge to find new oil and gas supplies is ONGC, with $11 billion in annual revenues. Through subsidiary ONGC Videsh Ltd., the government has been scouring the world, acquiring stakes in existing oil fields, and securing the rights into the future. The strategy is to go to oil-rich countries where U.S. companies cannot go or to developing nations with which India has long-standing diplomatic ties. Thus, since 2001, ONGC Videsh has spent an estimated $11 billion investing in 14 oil and natural gas projects in Sudan, Russia, Vietnam, Iran, Iraq, and Burma.

Everywhere it goes looking for petroleum, India is shadowed by China. It is sometimes outbid for oil concessions by China's three largest oil companies, which have more money to spend. So the Indian government is now starting to use its diplomatic clout. While bidding for a 20%, $1.7 billion share in Sakhalin I, an offshore oil and natural gas field, in 2001, New Delhi exploited its 50-year-old diplomatic alliance with Russia to win the deal.

If good diplomacy makes good economics, it works the other way too. The "peace pipeline" that is to run from Iran through Pakistan will cost billions but is expected to save India $300 million a year in energy transport costs. Pakistan will get its transit fee, a share of the pipeline gas, plus the right to buy diesel fuel from India. Meanwhile, India also wants to trade Indian power for Bangladeshi gas, an energy swap that could serve to relieve border tensions. And Nepal has extra hydroelectric energy it could sell to its neighbors. The implications of the various proposed energy deals are vast, since they will connect South Asia to new road and power grids in Southeast Asia. "Once roads, an electricity grid, and a natural-gas pipeline are linked, India will be a welcome addition to ASEAN," says TERI's Srivastava, referring to the Association of Southeast Asian Nations. "It will really open up Asia."

Skeptics doubt that the energy linkups will do more than paper over long-standing enmities. Still, in India's case, neither the government nor the business establishment is willing to let a shortage of energy curb the country's rise as an economic power. So whatever geopolitical obstacles may get in the way, the diplomacy of energy will continue.

# 11

# The New Competitive Challenge

THE REST OF THE WORLD JUST now is starting to fathom the long-term implications of the rise of China and India. Globally minded business people have naturally tended to view both nations as tremendous opportunities for growth. But as also can be expected with the arrival of any new superpowers, the general public, politicians, and many traditional businesses in the U.S., Europe, and Japan have tended to perceive them as threats. Especially worrying to pessimists, China and India are becoming the first giant developing nations capable of dominating not only low-wage assembly industries but also competing in high-pay technology and service work requiring advanced education and training.

As "Shaking Up Trade Theory" explains, India and China are prompting even prominent mainstream economists to reexamine assumptions about the benefits to the U.S. of free trade. China's seemingly unbeatable advantage in manufacturing evokes fears that damage to U.S. jobs is deeper than most optimists assume.

There also is the issue of the fairness of competition with China. "Fakes!" unveils the growing scale and sophistication of rampant intellectual-property theft, for example, while "Did Spark Spark a Copycat?" examines allegations by GM that one of its popular economy cars was counterfeited by a domestic Chinese automaker.

"Software: Will Outsourcing Hurt America's Supremacy?" explores whether India's software success and wealth of information technology graduates earning a fraction of U.S. salaries are threats to one of America's strongest industries. "Jobs That Could Swim Offshore" examines which types of skilled jobs are most vulnerable to offshore competition.

But will the rise of India and China really translate into lower living standards for the U.S.? Or will the American economy and workforce, as they have done so many times, simply adjust to the new competitive realities and move on to an even higher level of prosperity? "Does It Matter If China Catches Up to the U.S.?" puts these questions in historical perspective. "America's New Competition" sums up the new sets of challenges that the U.S. faces in maintaining its global leadership and ways in which policymakers should respond. Finally, the commentary "How to Level the Playing Field" offers ways in which the U.S. could more aggressively press its trade interests with China within the legal confines of the World Trade Organization.

---

## Shaking Up Trade Theory

*For decades economists have insisted that the U.S. wins from globalization. Now they're not so sure.*

Ever since Americans began fretting about globalization nearly three decades ago, economists have patiently explained why, on balance, it's a boon to the U.S. Yes, some Americans lose their jobs, either to imports or because factories move to cheap-labor countries such as China or India. But the bulk of this work is labor-intensive and lower skilled and can be done more efficiently by countries that have an abundance of less-educated workers. In return, those countries buy more of our higher-value goods made by skilled workers—for which the U.S. has a comparative advantage. The lost jobs and lower wages in the U.S., economists say, are more than offset when countries specialize like this, leading to more robust exports and lower prices on imported goods.

Now this long-held consensus is beginning to crack. True, China is emerging as a global powerhouse, realigning many economic relationships. But in the long run a more disruptive trend may be the fast-rising tide of white-collar jobs shifting to cheap-labor countries. The fact that programming, engineering, and other high-skilled jobs are jumping to places such as China and India seems to conflict head-on with the 200-year-old doctrine of comparative advantage. With these countries now graduating more college students than the U.S. every year, economists are increasingly uncertain about just where the U.S. has an advantage anymore—or whether the standard framework for understanding globalization still applies in the face of so-called white-collar offshoring. "Now we've got trade patterns that challenge the common view of trade theory, which might not be so true anymore," says Gary C. Hufbauer, a senior fellow at the Institute for International Economics (IIE), a Washington (D.C.) think tank. A leading advocate of free-trade pacts, he still thinks white-collar job shifts are good for the U.S.

The great debate percolating among the country's top trade economists gained new prominence with a 2004 article by Nobel laureate Paul A. Samuelson in the Journal of Economic Perspectives (JEP). In the piece, the 91-year-old professor emeritus at Massachusetts Institute of Technology, who largely invented much of modern-day economics, questions whether rising skills in China and India necessarily will benefit the U.S.

The reaction was swift. Experts such as Columbia University trade economist Jagdish N. Bhagwati, who countered Samuelson in the next JEP issue, resist the notion that the new offshoring could lower U.S. wages or slow growth of gross domestic product. After all, these economists have spent their professional lives ridiculing such conclusions as so much protectionist nonsense. Nevertheless, they aren't yet able to reconcile what's happening on the ground with the ideas they have so passionately defended. "This is a whole unexplored question that is very controversial, and nobody has a clue about what the numbers are," says Robert C. Feenstra, a prominent trade economist at the University of California at Davis.

## Global Labor Pool

The central question Samuelson and others raise is whether unfettered trade is always still as good for the U.S. as they have long believed. Ever since British economist David Ricardo spelled out the theory of comparative advantage in the early 1800s, most economists have concluded that countries gain more than they lose when they trade with each other and specialize in what they do best. Today, however, advances in telecommunications such as broadband and the Internet have led to a new type of trade that doesn't fit neatly into the theory. Now that brainpower can zip around the world at low cost, a global labor market for skilled workers seems to be emerging for the first time—and has the potential to upset traditional notions of national specialization.

There are three ways this new development could disrupt the U.S. economy. If enough cheap, high-skilled workers become available around the world, competition may drive down U.S. wages for a wide swath of white-collar workers. Even economists who still see overall net gains agree that this is a potential problem. "For the first time, high-skilled U.S. workers are going to be exposed to international competition, though it's not clear how much it will hurt their wages," says Bhagwati.

A second concern is how much of the gains from trade will flow through to U.S. consumers. Until now the pain of globalization has been borne by less than a quarter of the workforce, mostly lower-skilled workers, whose wage cuts outweighed the cheaper-priced goods globalization brings. But the other three-quarters of American workers still came out ahead, since they weren't affected by foreign wage competition. If blue- and white-collar employees alike are thrown into the global labor pool, a majority of workers could end up losing more than they gain in lower prices. Then the benefits of increased trade would go primarily to employers. "It's entirely possible that all workers will lose and shareholders will gain; you have to be concerned about that," says Harvard University trade economist Dani Rodrik.

Even that wouldn't be enough to completely derail comparative-advantage theory, which holds that higher profits from trade should more than offset the lower wages. But again, for the first time, economists see another factor at play. As skill levels improve in cheap-labor countries—for example, the new engineering class in India—competition is coming on in the very products for which the U.S. has had a global advantage, such as software. If the new competition drives down prices too much, U.S. export earnings will suffer, and the entire U.S. economy could end up worse off.

While experts such as Hufbauer and Bhagwati doubt it will ever come to this, the fact that they're even entertaining such concepts is an intellectual sea change on a subject long considered settled. When countries such as China can perform tasks in which the U.S. previously had a clear edge, "Comparative advantage cannot be counted on to create . . . net gains greater than the net losses," Samuelson asserts in his paper.

The rethinking among economists could soon spill over into the policy arena. No one is advocating new trade barriers, which could be a cure that's worse than the disease. Nonetheless, the shaken views of so many prominent economists could prove to be critical. Throughout the 1990s, Washington embraced new trade deals in large part because of the virtual unanimity among experts that trade always benefits the U.S. If they're not so sure anymore, the public consensus that was unsteady to begin with could start to unravel.

"I'm worried that rising anxiety among higher-skilled workers will erode support for continued globalization in the U.S.," says Dartmouth University economics professor Matthew J. Slaughter.

## "A Right to Be Scared"

How large might the white-collar offshoring trend become? The more jobs that go, the greater the impact on U.S. wages. Consultant Forrester Research Inc. in Cambridge, Mass., was among the first to spot the white-collar job shifts and has done the most detailed projections so far. It sees the pace of U.S. job flows abroad averaging 300,000 a year through 2015. This is probably conservative since Forrester has also found that the number of U.S. companies among the 1,000 largest that engage in some level of white-collar offshoring will rise sharply—from 37% in 2004 to 54% by 2008. Already, some 14 million white-collar jobs involve work that can be shipped electronically and thus in theory could be moved offshore, according to a study by economists Ashok D. Bardhan and Cynthia A. Kroll at the University of California at Berkeley's Haas School of Business.

The hit to wages could be powerful if that happens. Forrester analyst John C. McCarthy identified 242 service jobs as likely to be affected among the 500-plus major occupations tracked by the Bureau of Labor Statistics (BLS). He ranked each by the share of jobs employers are likely to shift abroad by 2015. His conclusion: The cumulative job outflow will total 3.4 million over that period. That comes to 6% of the 57 million people who work in these 242 occupations today.

If that's in the ballpark, U.S. white-collar wages would get whacked, says Harvard University labor economist Lawrence F. Katz. Every 1% drop in employment due to imports or factories gone abroad shaves 0.5% off pay for remaining workers, he found in a study with Harvard colleagues Richard B. Freeman and George J. Borjas. So if job losses rise to 6% of the white-collar total, these workers' pay could be depressed by 2% to 3% through 2015, figures Katz. While a few percentage points over a decade or so may not sound dire, it's roughly as much as blue-collar workers lost to globalization in recent decades. "White-collar workers have a right to be scared," says Katz.

Another way economists gauge the potential wage impact is to look at examples of how people fare when they lose a job and extrapolate for those who might get displaced by offshoring. Turns out that just 30% of laid-off workers earn the same or more after three years, according to a study of 22 years of BLS data by economics professor Lori G. Kletzer of the University of California at Santa Cruz. Only 68% even hold a job at that point, while the rest are unemployed, retired, or perhaps at home with children. On average, those reemployed earn 10% less than before, Kletzer found. "Clearly, offshoring will be bad for U.S. wages, given what the job displacement numbers tell us," says Princeton University economics professor Henry S. Farber, who has written extensively about displaced workers.

But even if the incomes of more U.S. workers fall, won't the rest of American consumers benefit from the lower-priced goods and services globalization brings? Not necessarily, some economists now believe. Most studies of trade's impact on pay, including Katz's, assume that factory-job losses simply shift the demand for labor from one kind of worker to another higher up the value chain. So higher-educated workers gained much of what the less-schooled lost.

But if white-collar offshoring swells enough, the resulting job losses could undercut a large swath of U.S. consumers. In part, this is a question of scale. There's little doubt that globalization is likely to continue to cut into the country's 14.5 million factory hands. Add in 57 million white-collar workers suddenly facing global competition, too, and more than half the U.S. workforce of 130 million could feel the impact. Then, economists conclude, the benefits of globalization would flow mostly to companies and shareholders who profit from the cheaper labor, with little pass-through to workers and consumers. "If a majority of Americans have lower wages from outsourcing, then capital would be the prime beneficiary, even if U.S. GDP goes up," says Harvard's Freeman.

## Domestic Disturbance

Could the offshore phenomenon even dent America's overall GDP? Standard theory suggests not, but it's now another question nagging economists. Ricardo's insight that all countries come out ahead when they trade more with each other was updated in the early 1900s by two Swedish economists, Eli F. Hecksher and Bertil Olin. They showed that Ricardo's idea holds even if high-skilled countries such as the U.S. trade more with low-skilled ones such as India, with each country specializing in products in which they have a relative advantage. Thus, it's more efficient for the U.S., where about 60% of the workforce has some college education, to export products that use their skills and import low-end ones from cheap-labor countries. Conversely, India, where just a fraction of its 400 million-plus workers have gone to college, should grab the low-skilled work and leave higher-end products to the U.S.

This theory doesn't square with today's outflows of programming and other higher-skilled jobs. "According to the Hecksher-Olin model, we shouldn't be sending these jobs to countries with [so few skilled workers]," says University of California at Los Angeles trade economist Edward E. Leamer. But U.S. companies are doing just that because labor is cheaper and the Net makes it feasible to transport work done abroad back to the U.S.

Still, most economists think the new offshoring is an overall plus. For one thing, they say, employers' cost savings should more than compensate for any wage damage. And by slashing the price of software and other goods, offshoring could power a new wave of U.S. productivity gains similar to those triggered by falling computer-hardware prices in the 1990s, says a study by Hufbauer's colleague, IIE senior fellow Catherine L. Mann.

She and others argue that countries will continue to specialize in what they do best. Sure, India or China are taking high-skilled jobs in programming, but the U.S. will still outperform them in, perhaps, drug research or nanotechnology. Instead of thinking about comparative advantage in broad strokes such as high-skilled and low-skilled, they say, it makes more sense to make finer distinctions and look at areas in which countries have industry- or occupation-specific advantages. "There will be specialization within industries, [which will bring] a lot of demand from India for our higher skills," says Bhagwati.

Other economists, however, such as Leamer and Rodrik, believe that in the new global economy, advantages from these kinds of microlevel specialties will be fleeting. After all, if the U.S. is better at aerospace research, there's no reason why China couldn't quickly ramp up college grads in that area too. It's already doing that in telecom and servers.

Leamer and other trade experts say the resulting price competition from rising stars such as China and India could overpower any economywide gains companies get from global sourcing. They point to a famous 1968 paper by, of all people, Bhagwati, who argued that a country can be made worse off if trade lowers the price of products in which it has a comparative advantage. Bhagwati called it the "immiserating" effects of trade. In discussing the idea with *BusinessWeek*, Leamer wrote a short proof showing how a downward spiral of lower labor costs leads to lower export prices, causing immiseration. Even Bhagwati concedes that his insight could apply to the U.S. today, though he thinks the chances are slim that it will. "Bhagwati showed back then that a country can grow and get poorer, which might be this story, though I doubt it," says Hufbauer.

Indeed, it's possible that the U.S. already has suffered immiseration. Mann's study found that the offshore exodus of U.S. chip factories accounted for 10% to 30% of the decline in the prices of personal computers and memory chips in the early 1990s. These savings boosted U.S. multinationals' net exports of these products, and by 2000 the companies saw a $10 billion trade surplus in them.

But did the U.S. as a whole come out ahead? Mann's study also shows that the country's overall trade deficit in these products plunged into negative territory in 1992 and has remained there ever since. So while large U.S. companies gained from moving chip factories abroad, the overall U.S. economy may have lost. "This looks like immiseration to me," says Leamer.

Globalization, say most trade economists, ultimately should benefit the U.S. more than it hurts. But they can't yet show that to be true. Until someone comes up with a convincing explanation for what happens when the highest-skilled jobs move offshore, battles over globalization are likely to rage even hotter.

---

# Fakes!

*The global counterfeit business is out of control, targeting everything from computer chips to life-saving medicines. It's so bad that even China may need to crack down.*

In late 2003, Pfizer Inc. got a disturbing call on its customer hotline. A woman who had been taking its cholesterol-lowering drug Lipitor complained that a new bottle of tablets tasted bitter. She sent the suspicious pills to the company, which tested them at a lab in Groton, Conn. The white oblong tablets looked just like the real thing—and even contained some of the active ingredient in Lipitor. But Pfizer soon determined that they were counterfeits. Over the next two months, distributors yanked some 16.5 million tablets from warehouses and pharmacy shelves nationwide.

An isolated case? Hardly In October 2004, Brazilian police got a tip-off about a hoard of bogus Hewlett-Packard Co. inkjet cartridges and seized more than $1 million worth of goods. Chinese police that same year conducted raids confiscating everything from counterfeit Buick windshields to phony Viagra; while in Guam, the Secret Service uncovered a network selling bogus North Korean–made pharmaceuticals, cigarettes, and $100 bills. French customs seized more than 11,000 fake parts for Nokia Corp. cell phones—batteries, covers, and more. In January 2005, U.S. Commerce Secretary Donald Evans blasted the Chinese on a visit to Beijing, demanding they step up efforts to police intellectual-property violations. Evans singled out the case of a General Motors Corp. subsidiary that is suing Chinese carmaker Chery Automotive for ripping off the design of its Chevrolet Spark minicar. The uncanny resemblance between the two cars, said Evans, "defies innocent explanation."

## Critical Mass

Kiwi shoe polish, Callaway golf clubs, Intel computer chips, Bosch power drills, BP oil. Pick any product from any well-known brand, and chances are there's a counterfeit version of it out there. Of course, as anyone who has combed the back alleys of Hong Kong, Rio, or Moscow knows, fakes have been around for decades. Only the greenest rube would actually believe that the $20 Rolex watch on Silom Road in Bangkok or the $30 Louis Vuitton bag on New York's Canal Street is genuine.

But counterfeiting has grown up—and that's scaring the multinationals. "We've seen a massive increase in the last several years, and there is a risk it will spiral out of control," says Anthony Simon, marketing chief of Unilever Bestfoods. "It's no longer a cottage industry." The World Customs Organization estimates counterfeiting accounts for 5% to 7% of global merchandise trade, equivalent to lost sales of as much as $512 billion in 2004—though experts say this is only a guess. Seizures of fakes by U.S. customs jumped by 46% in 2004 as counterfeiters boosted exports to Western markets. Unilever Group says knockoffs of its shampoos, soaps, and teas are growing by 30% annually. The World Health Organization says up to 10% of medicines worldwide are counterfeited—a deadly hazard that could be costing the pharmaceutical industry $46 billion a year. Bogus car parts add up to $12 billion worldwide. "Counterfeiting has gone from a local nuisance to a global threat," says Hanns Glatz, DaimlerChrysler's point man on intellectual property.

The scale of the threat is prompting new efforts by multinationals to stop, or at least curb, the spread of counterfeits. Companies are deploying detectives around the globe in greater force than ever, pressuring governments from Beijing to Brasília to crack down, and trying everything from electronic tagging to redesigned products to aggressive pricing in order to thwart the counterfeiters. Even some Chinese companies, stung by fakes themselves, are getting into the act. "Once Chinese companies start to sue other Chinese companies, the situation will become more balanced," says Stephen Vickers, chief executive of International Risk, a Hong Kong–based brand-protection consultant.

China is key to any solution. Since the country is an economic gorilla, its counterfeiting is turning into quite the beast as well—accounting for nearly two-thirds of all the fake and pirated goods worldwide. Daimler's Glatz figures phony Daimler parts—from fenders to engine blocks—have grabbed 30% of the market in China, Taiwan, and Korea. And Chinese counterfeiters make millions of motorcycles a year, with knockoffs of Honda's workhorse CG125—selling for about $300, or less than half the cost of a real Honda—especially popular. It's tales like this that prompt some trade hawks in the U.S. to call for a World Trade Organization action against China related to counterfeits and intellectual-property rights violations in general. Such pressure is beginning to have some effect. "The Chinese government is starting to take things more seriously because of the unprecedented uniform shouting coming from the U.S., Europe, and Japan," says Joseph Simone, a lawyer specializing in IPR issues at Baker & McKenzie in Hong Kong.

Yet slowing down the counterfeiters in China and elsewhere will take heroic efforts. That's because counterfeiting thrives on the whole process of globalization itself. Globalization, after all, is the spread of capital and know-how to new markets, which in turn contribute low-cost labor to create the ideal export machine, manufacturing first the cheap stuff, then moving up the value chain. That's the story of Southeast Asia. It's the story of China. Now it's the story of fakes. Counterfeiting packs all the punch of skilled labor, smart distribution, and product savvy without getting bogged down in costly details such as research and brand-building.

The result is a kind of global industry that is starting to rival the multinationals in speed, reach, and sophistication. Factories in China can copy a new model of golf club in less than a week, says Stu Herrington, who oversees brand protection for Callaway Golf Co. "The Chinese are extremely ingenious, inventive, and scientifically oriented, and they are becoming the world's manufacturer," he says. The company has found counterfeiters with three-dimensional design software and experience cranking out legitimate clubs for other brands, so "back-engineering a golf club is a piece of cake" for them, he says. And counterfeiters are skilled at duplicating holograms, "smart" chips, and other security devices intended to distinguish fakes from the genuine article. "We've had sophisticated technology that took years to develop knocked off in a matter of months," says Unilever marketing boss Simon.

The ambition of the counterfeiters just keeps growing. In China, raids have turned up everything from fake Sony PlayStation game controllers to Cisco Systems router interface cards. "If you can make it, they can fake it," says David Fernyhough, director of brand protection at investigation firm Hill & Associates Ltd. in Hong Kong. Don't believe him? Shanghai Mitsubishi Elevator Co. discovered a counterfeit elevator after a building owner asked the company for a maintenance contract. "It didn't look like our product," says Wang Chung Heng, a lawyer for Shanghai Mitsubishi. "And it stopped between floors."

Many fakes, though, are getting so good that even company execs say it takes a forensic scientist to distinguish them from the real McCoy. Armed with digital technology, counterfeiters can churn out perfect packaging—a key to duping unwitting distributors and retail customers. GM has come across fake air filters, brake pads, and batteries. "We had to cut them apart or do chemical analysis to tell" they weren't real, says Alexander Theil, director of investigations at General Motors Asia Pacific. The parts might last half as long as the real thing, but that's not apparent until long after the sale.

The counterfeiters even ape the multinationals by diversifying their sourcing and manufacturing across borders. In August 2004, Philippine police raided a cigarette factory in Pampanga, two hours outside of Manila. What they found was a global operation in miniature. The factory was producing fake Davidoffs and Mild Sevens for export to Taiwan. The $6 million plant boasted a state-of-the-art German cigarette-rolling machine capable of producing some 3 billion fake smokes, worth $600 million, annually. The top-quality packaging came from a printer in Malaysia. The machinery itself was manned by 23 Chinese brought in by a Singapore-based syndicate, says Josef Gueta, director of Business Profiles Inc., a Manila firm that tracks counterfeit rings for multinationals. "They have shipping, warehousing, and the knowledge and network to move things around easily," he says.

As such counterfeiters get more entrenched and more global, they will be increasingly hard to eradicate. Financing comes from a variety of sources, including Middle East middlemen, local entrepreneurs, and organized crime. Sometimes the counterfeiters are fly-by-night operations, but just as often they're legitimate companies that have a dark side. In fact, many are licensed producers of brand-name goods that simply run an extra, unauthorized shift and sell out the back door. Or they are former licensees who have kept the molds and designs that allow them to go into business for themselves. Shoemaker New Balance Athletic Shoe Inc. is suing a former contract manufacturer in Guangdong Province for selling unauthorized New Balance sneakers that have turned up as far away as Australia and Europe. In the Philippines, semiconductor distributor Sardido Industries says it has been burned by counterfeiters that have sold it microprocessors rejected by inspectors from the likes of Intel and Advanced Micro Devices. These are doctored with logos and serial numbers to look like genuine parts and sold off cheaply as returns or production overruns. Other counterfeiters are generic manufacturers who moonlight as makers of fakes. Yamaha Corp. has licensed five plants in China to make its motorcycles, but almost 50 factories have actually produced bikes branded as Yamaha.

It's easy to find the counterfeiters too. The Ziyuangang market in the sprawling city of Guangzhou, two hours north of Hong Kong, looks pretty much like any recently built Chinese shopping mall. But venture inside, and you'll find row upon row of shops offering bogus Gucci, Versace, Dunhill, Longines, and more. Each shop has just a few dozen samples but offers vast catalogs of goods that can be made and delivered in less than a week. At one outlet, a clerk offers counterfeit Louis Vuitton bags in various sizes. "Even fakes have many grades of quality, and these fakes are really, really good," she boasts. Exports? She's happy to arrange shipping to the country of your choice.

Once those goods leave China, they can sneak into the legitimate supply chain just about anywhere. Sometimes, phony components get used in authentic products. In 2004, for example, Kyocera Corp. had to recall a million cell-phone batteries that turned out to be counterfeit, costing the company at least $5 million. Unscrupulous wholesalers will fob off fakes on small auto-repair shops, office-supply stores, or independent pharmacies by saying they have bargain-priced—but not suspiciously cheap—oil filters, printer cartridges, or bottles of shampoo that another retailer returned, or which are close to their sell-by date. Some traders mix phonies in with authentic goods. "It's easy to slide a stack of fake Levis under the real ones," says one investigator based in Shanghai. "Most inspectors and buyers can't tell the difference."

Counterfeiters can also disguise their wares before they reach their final destination. Some ship unmarked counterfeit parts in several consignments to be assembled and labeled at their destination. And in May 2004, Shanghai customs officials were inspecting a Dubai-bound shipment of 67 100cc motorcycles labeled with the brand name Honling. But when they peeled back stickers on the machines' crankcases, they found "Yamaha" engraved on the casting. "They are very sneaky and cunning, and that's very frustrating," laments Masayuki Hosokawa, chief representative of Yamaha Motor Co. in Beijing.

## Strategic Defense

They are also making big bucks. Counterfeiting has become as profitable as trading illegal narcotics and is a lot less risky. In most countries, convicted offenders get off with a slap on the wrist and a fine of a few thousand dollars. Counterfeiters, after all, don't have to cover research and development, marketing, and advertising costs, and most of the expense goes into making goods look convincing, not performing well. Fake Marlboros that cost just pennies a pack to make in China could end up selling for $7.50 in Manhattan. Phony New Balance shoes can be stitched together for about $8 a pair and retail for as much as $80 in Australia, while real ones cost between $11 and $24 to make, and sell for up to $120. Gross margins for knockoff printer cartridges are north of 60%. Counterfeiters "use low-paid employees and cut corners on safety," says Richard K. Willard, general counsel for Gillette Co., which turns up hundreds of thousands of imitation Duracell batteries every week. "If they can push them off as a high-quality product, there is a big margin for them."

While the counterfeiters are piling up profits, the multinationals are spending ever more on stopping them. Luxury house LVMH Möet Hennessy Louis Vuitton spent more than $16 million in 2004 on investigations, busts, and legal fees. GM has seven full-time staffers sleuthing the globe, and Pfizer has five people working in Asia alone. Nokia now makes batteries with holographic images and 20-digit identification codes that can be authenticated online. Cigarette maker JT International has boosted its anti-counterfeiting budget from $200,000 to $15 million since 1999, spending the money on a network of investigators, lawyers, and informants in factories suspected of making fakes.

Pfizer will soon introduce radio-frequency ID tags on all Viagra sold in the U.S., which will enable it to track drugs all the way from the laboratory to the medicine cabinet. Other companies simply try to make life as difficult as possible for manufacturers and distributors by raiding factories and warehouses or by slightly altering the look of products, making it tough for counterfeiters to keep up with the changes. JT International—which sells Camels and Winstons outside the U.S.— sometimes digs through dumpsters at suspect factories looking for counterfeit packaging. Callaway patrols the Web looking for suspiciously cheap clubs bearing its brand—though as soon as it shuts one dealer down, another is sure to pop up. "Getting rid of the problem altogether is too much to ask," says Callaway's Herrington. "We just try to do our best and give the counterfeiters a really bad day."

One tactic is to outwit the counterfeiters in the marketplace. Anheuser-Busch Cos., for instance, was plagued by knockoff Budweiser in China. A big problem was that counterfeiters were refilling old Bud bottles, so the company started using expensive imported foil on the bottles that was very hard to find in China. The company also added a temperature-sensitive label that turned red when cold. The result: "We've been able to keep [counterfeiting] at a pretty low level," says Stephen J. Burrows, chief executive and president of Anheuser-Busch International. Yamaha, meanwhile, overhauled the way it manufactures and designs motorcycles to lower costs. Now it charges $725 for its cheapest bikes in China, down from about $1,800. To stay competitive, counterfeiters have since lowered their prices from around $1,000 to roughly half that.

The biggest challenge is getting cooperation from China. For years, Chinese authorities turned a blind eye to the problem, largely because most of the harm was inflicted on foreign brand owners and most counterfeiting was seen as a victimless offense. The only time China got tough on counterfeiters was when there was a clear danger to Chinese. In 2004, for example, 15 infants died from phony milk powder. The ringleader was sentenced to eight years in prison. But when the victim is a company not an individual, the courts are far less severe. In June 2004, a Guangdong businessman was found guilty of producing fake windshields under 15 different brand names, including General Motors, DaimlerChrysler, and Mitsubishi Motors. He was fined just $97,000 and given a suspended sentence. It's unclear just how much he made selling fakes, but GM gumshoe Theil says "there is no way the fine is commensurate with the profits he made."

But more Chinese corporate interests have seen profits hit because of counterfeiting—which may lead to a tougher response from Beijing. Li-Ning Co., China's No. 1 homegrown athletic footwear and apparel company, has gotten the ultimate compliment from counterfeiters: They're faking its shoes. So today, Li-Ning has three full-time employees who track counterfeiters. The state tobacco monopoly is conducting joint raids with big international tobacco companies, since counterfeiters have started cranking out Double Happiness, Chunghwa, and other Chinese smokes. The crackdown, investigators believe, has forced some cigarette counterfeiters to decamp to Vietnam and Burma. And the government is finally realizing that piracy—which accounts for 92% of all software used in the mainland—isn't just setting back the likes of Microsoft Corp. "Piracy is a big problem for the development of the local software industry," says Victor Zhang, senior representative for China of the Business Software Alliance, an industry group. Some fear that Western companies may cut research spending in China if the mainland doesn't crack down.

Now, China is toughening its legal sanctions. In December 2004, Beijing lowered the threshold for criminal prosecution of counterfeiters. Prior to the changes, an individual needed to have $12,000 worth of goods on hand before police could prosecute. It was easy to skirt that rule by spreading the wares around. That threshold now stands at $6,000 for counterfeiters caught with one brand and $3,600 for those with two or more. And in late January 2005, Beijing began the trial of two

Americans who are accused of selling $840,000 in knockoff CDs and DVDs made in China over the Internet. The two could face up to 15 years in jail if convicted.

One big problem: Too many scammers have ties to local officials, who see counterfeit operations as a major source of employment and pillars of the local economy. "Two or three of our raids have failed because of local protection," says Joseph Tsang, chairman of Marksman Consultants Ltd., a Hong Kong–based company that has helped conduct raids on behalf of Titleist and Nike Golf. Take the example of a raid in August 2004 in Fujian Province. The police found a dirt-covered hatch hiding a stairway that led into a pitch-black cave. Inside was a rolling machine, cigarette paper, and a die for stamping Marlboros and Double Happiness packaging. But the counterfeiters themselves had cleared out and taken the smokes with them. "They knew we were coming," sighs a Hong Kong–based investigator who participated in the raid.

## Embattled Beijing

Beijing says it's doing what it can. The government has raised intellectual-property issues to the highest levels: Trade czar and Vice-Premier Wu Yi, for instance, has held regular meetings with the Quality Brands Protection Committee since 2003. "China customs is taking the fight seriously," says Meng Yang, director general for the Policy & Legal Affairs Dept. of the General Administration of Chinese Customs. The agency in November 2004 held a conference in Shanghai with brand owners and customs officers from around the world to map out strategies. But delegates acknowledged their biggest challenge is finding the funds to fight counterfeiting, as most governments are more concerned with preventing the smuggling of drugs and arms.

Could the U.S. apply stronger pressure to get China to crack down? "The answer is for the Administration to bring a WTO case against the Chinese," says one leader of the intellectual-property bar in Washington. The challenge is to secure evidence from U.S. companies, which desperately want relief but don't want to anger Beijing.

Hard as it is, there's every reason to try to keep up the fight to stop counterfeiting. One is safety. Novartis says counterfeiters have used yellow highway paint to get the right color match for fake painkillers. And in some African countries, counterfeit or illegal medicines account for as much as 40% of the drugs on the market. "You even have antibiotics without the ingredients," says Daniel L. Vasella, chairman of Novartis. Pfizer says police and regulators in Asia uncovered more than 1.5 million counterfeit doses of its hypertension drug Norvasc in 2003. "You are seeing counterfeiters exploit a loose supply chain and moving from lifestyle drugs to life-saving drugs," says Pfizer's vice-president for global security, John Theriault. "That should make people nervous."

The other reason to mount an offensive against the counterfeits is, obviously, the hit to corporate profits—and the likelihood that developed markets will one day be seriously contaminated. It's already happening. In June 2003, Tommy Hilfiger Corp. successfully sued Goody's Family Clothing Inc. for $11 million for carrying fake shirts. The incidence of fake prescription drugs in the U.S., though small, is rising sharply. The U.S. Food & Drug Administration began 58 investigations of counterfeit drugs in fiscal 2004, up from 22 in 2003.

More alarming, say police, is counterfeiting's connection to the underworld. "Organized crime thrives on counterfeiting," says Ronald K. Noble, Secretary General of Interpol. So does terrorism. Noble says profits from pirated CDs sold in Central America have funded Hezbollah in the Middle East. One cigarette executive estimates North Korea earns $100 million per year in fees from pirates producing there. That kind of activity proves that buying fakes "isn't innocent, and it's not a game," says Bernard Arnault, chairman of luxury goods maker LVMH.

The counterfeiting scourge, meanwhile, continues to spread. Pakistan and Russia are huge producers of fake pharmaceuticals. In Italy an estimated 10% of all designer clothing is fake, much of it produced domestically. Gangs in Paraguay funnel phony cosmetics, designer jeans, and toys from China to the rest of South America. Bulgarians are masters at bootlegging U.S. liquor brands. This is one fight that will take years to win.

# Did Spark Spark a Copycat?

It's close to noon on a sunny January day, and the Chery dealership at the Asian Games Village car market in north Beijing is bustling. That's because the price of the popular Chery QQ minicar was just slashed by as much as $725, to a highly affordable $3,600. "The best thing is the low price," says one customer preparing to buy a gray QQ, which he says has "a fashionable shape."

General Motors Corp. execs would agree with that—which is why they're apoplectic. GM Daewoo Auto & Technology Co., the Korean subsidiary of GM, says the QQ is a knockoff of its own Matiz minicar, sold in China as the Chevrolet Spark since 2003. "The cars are more than similar," says Rob Leggat, vice-president for corporate affairs at GM Daewoo. "It really approaches being an exact copy." Same cute, snubby nose. Same bug-eyed headlights. Same rounded, high back. And most components in the QQ, Leggat says, can easily be interchanged with parts on the Spark. In December 2004, GM Daewoo filed suit in a Shanghai court alleging that Chery Automobile Co. stole its trade secrets to make the QQ. Chery declined to comment.

This isn't the first time a foreign automaker has felt ripped off in China. In 2003, Toyota Motor Corp. sued Hangzhou-based Geely Group Co. for copying the Japanese company's logo and slapping it on Geely models. Toyota lost the case. Yet Honda Motor Co. in December 2004 won a ruling that bars Chongqing Lifan Industrial from selling motorcycles under the "Hongda" brand. Honda is also suing Shuanghuan Automobile Co., saying the Chinese company's Laibao SRV is a copy of the Honda CR-V sport-utility vehicle. "Chinese car companies still have limited [design] capabilities," says Jia Xinguang, an analyst at China National Automotive Industry Consulting & Developing Corp., a consultancy. "That is why so many copy bigger car companies' models."

Some, though, believe China will need to clean up its act on intellectual property if Chery and other automakers hope to be successful overseas. "Intellectual-property rights violations will be a major impediment to the aspirations" of Chinese car companies looking to export, says Charlene Barshefsky, former U.S. Trade Representative and now a Washington attorney.

Chery already has global ambitions. In 2004 the company exported 8,000 vehicles to Cuba, Malaysia, and elsewhere and started assembling cars in Iran. In January 2005, Chery announced plans to export five models, ranging from a compact sedan to an SUV, to the U.S. by 2007—though the QQ isn't part of the mix.

At home, the QQ is Chery's mainstay. The model made up 57% of the 87,000 cars it sold in China in 2004—outselling the Chevy Spark nearly five to one, according to researcher CSM Asia.

And sales show no sign of slowing. In the first three weeks of January 2005, the Asian Games dealership sold 118 QQs, says manager Zhang Ying, noting that the model costs about $1,000 less than the Spark after the recent discount. With such a price gap, it's unlikely that the Spark will outsell the QQ anytime soon. So GM had better hope it outmaneuvers Chery in court.

---

# Software: Will Outsourcing Hurt America's Supremacy?

*Programming jobs are heading overseas by the thousands. Is there a way for the U.S. to stay on top?*

Stephen Haberman was one of a handful of folks in all of Chase County, Neb., who knew how to program a computer. At the height of the Internet boom, the 17-year-old whiz wanted to strut his stuff outside of his windswept patch of prairie. He was too young for a nationwide programming competition sponsored by Microsoft Corp., so an older friend registered for him. Haberman wowed the judges with a flashy Web page design and finished second in the country. Emboldened, Stephen came up with a radical idea: Maybe he would skip college altogether and mine a quick fortune in dot-com gold. His mother, Cindy, put the kibosh on his plan. She steered him to a full scholarship at the University of Nebraska at Omaha.

Half a world away, in the western Indian city of Nagpur, a 19-year-old named Deepa Paranjpe was having an argument with her father. Sure, computer science was heating up, he told her. Western companies were frantically hiring Indians to scour millions of software programs and eradicate the much-feared millennium bug. But this craze would pass. The former railroad employee urged his daughter to pursue traditional engineering, a much safer course. Deepa had always respected her father's opinions. When he demanded perfection at school, she delivered nothing less. But she turned a deaf ear to his career advice and plunged into software. After all, this was the industry poised to change the world.

As Stephen and Deepa emerge from graduate school—one in Pittsburgh, the other in Bombay—they'll find that their decisions of a half-decade ago placed their dreams on a collision course. The Internet links that were being pieced together at the turn of the century now provide broadband connections between multinational companies and brainy programmers the world over. For Deepa and tens of thousands of other Indian students, the globalization of technology offers the promise of power and riches in a blossoming local tech industry. But for Stephen and his classmates in the U.S., the sudden need to compete with workers across the world ushers in an era of uncertainty. Will good jobs be waiting for them when they graduate? "I might have been better served getting an MBA," Stephen says.

U.S. software programmers' career prospects, once dazzling, are now in doubt. Just look at global giants, from IBM and Electronic Data Systems to Lehman Brothers and Merrill Lynch. They're rushing to hire tech workers offshore while liquidating thousands of jobs in America. From 2001 to 2004, offshore programming jobs have nearly tripled, from 27,000 to an estimated 80,000, according to Forrester Research Inc. And Gartner Inc. indicated that 1 of every 10 jobs in U.S. tech companies had moved to emerging markets by the end of 2004. In other words, recruiters who look at Stephen will also consider someone like Deepa—who's willing to do the same job for one-fifth the pay. U.S. software developers "are competing with everyone else in the world who has a PC," says Robert R. Bishop, chief executive of computer maker Silicon Graphics Inc.

For many of America's 3 million software programmers, it's paradise lost. Just a few years back, they held the keys to the Information Age. Their profession not only lavished many with stock options and six-figure salaries but also gave them the means to start companies that could change the world—the next Microsoft, Netscape, or Google. Now, these veterans of Silicon Valley and Boston's Route 128 exchange heart-rending job-loss stories on Web sites such as yourjobisgoingtoindia.com. Suddenly, the programmers share the fate of millions of industrial workers, in textiles, autos, and steel, whose jobs have marched to Mexico and China.

## "Leap of Faith"

This exodus throws the future of America's tech economy into question. For decades, the U.S. has been the world's technology leader—thanks in large part to its dominance of software, now a $200 billion-a-year U.S. industry. Sure, foreigners have made their share of the machines. But the U.S. has held on to control of much of the innovative brain-work and reaped rich dividends, from Microsoft to the entrepreneurial hotbed of Silicon Valley. The question now is whether the U.S. can continue to lead the industry as programming spreads around the globe from India to Bulgaria. Politicians are jumping on the issue in the election season. And it will probably rage on for years, affecting everything from global trade to elementary-school math and science curriculums.

Countering the doomsayers, optimists from San Jose, Calif., to Bangalore see the offshore wave as a godsend, the latest productivity miracle of the Internet. Companies that manage it well—no easy task—can build virtual workforces spread around the world, not only soaking up low-cost talent but also tapping the biggest brains on earth to collaborate on complex projects. Marc Andreessen, Netscape Communications Corp.'s co-founder and now chairman of Opsware Inc., a Sunnyvale (Calif.) start-up, sees this reshuffling of brainpower leading to bold new applications and sparking growth in other industries, from bioengineering to energy. This could mean a wealth of good new jobs, even more than U.S. companies could fill. "It requires a leap of faith," Andreessen admits. But "in 500 years of Western history, there has always been something new. Always always always always always."

This time, though, there's no guarantee that the next earth-shaking innovations will pop up in America. Deepa, for example, has high-speed Internet, a world-class university, and a venture-capital industry that's starting to take shape in Bombay. What's more, her home country is luring back entrepreneurs and technologists who lived in Silicon Valley during the bubble years. Many came home to India after the crash and now are sowing the seeds of California's start-up culture throughout the subcontinent. What's to stop Deepa from mixing the same magic that Andreessen conjured a decade ago when he co-founded Netscape? It's clear that in a networked world, U.S. leadership in innovation will find itself under siege.

The fallout from this painful process could be toxic. One danger is that high-tech horror stories—the pink slips and falling wages—will scare the coming generation of American math whizzes away from software careers, starving the tech economy of brainpower. While the number of students in computer-science programs is holding steady—for now—the elite schools saw applications fall by as much as 30% between 2002 and 2004. If that trend continues, the U.S. will be relying more than ever on foreign-born graduates for software innovation. And as more foreigners decide to start careers and companies back in their home countries, the U.S. could find itself lacking a vital resource. Microsoft CEO Steven A. Ballmer says the shortfall of U.S. tech students worries him more than any other issue. "The U.S. is No. 3 now in the world and falling behind quickly No. 1 [India] and No. 2 [China] in terms of computer-science graduates," he said in late 2003 at a forum in New York.

Fear in the industry is palpable. Some of it recalls the scares of years past: OPEC buying up the world in the 1970s and Japan Inc. taking charge a decade later. The lesson from those episodes is to resist quick fixes and trust in the long-term adaptability of the U.S. economy. Job-protection laws, for example, may be tempting. But they could hobble American companies in the global marketplace. Flexibility is precisely what has allowed the U.S. tech industry to adapt to competition from overseas. In 1985, under pressure from Japanese rivals, Intel Corp. exited the memory-chip business to concentrate all its resources in micro-processors. The result: Intel stands unrivaled in the business today.

While the departure of programming jobs is a major concern, it's not a national crisis yet. Unemployment in the industry is 7%. So far, the less-creative software jobs are the ones being moved offshore: bug-fixing, updating antiquated code, and routine programming tasks that require many hands. And some software companies are demonstrating that they can compete against lower-cost rivals with improved programming methods, more automation, and innovative business models.

For the rest of the decade, the U.S. will probably maintain a strong hold on its software leadership, even as competition grows. The vast U.S. economy remains the richest market for software and the best laboratory for new ideas. The country's universities are packed with global all-stars. And the U.S. capital markets remain second to none. But time is running short for Americans to address this looming challenge. John Parkinson, chief technologist at Capgemini Ernst & Young, estimates that U.S. companies, students, and universities have a few years to come up with responses to global shifts. "Scenarios start to look wild and wacky after 2010," he says. And within a decade, "the new consumer base in India and China will be moving the world."

## People Skills

To thrive in that wacky world, programmers like Stephen must undergo the career equivalent of an extreme makeover. Traditionally, the profession has attracted brainy introverts who are content to code away in isolation. With so much of that work going overseas, though, the most successful American programmers will be those who master people skills. The industry is hungry for liaisons between customers and basic programmers and for managers who can run teams of programmers scattered around the world. While pay for basic application development has plummeted 17.5% between 2001 and 2003, according to Foote Partners, a consultant in New Canaan, Conn., U.S. project managers saw their pay rise an average of 14.3% since 2002.

Finding those high-status jobs won't be easy. In the summer of 2003, 34-year-old Hal Reed was so hungry for a programming job that he answered an ad in the *Boston Globe* for contract work at cMarket, a Cambridge (Mass.) start-up. The pay was $45,000—barely more than an outsourcing company charges for Indian labor. But he took it. Fortunately for him, he was able to convince his new boss quickly that he was much more than a programmer. He could lead a team. Within weeks, his boss nearly doubled Reed's pay and made him the chief software architect. "He had great strategic thinking skills," says Jon Carson, cMarket's chief executive. "You can't outsource that."

To prepare students for the hot jobs, universities may need to revamp their computer-science programs. Carnegie Mellon University in Pittsburgh, where Stephen now studies, has already begun that process. His one-year master's program focuses on giving students the skills needed to manage teams and to play the role of software architect. Such workers are the visionaries who design massive projects or products that hundreds or even thousands of programmers flesh out.

The key players in the drama, including these two master's students, Stephen and Deepa, don't have the luxury to wait and see how it turns out. Their time is now. Deepa graduated in 2004 from the Bombay campus of the elite Indian Institute of Technology.

The options they're eyeing illustrate the unfolding map of an industry in full mutation. A software career is no refuge for the faint of heart. Deepa, for example, could suffer if the U.S. government moves to block offshore development or if rocky experiences in foreign lands spark an industry backlash. And Stephen, if he misplays his hand, could find himself competing with lowballing Filipinos or Uruguayans.

For now, their stories reflect the moods in their two countries—one with lots to lose, the other with a world to win. Deepa is brimming with optimism about the future, convinced that her opportunities are limited by nothing more than her imagination. She is thinking not only about the next job but about the start-up that she'll found after that. Stephen, by contrast, is cautious. Even at 22, he's attuned to the risks of a global market for software talent. While confident he'll make a good living, he's plotting out a career that sacrifices opportunities for a measure of safety. Self-protection, an afterthought a few years ago, is a pillar of his strategy.

## Seeking a Niche

It's midday in the windowless basement labs at CMU's Wean Hall. Stephen, tall and lanky, wearing a white T-shirt tucked into jeans, leans back in his chair and ponders his future. He signed up for the master's program at CMU on the advice of a professor in Omaha who told him that graduates with an MS could land more interesting jobs and make more money. But now the big recruiters coming onto the snowy Pittsburgh campus—companies such as Microsoft and Amazon.com Inc.—are hiring cheaper undergrads, he says, and barely giving the masters a look. Sure, other recruiters come knocking. Banks, he says with a grimace. Insurance companies. But the idea of working in a finance-industry tech shop leaves him cold. "I'm not even interviewing," he says.

The 17-year-old hotshot who was ready to skip college and make a mint has undergone quite a change. He's married, has witnessed the bumps in the world of software, and plans to establish "an upper-middle-class lifestyle, and maybe more" as a businessman. His plan is to carve out a niche for himself back in Omaha. He'll gather three or four colleagues and produce custom software for businesses in town, from hospitals and steakhouses to law firms. Omaha is plenty big, he says, for a good business, but it's remote enough to insulate his start-up from off-shore competition—and even from the bigger competitors in Chicago.

Stephen understands the threat posed by smart and hungry programmers in distant lands. He was once such a programmer himself. From his senior year in high school all the way through college, he worked as a freelancer for a New York software-development company, Beachead Technologies Inc. Geoff Brookins, Beachead's young founder, spotted Stephen's prize-winning entry in the Microsoft Web site design contest. He called Nebraska, sent Stephen some work, and was blown away. "He did two months of work in three days," he recalls. Brookins quickly signed him on at $15 an hour, ultimately paying him $45 an hour. Like the Indians, Stephen provided a low-cost alternative to big-city programmers—but he had an advantage because he spoke American English and was only one time zone away from New York.

The job let Stephen work on projects that normally would have been far beyond the reach of a student. One was to create IBM's Web page for its Linux operating-system technology—a crucial arm of Big Blue's business. "Stephen was lead engineer on that project," Brookins says. The student also got to spend much of one summer working at Beachead's office in New York City. It was a fun contrast to Nebraska, he recalls. But he stopped working for Beachead after he moved to Pittsburgh.

It was there that Stephen got a strong signal that the prospects were dimming for programmers. When his wife, Amy, a fellow computer-science student from Nebraska, began looking for programming work, she came back to their suburban apartment disheartened. The only available jobs, she says, "would have paid me interns' rates." She ditched the profession and is now writing a Christian-themed novel.

Then, Stephen's old boss hammered home the dangers of coding for a living in a wired world. Beachead's competitors were finding cheaper labor offshore, and Brookins, to win contracts, had to match them. He logged on to a Web site, RentACoder, a matchmaking service between employers and some 30,000 programmers around the world. There, Brookins found a 27-year-old Romanian named Florentin Badea, a star from Bucharest's Polytechnic University and the 11th-ranked programmer on the whole site. Badea was willing to charge just $250 for a project that would have cost $2,000, Brookins estimates, if Stephen had done it.

Those same global forces, Stephen admits, could eventually hollow out his business in Omaha. Already, Indian tech-services outfits such as Infosys and Wipro are competing head-to-head with U.S. companies in this country. But Stephen is betting that by working closely with customers, he can whip bigger firms on quality and service. He says he'll give the venture six months to a year and then see what happens.

## Ultrafast Track

Deepa sees a reverse image of Stephen's worldview. Where the prospects for U.S. tech grads seem to narrow as they peer into the future, she's looking down an eight-lane highway. Yet she faces her own set of challenges, she acknowledges, while sipping tea with her classmates. She and her IIT classmates don't want to be cogs in a software-programming factory—India's role to date. Instead, they want India to be a tech powerhouse in its own right. "Good Indian engineers can do good design work, but we need a venture industry" so Indians can start their own companies, says Deepa. Her pals nod in agreement.

Deepa is positioned on India's ultrafast track. The country pins high hopes on the 3,000 students in the six Institutes of Technology. Their alumni are stars locally and worldwide—including Yogen Dalal, a top venture capitalist at Mayfield, and Desh Deshpande, founder of Sycamore Networks and Cascade Communications. Within this elite, Deepa and her friends are a rarified breed. They aced the grueling national exams, ranking in the top 0.2% and winning places in the school of computer science. They're known as "toppers." The challenge for Deepa's small crowd is to move beyond the achievements of Dalal and Deshpande, who notched their successes for U.S. companies, and to make their mark with new Indian companies.

That means bypassing the bread-and-butter service giants, such as Tata, Infosys, and Wipro, that dominate the Indian stage. The jobs they offer, says Deepa, sound boring. To get their hands on exciting research and more creative programming, she and her friends are banking mostly on U.S. companies in India, including Intel, Texas Instruments, and Veritas. Deepa lined up a job as a software engineer at the Pune operations of Veritas Software Corp., a Silicon Valley storage-software maker, after graduation. Her pay started at $10,620 a year—plenty for a comfortable middle-class life in India. "I'm living my dream," she says.

And thrilling her family. Her father, Arun Paranjpe, who grew up in Mhow, a tiny army-base town in central India, could afford only a bachelor's degree, which prepared him for work as an officer in India's railways. He regretted not advancing further, and along with Deepa's homemaker mother, he pushed his two daughters toward advanced professional degrees. She studied Indian classical vocal music for nine years and escaped, when she could, to the cricket field. Deepa always finished at the top of her class in mathematics. That helped her land a plum spot in the computer-science program at Nagpur University.

Now Deepa is IIT–Bombay's star in search technology—and she's hoping that this specialty will be her ticket to a rip-roaring career. She routinely works till 3 a.m. in the department's new 20-pod computer lab, doing research on search engines. She admits the work at Veritas, at least initially, will involve more routine database tasks than the cutting-edge work she's hoping for. But if Veritas disappoints, a topper like Deepa will have plenty of other options. Both the search giant Google Inc. and the Web portal Yahoo! set up research and development centers in India in 2004. Deepa hopes to manage a research lab some day, and ultimately, she says, "I'd like to be an entrepreneur."

But she's an entrepreneurial revolutionary and family traditionalist at the same time. It's part of her balancing act. Consider her eventual marriage. As an attractive, professional woman, she'll make a prize catch in India's conservative marriage market. Deepa expects she will have an arranged marriage: Her parents will choose a suitable husband for her from within her own caste. But she is firm: Her husband would have to be an entrepreneur, or a tech whiz, and preferably in the same field, "so we can have a common platform, and he can understand my work," she says.

Maybe one day the couple will be able to raise venture money together. While venture-capital investing didn't exist in India until a few years ago, the industry is starting to take root. In 2003, India's 85 venture-capital firms invested about $162 million in tech companies, according to estimates from the India trade group National Association of Software & Services Cos. That's up from zero in 1998. Still, it's miles short of the financial support available to Stephen and his classmates. The 700 U.S. venture-capital firms poured $9.2 billion into tech start-ups in 2003, according to market researcher VentureOne.

## Multicultural Edge

Diversity is another advantage the U.S. has over India. Take a stroll with Deepa through the leafy IIT campus, and practically everyone is Indian. Stephen's scene at CMU, by contrast, feels like the U.N. Classmates joke in Asian and European languages, and a strong smell of microwaved curry floats in the air. This atmosphere extends to American tech companies. With their diverse workforces, American companies can field teams that speak Mandarin, Hindi, French, Russian—you name it. As global software projects take shape, with development ceaselessly following the path of daylight around the globe, multicultural teams have a big edge. Who better than U.S.-based workers to stitch together these projects and manage them? "These people can act as bridges to the global economy," says Amar Gupta, a technology professor at Massachusetts Institute of Technology's Sloan School of Management.

The question is whether the technology industry can respond quickly enough to a revolution that's racing ahead on Internet time. Stephen's former boss, Brookins, frets that the pace could overwhelm the coming generation of U.S. programmers, including his former Nebraska star. "He's a genius. He's the future of the country. [But] if the question is whether there's going to be a happy ending for Stephen, there's a big question mark there," Brookins says. Stephen is betting that quality and customer service will offset the cost advantage of having computer programmers 10 time zones away. He still sees software in the U.S. as a path to wealth—"though I won't really know until I get out there," he says.

While Stephen is busy mounting his defenses, Deepa is setting out on the hard climb to build Silicon India. Much like their two countries, the leader is looking cautiously over his shoulder while the challenger is chugging single-mindedly ahead. No matter which way they may zig or zag, both of them are prepared to encounter rough competition from every corner of the globe. There's no such thing as a safe distance in software anymore.

---

## Jobs That Could Swim Offshore

*Nurses and barbers don't need to fear for their livelihoods, say two researchers. Most everyone else, don't be so confident.*

Which American jobs are in jeopardy of being shipped offshore? Sure, barbers are safe. But lots of others—radiologists, accountants, and architects among them—are discovering to their great unease that overseas residents can do what they do for American customers.

Economists J. Bradford Jensen and Lori G. Kletzer have come up with an inventive way of figuring out whose jobs are vulnerable and whose aren't.

### Bunch Factor

The two hold positions at the Institute for International Economics, a Washington, D.C., think tank, and Kletzer is also on the faculty of the University of California at Santa Cruz.

Jensen and Kletzer came up with a simple test: If a worker has to be located close to the customer, then the job can't be sent offshore. If the worker can be located far from the customer, the job might qualify for offshoring. After all, they reason, if you can serve a customer in

Alabama from New York, you can probably serve her almost as easily from Shanghai or Mumbai.

Next, they assume that customers for most kinds of businesses are spread uniformly across the U.S. If the people serving them are spaced just as thinly and evenly (as, say, barbers and mechanics are), then the work likely requires geographic proximity to the customer. But employees of other businesses are highly bunched—auto workers in Detroit, stock traders in New York City, moviemakers in Los Angeles. Those people clearly can get their jobs done from afar.

Jensen and Kletzer classify every worker two ways: by occupation and by industry. For example, an in-house counsel for GM would fall into the "lawyer" and "auto industry" categories. Want to determine your job and industry's vulnerability? The following table demonstrates how Jensen and Kletzer categorize the U.S. workforce.

|  | Nontradable occupations | Tradable occupations |
|---|---|---|
| **Nontradable industries** | 50.03% | 10.79% |
| **Tradable industries** | 21.64% | 17.54% |

Here's what Jensen told *BusinessWeek* Economics Editor Peter Coy in an interview about his work with Kletzer:

**Q: What gave you the idea of looking for geographic clusters of workers?**
**A:** We used this geographical approach, because doing research on this is hampered by the lack of good detailed data from government sources on what is actually being traded.

**Q: Where did you tend to find lots of clusters—indicating that the jobs are potentially offshorable?**
**A:** In professional and business services, 70% of employment is in the tradable range. It's very concentrated. The most concentrated are software